S0-BRJ-313

Practical Marketing for Your Small Retail Business

WILLIAM H. BRANNEN

Professor of Marketing,
Creighton University

63626

A SPECTRUM BOOK

PRENTICE-HALL, INC., Englewood Cliffs, New Jersey 07632

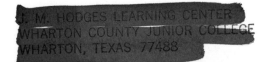

Library of Congress Cataloging in Publication Data

BRANNEN, WILLIAM H.
   Practical marketing for your small retail business.

  (A Spectrum Book)
  Includes bibliographical references and index.
   1. Marketing.   2. Marketing management.   3. Small
business.   I. Title.
HF5415.B633   658.8′0024381   81-92
ISBN 0-13-692764-5   AACR2
ISBN 0-13-692756-4 (pbk.)

Dedicated to Kathy

10 9 8 7 6 5 4 3 2 1

Editorial/production supervision
by Maria Carella and Alberta Boddy
Interior design by Maria Carella
Cover design by Honi Werner
Manufacturing buyer: Cathie Lenard

PRENTICE-HALL INTERNATIONAL, INC., *London*
PRENTICE-HALL OF AUSTRALIA PTY. LIMITED. *Sydney*
PRENTICE-HALL OF CANADA, LTD., *Toronto*
PRENTICE-HALL OF INDIA PRIVATE LIMITED, *New Delhi*
PRENTICE-HALL OF JAPAN, INC., *Tokyo*
PRENTICE-HALL OF SOUTHEAST ASIA PTE. LTD., *Singapore*
WHITEHALL BOOKS LIMITED, *Wellington, New Zealand*

Contents

15

Preface

If you are interested in small business retailing, this book was written for you. It is a marketing book for small retailers of consumer goods and services. It *adapts* the consumer-oriented marketing concept (which has proven so successful for many large firms) to fit the needs of small retailers. This is new!

Just as the basic principles of navigation apply to both large ocean liners and small canoes, the basic principles of retail marketing apply to retailers of all sizes. Because many important differences exist between large and small retailers, however, such principles must be *adapted* for small retail firms. As a present or future small retailer, you are invited to use these adapted principles. To help you do so, the book gives you a framework for planning, implementing, and controlling your own retail marketing strategy. The book does not preach to you

or try to tell you how to run your business. It does tell you how you can use your knowledge and experience in a line of retail trade to formulate a unique marketing strategy and become a more successful retailer.

An eight-step process is given for building your retail marketing strategy. You will find this process easy to understand and easy to use. Many examples are presented to illustrate its use. Readers interested in small business marketing for the nonretail firm are referred to my previous book, *Successful Marketing for Your Small Business,* published by Prentice-Hall.

The researching and writing of this book were enjoyable and educational for the author. Reading and using the book should provide enjoyment and education for you. The payoff for all of us is an increased number of more successful small retailers. Our modern society desperately needs such successes.

You are invited to judge this book in your own way, and your comments to the author will be appreciated. Eventually, the market judges us all.

Although I accept the full responsibility of authorship, I do wish to acknowledge the help of others. In addition to the many sources and authors given credit in the text, I also wish to thank my teaching colleagues and students. Graduate students who were especially helpful in securing practical examples from successful small retailers are Bruce Deines, Pat McGowan, Ron Mor-

tensen, Jim Norman, and Bill Walker. The College of Business Administration and the Graduate School at Creighton University provided me time and resources for completing this book. Dr. J. L. Carrica, Dean of the College of Business Administration, was especially supportive. For an excellent job of typing and otherwise preparing the manuscript, I with to thank Ms. Vicki Gangestad. For her constructive criticism, editorial assistance, encouragement, and many other ways of helping, I thank my wife, Dr. Kathleen C. Brannen. Finally, to our children, Julie and Patrick: thank you for making it all worthwhile.

1

You and Small Business Retailing

The most important element in the success of your small retail business is **YOU.** In a small retail business the responsibility for a successful marketing program belongs to the owner/manager. You must ask yourself, "Am I genuinely interested in becoming a successful small retailer and am I willing to pay the price to do so?"

The field of retailing abounds with opportunities for professional small marketers who are willing to perform and are personally suited to the task. Retailing in small business requires a philosophy and a way of life that include hard work and long hours. The commitment often includes evenings and weekends. Certain personal characteristics also are found among successful small retailers; your chances for success are greater if you have a generous degree of the following:

1. Ability to organize.
2. Effective communication skills.
3. Good human relations ability.
4. Leadership qualities.
5. Ability to adapt quickly to change.
6. An outgoing personality.
7. Good judgment and thinking ability.
8. Physical and mental health.
9. Energy.
10. Effectiveness in making use of time.
11. Technical and managerial preparation and experience.
12. Initiative beyond a mere willingness to work.

To the extent that you possess some or all of the above personal characteristics, the retail marketing you learn from this book can help you become a more successful small business retailer.

An Overall View of Small Business Retailing

The Scope of Small Business Retailing. Are you a small retailer? Most businesses are small, and most retail businesses are small. You are a small retailer if you are both (a) **small** and (b) a **retailer.** Without discussing the many definitions for these terms, let us simply agree that a small business usually is one that is independently owned and operated and is not dominant in its field of operations. A retailer is one who offers goods and/or services for sale primarily to individuals for ultimate consumption.

Retail trade in the United States is composed of slightly less than two million establishments. By most definitions, a majority of these retailers are small. Figure 1-2

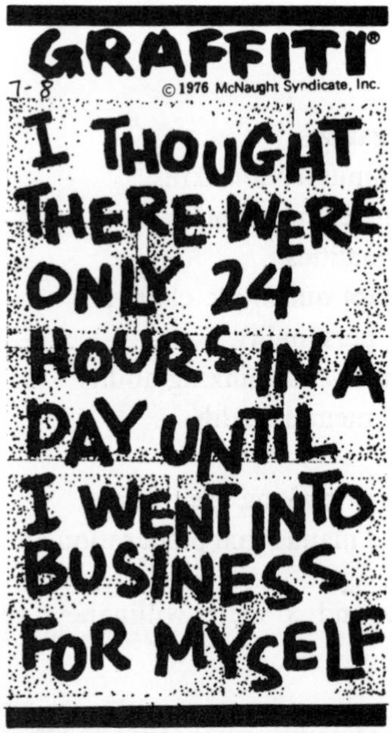

Figure 1-1 A newspaper feature comments on small business. (Source: Reproduced with permission of McNaught Syndicate, Inc.)

shows the percentage distribution of sales (1972) by sales size of firm and for selected kinds of business. Firms with less than $1 million annual sales account for 38.2 percent of all retail sales. Sales in Figure 1-2 are based on total sales of all units of the firm.

Another measure of the importance of small retailing in the economy is provided in Figure 1-3. Shown here is the percentage distribution of sales (1972) of single-unit and multiunit firms. Most small retailers would be included as single-unit establishments. A few small retailers would be in the "two to ten establishments" category. Figure 1-3 points out that 54.8 percent of all retail trade is done by single-unit establishments. About two-thirds of all retail trade sales are by firms with ten or fewer establishments. Although the statistics are not applied to an exact definition of small retailing, the message is quite clear: small retailing is a major force in the economy. One estimate of the Small Business Administration states that 99 percent of the total 2.3 million retail trade businesses in the United States are small and that these small businesses account for 73 percent of total retail sales receipts.[1]

In addition to size, retailing could also be classified along such dimensions as (1) instore or nonstore, (2) merchandise carried, (3) services offered, (4) ownership or affiliation, (5) geographic location, and so on. The marketing strategy planning discussed in this book will be applicable for small retailers regardless of where they fit into these dimensions. Our only requirements are that you are *small,* are a *retailer,* and are interested in implementing the customer-oriented marketing concept in your business.

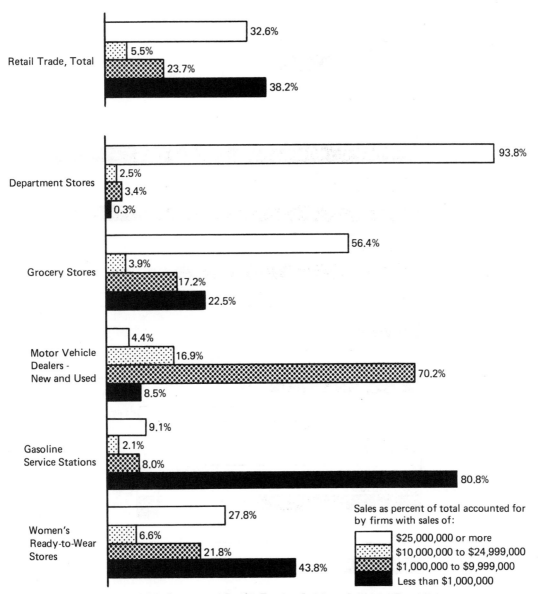

RETAIL TRADE
Percent Distribution of Sales: 1972

by Sales Size of Firm and for Selected Kinds of Business

Retail Trade, Total
- 32.6%
- 5.5%
- 23.7%
- 38.2%

Department Stores
- 93.8%
- 2.5%
- 3.4%
- 0.3%

Grocery Stores
- 56.4%
- 3.9%
- 17.2%
- 22.5%

Motor Vehicle Dealers - New and Used
- 4.4%
- 16.9%
- 70.2%
- 8.5%

Gasoline Service Stations
- 9.1%
- 2.1%
- 8.0%
- 80.8%

Women's Ready-to-Wear Stores
- 27.8%
- 6.6%
- 21.8%
- 43.8%

Sales as percent of total accounted for by firms with sales of:
- $25,000,000 or more
- $10,000,000 to $24,999,000
- $1,000,000 to $9,999,000
- Less than $1,000,000

Figure 1-2. (*Source: 1972 Census of Retail Trade: Subject Series,* "Establishment and Firm Size," pp. 1-4)

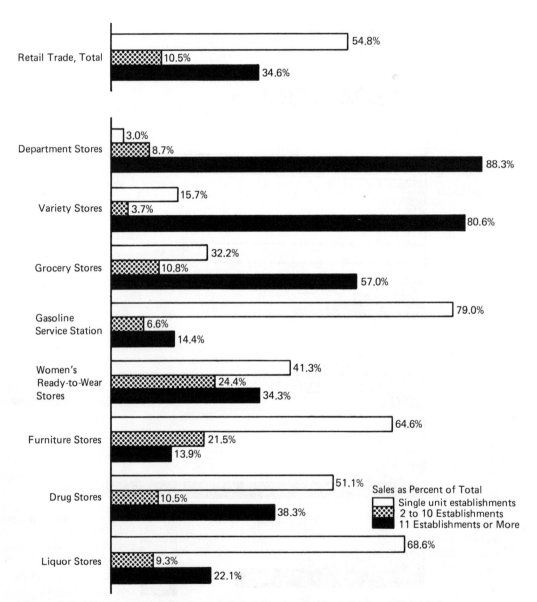

RETAIL TRADE

Percent Distribution of Sales by Firm Size: 1972

for Selected Kinds of Business

Retail Trade, Total — 54.8% / 10.5% / 34.6%

Department Stores — 3.0% / 8.7% / 88.3%

Variety Stores — 15.7% / 3.7% / 80.6%

Grocery Stores — 32.2% / 10.8% / 57.0%

Gasoline Service Station — 79.0% / 6.6% / 14.4%

Women's Ready-to-Wear Stores — 41.3% / 24.4% / 34.3%

Furniture Stores — 64.6% / 21.5% / 13.9%

Drug Stores — 51.1% / 10.5% / 38.3%

Liquor Stores — 68.6% / 9.3% / 22.1%

Sales as Percent of Total
Single unit establishments
2 to 10 Establishments
11 Establishments or More

Figure 1-3. (*Source: 1972 Census of Retail Trade: Subject Series,* "Establishment and Firm Size," pp. 1-2)

Marketing Advantages and Disadvantages of Small Retailers. As a small retailer, you have no shortage of competition. Besides the large retailers, such as Sears, Safeway, Woolco, K-Mart, and Penney's, you have numerous small and medium-sized competitors. What advantages and disadvantages should you consider in such a competitive market situation?

The advantages and disadvantages of anything are not automatic. Although some may appear to be unique to a specific situation such as small retailing, other advantages may be unrealized while some disadvantages are unnecessarily self-imposed. As a small retailer, you will want to capitalize on all the potential advantages and recognize the disadvantages only in order to avoid them.

Large and small retailers do not face the same sets of problems. Large retailers spend much time and energy coordinating activities of various parts of their large organizations. Small retailers tend to have more problems in marketing and creating sales than in managing people.

Marketing advantages of small retailers (and conditions under which small retailers can advantageously operate) often include the following:

1. *Less goal conflict* should exist in a small retail firm. The overall company goals of the small retailer are usually (or should be) quite compatible with the marketing goals. By contrast, in the large retail firm, both overall goals and marketing goals are likely to be interpreted differently by different persons and in different parts of the organization. Firm goals and personal goals are also more likely to be compatible in the small firm.

2. *Smaller, more limited markets* represent opportunities for small retailers but not for large retailers. By successfully segmenting markets, small retailers may profitably serve markets that are too limited to be of interest to large retailers. Some markets are not worth the bother and the required investment to large retailers, who must cover high overhead to obtain the required return on investment.

3. *Product characteristics* sometimes favor small retailers—for example, perishable products, customized products, and products involving a significant amount of personal service.

4. *Flexibility* is often cited as an advantage of the small retailer. This usually means the ability to react quickly to change by making decisions on the spot without needing approval from headquarters.

5. *Closer customer contact* and the informality of the small firm make it possible (though not inevitable) for the small retailer to personally communicate with and better judge the needs of the customers. Also, close customer contact provides an added dimension to the marketing strategy of many small retailers. This dimension, called *people strategy,* is the topic of Chapter 10. This individualized people strategy cannot be duplicated by large retailers.

6. *Cost advantages* such as low overhead are sometimes enjoyed by small retailers. This does not mean that such a retailer necessarily will have lower selling prices, but it does provide an opportunity to differentiate the marketing mix.

7. *Growth potential* could also be cited as an advantage of many small retailers. Small retailers, especially those with innovative ideas and growth goals, have more to gain and less to lose than do their larger rivals. For example, a small pizza retailer with only two stores has many untapped potential markets, but many of the best markets for a larger, established firm such as Pizza Hut already have their Pizza Hut.

Marketing disadvantages of small retailers (and conditions under which small retailers might operate at a disadvantage) include the following:

1. *Competing head-on* with large mass retailers for mass markets is extremely difficult. In fact, many large retailers attempt to segment the overall market and serve only certain target markets. Small retailers must almost always be target marketers.

2. *Some discrimination* against small retailers does exist. Examples are the favored treatment given national chains by shopping-center developers, quantity discount structures, and mass-media advertising rates that favor large advertisers.

3. *Limited resources* can exclude small retailers from considering certain marketing opportunities. For example, limited financial and managerial resources may prevent an existing small retailer from expanding or opening at an additional location. Competition from other small retailers or large retailers will make such opportunities short-lived.

4. *Costs are sometimes higher.* For example, cost of merchandise may be higher because of purchase of smaller quantities and because of lack of bargaining power with suppliers.

5. *Lack of effective marketing techniques* is a major disadvantage of many small retailers. One study of small retailers in small towns revealed that (a) marketing was the major problem of these retailers and (b) advertising was their major marketing problem.[2] Small retailers cannot afford specialized managers and professionals for all areas of the business. The solution often used to overcome this disadvantage is to hire such expertise from outside the firm.

The above list of marketing advantages and disadvantages is a general one. As a small retailer, you should be able to note which items apply specifically to your business and exactly how they apply. You might also expand the list and make it more specific in relation to your business situation. Also, re-member that so-called inherent advantages are not automatic, and disadvantages should not be unnecessarily self-imposed.

People and Small Retail Marketing. A fundamental difference between small and large retailers is that small retail organizations tend to be built around people. Large retailers employ many people, but for the most part the people are required to fit into the large retail organization much as cogs fit into a machine. Small retail firms, on the other hand, usually exhibit a lack of hierarchy and formal bureaucratic organization. They place a special emphasis on the people who make up the firm. These people include the owner/manager, other managers, employees, and cooperating outside people such as the firm's accountant or advertising agency. As a small retailer, you can either recognize or ignore the emphasis on people as a fundamental distinction between your firm and other retailers.

A second fundamental way in which you can distinguish your retail business is by the implementation of the customer-oriented marketing concept. Don't think of yourself as a retailer who sells products to customers. Think of yourself as a retail marketer who serves a selected group of customers by helping them to satisfy their wants and needs. Marketing should not be merely selling products; that would be a product or sales orientation. A broader customer-oriented approach is advocated here.

Many small retailers have succeeded without using an effective people strategy as part of an overall marketing strategy. In fact, many small retailers have only a vague notion of what is meant by *marketing*. Perhaps you or some of the retailers you know fit this description. You will, however, be a more successful small retailer if you plan, implement, and control an overall retail marketing program that includes strategies for serving target customers at a profit with the right *products,* at the right *place,* at the right *price,* with the right *promotion,* and by the right *people.* How to do this is what this book is all about. Before constructing a framework for this activity (in Chapter 2), let us first look more closely at *success* in small retailing.

Success and Failure in Small Retailing. We mention failure here, but we stress **SUC-CESS.** If you are interested in failing, many prophets of doom are waiting with failure statistics from Dun and Bradstreet to demonstrate both the reasons and the supposed high probabilities of failing in small business. However, if you wish to succeed, concentrate on success and study ways of becoming successful.

Many books, articles, and speeches on small business begin by discussing failure rates and failure reasons among new and small businesses. For example, Dun & Bradstreet lists the following major pitfalls of starting and owning your own business:

Lack of experience
Lack of capital
Poor location
Too much inventory, particularly of the wrong kind
Excessive purchase of fixed assets
Poor credit granting practice
Personal expenses too high
Unplanned expansion
What might be called faulty attitudes[3]

These pitfalls are certainly to be avoided by the astute small retailer. However, the warnings of failure can sometimes be misleading. In an article titled "It's Easier to Slay a Dragon than Kill a Myth," Michael Massel suggests that Dun & Bradstreet business-failure data could also logically be interpreted to infer that businesses have been and are healthy.[4] Four submyths of the failure myth are explored in this article. These submyths are:

1. D&B's Rate of Failure statistics indicate a high mortality rate in business enterprises.
2. D&B states that the mortality rate among small businesses is greater than among large businesses.
3. D&B reports that a large percent of all firms fail during the early years.
4. Don't go into business; the statistical odds are against success.[5]

Massel presents a "myth killer" in an attempt to "kill" each of the above submyths. For example, the "killer" to submyth 4 points out that the statistical odds *against* failure are 230 to 1.[6] Do you know of any small retailer who would consider such odds to be risky? Statistical odds do not necessarily apply to individual cases, but they do suggest by the law of averages that small retailers may realistically share in a spirit of success. In the chapters that follow you will explore both why and how successful small retail marketers succeed. For some practical introductory suggestions, think about the six methods for success in a small store given in Figure 1-4.

 **SMALL BUSINESS ADMINISTRATION**
SMALL MARKETERS AIDS No. 127

FIRST PRINTED MAY 1967   **WASHINGTON D.C.**   REPRINTED FEBRUARY 1978

SIX METHODS FOR

SUCCESS IN A SMALL STORE

By ROBERT E. LEVINSON

Executive Vice President and General Manager The Steelcraft Manufacturing Company, Cincinnati, Ohio

You can increase your store's potential for success by using the methods discussed below. In addition, use outside advisers, such as your accountant, banker, and lawyer, to help you over the rough spots.

1. CATER to customers

Your number one job should be to please customers. Roll out the red carpet for them. They keep you in business.

Learn their likes and make them feel you are interested. Give an extra bit of service. People will remember and tell others.

Be an expert on your products. Tell the truth about them even if it means a lost sale.

Build on existing customers. It is easier to increase their purchases than to draw in new people. Always thank customers.

2. BUILD an image

A small retail or service firm needs steady and solid promotion. Part of building an image is using ads, handbills, radio or TV spots. They set the stage.

Yet many a store suffers because the owner fumbles his role at the point of sale. There, use your personality to encourage people to think

favorably of your store and its goods.

A clean, well-lighted store helps to create a favorable image of its merchandise.

Figure 1-4. (*Source:* U.S. Small Business Administration. Small Marketers Aids No. 127)

3. ENCOURAGE teamwork

The satisfaction customers get from trading with you will be only as good as your employees.

So don't keep secrets from your staff. Give them facts about merchandise. Let them help decide what to put on sale and how to display it.

In teamwork, employees do their jobs without prompting. Teach them to know: what to do, how to do it, and when to do it.

Praise employees in public. Correct them in private.

4. PLAN ahead

Teamwork makes it easy to plan ahead. Employees who can do a variety of jobs save your time for management work.

Watch the calendar for special events which need advance preparation. Use the 5-day weather forecast as a clue for planning special sales.

Train an assistant. Put him in charge and take a day off. This will help him learn.

Look ahead. Estimate your sales and cash flow for the next 5 years. Make plans for financing the store's growth.

5. LOOK for profit volume

The name of the game in a store is profit. A big sales volume does not necessarily mean a high profit volume. Profit depends on what is left after your pay your bills.

Keep expenses in line. Make a list of them—both fixed and variable expenses. Rent is an example of fixed expenses. You have to pay it even if you don't sell anything. Bags and wrapping paper are examples of expenses that vary with sales.

Determine your break-even point—the point at which sales volume and expenses are equal—and use it as a control tool. Your sales volume should be way beyond the point at which your revenue and expenses balance.

6. PAY your civic rent

A store's opportunities for expansion are tied up with the growth of the community in which it is located. When a city has a reputation for "being a good place to live," it is more apt to hold residents and attract new ones.

You "pay your civic rent" when you take part in local clubs and other organizations that work to build the community.

One caution: Take on only what you can handle. It is better to use your management skills effectively on a few projects than to squander them on many.

Copies of this Aid are available free from field offices and Washington headquarters of the Small Business Administration. Aids may be condensed or reproduced. They may not be altered to imply approval by SBA of any private organization, product, or service. If material is reused, credit to SBA will be appreciated. Use of funds for printing this publication approved by the Office of Management and Budget, March 20, 1975.

Figure 1-4 (continued)

2

A Framework for Your Retail Marketing Strategy

This chapter is an outline that summarizes the rest of the book. It gives you a framework within which you can formulate your retail marketing strategy. This framework will *not* tell you what your marketing strategy should be. Rather, it will be a step-by-step method that guides you. It is a "how to" framework, which you follow as an outline. But you must determine your own marketing strategy. No one else can do it for you. Because your retail business is unique, **YOU** must bring to this strategy-formulation process your knowledge of your target customers, your experience in your line of business, and your mix of the right product, place, price, promotion, and people strategies.

Marketing management of a small retail firm is composed of the continuous three-part process of (a) planning, (b) implementing, and (c) controlling. We will refer to this as the PIC (plan, implement, and control) process of retail marketing management. In Figure 2-1 the PIC process is shown as a continuous triangular path that encompasses the rest of the diagram. Additional references will be made later to other parts of Figure 2-1.

Briefly stated, the ten steps in our retail marketing strategy outline are:

1. How to set your company goals and objectives.
2. How to set your marketing goals and objectives.
3. How to identify your differential advantage.
4. How to define your target market(s).
5. How to plan for dealing with your business environment.
6. How to plan your overall marketing strategy (steps 1–8 of the strategy-formulation

process) by first planning each of the following parts of your retail marketing mix:

a. Product mix.

b. Place mix.

c. Price mix.

d. Promotion mix.

e. People mix.

7. How to integrate your overall marketing strategy plan into an overall retail marketing program.

8. How to implement your retail marketing program by:

a. Organizing.

b. Directing.

c. Tactical adjustments.

9. How to control your retail marketing program.

10. Your result is a successful retail firm that produces customer satisfaction at a profit.

How to Set Your Company Goals and Objectives

In a game such as football, soccer, or hockey the goals are already set. Each team member is assigned certain objectives in order that the team objectives (such as moving the ball toward the goal) can be

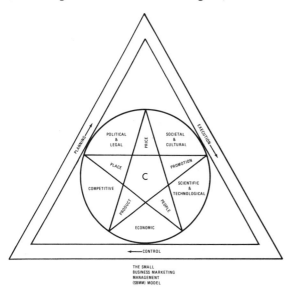

Figure 2-1. A visual model of retail marketing management. (*Source:* William H. Brannen, *Successful Marketing for Your Small Business,* Englewood Cliffs, N.J.: Prentice-Hall, Inc., 1978, p. 31. See Chapter 3 of *Successful Marketing* for a detailed description of this diagram. The term *execution* in this diagram means the same as *implementation* as used in the present volume.

accomplished. For the small retailer the goals are not set. As a small retailer you must set your own goals. You must then specify specific objectives that, if accomplished, will assure you of reaching your goals. The extent to which your goals are reached is the measure of your firm's success.

The goals of a small retail firm often reflect the retailer's own personal goals. For example, if a small retailer has a personal goal of providing retail management careers for sons and/or daughters, sufficient expansion of the family business is likely to be a goal of that retail firm.

Overall goals are typically set when the firm is founded, when major problems appear, or when major opportunities appear. Such goals may be implicit; however, it is better to have an explicit written goal statement. Because these overall goals are the basic identity of the small retail firm, they will not be revised frequently. But they certainly could and should be reviewed, reaffirmed, and restated at the beginning of each strategy-planning session. Once a year would not be too often.

As a small retailer your overall goal may be stated generally as satisfying the needs of customers, and the incentive for doing so is the resulting profit. But you must make a more specific statement. Your overall goal is composed of a specific goal in each of three areas: (a) a service goal, (b) a profit goal, and (c) a firm life-cycle goal.

Regarding your service goal, you answer such questions as types of customers to be served, needs to be fulfilled, and the ways in which your firm will do these things. In considering your profit goal you decide on how much profit you are seeking as a reward for the service you are providing. Are you trying to maximize profit—in both the short and long run? Are you looking for some target return on your investment? Or are you after a "satisfactory" level of profits based upon some calculation that takes into consideration alternate employment, a "fair" return, industry practice, and social responsibility? You must decide.

The firm life-span goal relates to questions of firm size, survival, stability, and growth. You should answer such questions as: Do I want to remain a small retailer? Do I want a slow but steady rate of growth? Do I want expansion at one site or am I interested in operating at several? Despite much thinking to the contrary, growth for its own sake is not an essential ingredient for success. However, if growth is to be important in your overall goals, you will encounter a unique set of problems and opportunities as a small retailer.

Set your overall goals, write them down, and communicate them to others in your retail firm.

How to Set Your Marketing Goals and Objectives

The ultimate goal of your marketing program is to advance the firm's overall goals and objectives. The old saying that "nothing happens unless something is sold" emphasizes the importance of marketing. Your overall marketing goal will be a *specifically stated, time-related, attainable* end toward which marketing activities can be directed. As will be shown in later chapters, the overall marketing goal is that goal toward which the total marketing program is directed. Just as the overall marketing strategy entails effective strategies in each of the elements of the marketing mix, so also the overall marketing goals and objectives can be thought of in terms of several subgoals. In other words, you will have advertising goals, pricing goals, and so on.

In setting your marketing goals, consider making goal statements for (a) target markets to be served, (b) sales to these markets, (c) market share or position within these markets, and (d) rewards (profits) for reaching these marketing goals. For example, what would be a specific, time-related, attainable marketing goal for a successful small retailer who has recently doubled his selling floor space from its previous crowded size? The target markets served would probably be the same unless the increased space involved a new location or substantially different product lines. However, current markets could be served better and more completely. This should help sales to expand. By how much? A dollar and/or unit sales goal should be set here, both for the next year and for shorter planning periods. If a dollar goal is set, it should take into account price increases (through upgrading or inflation) as well as the increased selling space. The market-share part of the goal refers to the relative competitive position within the market. Other marketing goals could also be set.

Before listing other types of marketing goals, let us give an illustrative goal statement for the small retailer in the above example. This is merely an example and is not necessarily the "right" goal. Our illustrative marketing goal statement is as follows:

To serve current customers well during the year so that average sales per customer is increased by 10 percent for present products and these same customers will purchase an additional $20,000 during the coming year from product lines added as a result of the expansion. To attract 200 new customers during the year in order to replace an estimated lost 100 customers and to expand the customer base. This will give the store an estimated market share goal of 25 percent at the end of the year. Because increased sales via new customers will take time to (a) get new customers over the year and (b) get these new customers to purchase up to the average of current customers, average sales per customer will be less for new customers. Therefore, the sales goal is in total $217,000 and the profit goal before taxes is $38,000.

This statement is actually quite brief and assumes that the retailer has a good set of records and knows how to use them. In a limited way it illustrated a specific, time-oriented, attainable goal. Several objectives, which are even more specific, are implied if the overall marketing goals are to be reached. These might be called performance objectives for all parts of the marketing mix. Following are a few isolated examples.

1. *Product objectives:*
   a. Increase stock turnover of brands carried in a certain product line.
   b. Increase store traffic (by adding an attractive product or service).
2. *Place objective:*
   a. Increase sales per square foot of floor space.
3. *Price objectives:*
   a. Give a low-price image for a competitive product grouping.
   b. Deemphasize the importance of price to the customer.
   c. Encourage repeat business (e.g., by giving a cumulative discount over time).
4. *Promotion objectives:*
   a. Increase store traffic by X percent.
   b. Sell X number of products this month.
5. *People objective:*
   a. Replace salesperson X with a person whose personal qualities and technical qualifications are . . . .

By this time, you have undoubtedly gathered that goals and objectives are present at various levels in the marketing management process. These must be meshed together in a compatible manner. Priorities must be given and conflicts must somehow be resolved. As a small retailer, you do not have the resources to accomplish all desirable objectives. Look to your strengths and keep in mind your weaknesses when attempting to identify your differential advantage.

How to Identify Your Differential Advantage

If you don't have some kind of differential advantage, and cannot identify one after considerable thought, don't become a small retailer. If you are already a small retailer and cannot identify your differential advantage, chances are that you are not very successful or you've been just plain lucky up to now.

A differential advantage is something, or some combination of things, that gives you a competitive edge in serving the needs of a specific target market. Every retailer, regardless of size, differs from all its competitors in some ways. If these differences are important to customers, they constitute a differential advantage. Most successful retailers have identified some sort of differential advantage. Examples of a place to look for a differential advantage are a superior store location, a product and service well suited to a specific group of target customers, knowledgeable and personable sales and service personnel, brands of merchandise carried, pricing policies, unique advertising and promotion, and the image projected by the firm. The question you ask is: Where in our total marketing program do our resources give us a competitive edge?

Some forms of differential advantage have more permanency than others, but all eventually fade in importance in a competitive and changing retail environment. For example, a small retailer whose differential advantage is a superior location may lose this advantage when his street is made one-way. Or a retailer who once offered excellent parking may suddenly have very mediocre parking when a street is widened.

The importance of identifying and periodically reviewing your differential advantage cannot be overestimated. It is what you are going to base your marketing strategy on. At this point, try to make a concise statement of the differential advantage for your own small retail business, or for a small retail firm with which you are familiar. Once you have done this, you are ready to define your target market(s) and begin forming a marketing strategy for serving them.

We shall now look briefly at a number of topics that will be discussed later in detail.

How to Define Your Target Market(s)

Retail markets are composed of (a) people who have needs with (b) purchasing power in the form of money or credit with (c) the willingness to buy. As a small retailer, you cannot serve all retail markets. Small retailers (and even large ones to some extent) specialize. You must decide what needs you are going to attempt to satisfy for what group of people. These people then become your target customers. Taken together, they constitute your target market. You will place primary emphasis on your target market customers in developing your total marketing program. You will, of course, sell to some people who are not a part of your target market, but the vast majority of your sales will be to target market customers.

Defining your target market(s) is one of your most basic decisions. It is the matching of your differential advantage with a market opportunity where that advantage can be put to good use in satisfying customers. For this reason, and because small retailers who believe in the marketing concept are customer-oriented, the target market is shown as a pentagon at the very center of our model of retail marketing management in Figure 2-1. In the diagram, the C in the pentagon stands for target market customer.

The process that many successful retailers use to define their target markets is called *market segmentation.* This is a process of dividing up the heterogeneous total market into small groups of customers. Each of these smaller groups possesses its own somewhat homogeneous characteristics. The market segmentation process is discussed in detail in Chapter 3. For now, we simply note that cetain market segments tend to be more attractive to small retailers. The determination of which market segments are the best or most appropriate target markets for a particular small retailer is a subjective process. Two principles you may wish to use in this process are those of *market simplification* and *market dominance*. These are discussed in Chapter 3. After you have conceptually defined your target market along several meaningful dimensions, several suggestions are given in Chapter 3 for making your definition operational by actually locating the target market customers.

How to Plan for Dealing with Your Business Environment

Your business environment is a given. You can't change it, at least not in the short run, so you adapt to it. However, the environment does change. We will discuss the environment in terms of five categories of uncontrollable variables. These are shown in Figure 2-1 as a circular area. Within this circle (called the environment) the small retailer formulates a marketing strategy involving a retail marketing mix of the "five P's" in an attempt to satisfy the target market. The environmental variables can be categorized under five headings: (a) the *economic* environment, (b) the *competitive* environment, (c) the *political and legal* environment, (d) the *societal and cultural* environment, and (e) the *scientific and technological* environment.

Your economic environment is comprised of the economic conditions of the markets in which you operate. National economic conditions are usually of interest to small retailers only insofar as they affect local conditions. For example, low unemployment nationally is of little interest to the small-town retailer whose major employer is closed due to a strike. Inflation, recession, depression, employment levels, tight money, and other factors are parts of the economic environment in which small retailers operate. Because these factors directly affect consumer behavior and the general level of business activity, small retailer marketing programs must take them into account.

Your competitive environment is defined by the nature and intensity of those firms that are competing to satisfy the needs of the same target markets you are serving. Are these competitors national chains or local independents? What are their basic competitive strategies? What are their differential advantages and disadvantages? What are your indirect forms of competition? For example, the retailer who sells lawn-care products to homeowners is indirectly competing with lawn-care services. What new forms of competition are on the horizon? Realistic answers to such questions as these will provide an understanding of the competitive environment. Such analysis may also reveal market gaps where market opportunities exist.

Your political and legal environment consists of government relations at all levels of government. This environmental area has become an increasing problem for small retailers. Big government is getting bigger, and the problems are not likely to go away. Often you will need outside help from attorneys and trade associations to successfully adapt to the changing political and legal environment.

Your societal and cultural environment

is reflected most directly in the attitudes and behavior of your potential customers. How are their life styles changing? In what ways have their values changed? How do changes in such basics as family, sex roles, marriage, divorce, educational levels, and religious practices affect your retail business? As a successful small retailer you will monitor such changes in order to adapt your marketing program accordingly.

Your scientific and technological environment tends to make old retailing opportunities obsolete while creating new ones. Small retailers can both affect and be affected by changing technology. For example, they may be affected by the micro-computer, which enables many alert small retailers to keep better records, but which simply wastes money and effort for those who do not know how to use the improved information. A small retailer who sells microcomputers to household consumers is affecting the scientific and technological environment.

What have we been saying? Successful small retailers attempt to *know* their environment and maintain some flexibility in their marketing plans in order to *adapt* to changes in it. And that is how you can successfully deal with the environment of your retail business. Details are given in Chapter 4.

How to Plan Your Overall Marketing Strategy

Your overall retail marketing strategy is composed of (1) a target market(s) and (2) a retail marketing mix designed to satisfy that target market at a profit. Target markets were briefly discussed earlier in this chapter. Your marketing mix is comprised of product, place, price, promotion, and people. These variables over which you have control are combined in such a way as to form a whole that is greater than the sum of its parts; this is known as the *synergetic effect.*

Each controllable variable will be planned, implemented, and controlled in such a way that product, place, price, promotion, and people strategies combine to form a compatible overall marketing strategy. In Figure 2-1 the five-pointed star represents the overall marketing strategy, and each triangular point of the star represents one of the five P's. The chapters that follow deal respectively with product strategy (Chapters 5 and 6), place strategy (Chapters 7 and 8), price strategy (Chapters 9 and 10), promotion strategy (Chapters 11 and 12), and people strategy (Chapter 13). In the present chapter a retail marketing strategy framework and an eight-step strategy planning process are introduced. In Chapter 4 the framework will be filled in. At that point you should be able to use the framework in your retail business.

The Five P's of Your Retail Marketing Mix. The five P's of your retail marketing mix are product, place, price, promotion, and people.

Product includes both goods and services. Product is broadly defined to include more than physical goods; it includes such things as the merchandise variety and selection offered by the retailer. The width, depth, and consistency of product lines carried are part of the product mix. Customer services (or the absence of certain customer services) are also part of the product mix. For example, refunds, exchanges, credit, delivery, extended store hours, and free customer parking are all part of the product mix that a small retailer might offer his customers.

Place as an element of the retail marketing mix refers to three areas of marketing activity that insure the customer of having the product available where he wants it. These three areas are (1) the site location of the retail facility, (2) the use of space within the retail facility, and (3) the physical distribution system employed for providing the desired level of customer service. The site-location question is one of the most important. Should you locate in a particular city, town, suburb, or along a highway? Should you locate in a regional shopping center, a neighborhood shopping center, a central business district, or some other type of location? Should your specific site have parking, easy access from high-traffic streets, pedestrian traffic? Space utilization within the store poses such questions as how much space you should devote to each department, product category, or item; the location of products within the store so you can increase impulse sales and maintain ideal customer traffic patterns; and which space should be used for nonselling activities such as storage and price-marking. Your physical distribution system deals with order size and frequency, the handling of incoming merchandise, an inventory control system that enables you to know the status of your merchandise, and related matters that enable you to minimize lost sales due to out-of-stocks and not having the right merchandise.

Price is the one element of your retail marketing mix that has a direct and measurable impact on your profits. Price is not simply how much the customer pays you for something. You can control or administer your prices in several ways to influence customers. For example, you can create either a prestige-price image or a low-price image. You can price in such a way as to de-emphasize the importance of price in the minds of your customers. A few of the pricing tools available to you are discounts of various kinds, special prices such as cents-off coupons or two-for-one pricing, seasonal price deals, announcements that you will meet or beat any advertised price of a competitor, and the offering of credit.

Promotion is a part of the marketing mix that many small retailers actively engage in but really do not understand. The problem is often that the small retailer has extensive advertising that could not be described as a unified program based on an overall promotion strategy. Advertising is one part of promotion. The other parts are (a) sales promotion activities such as coupons, trading stamps, contests, and deals, (b) personal selling, and (c) publicity and public relations. Ideally, all should work together to help the small retailer communicate effectively with customers.

People is the one element of a retail marketing mix that is unique to small retailers. It is more than the personality or image of the store. Also included are the matching of store people to the expectations of target customers, the proper organizing of store personnel to meet customer needs, the combining of people and machines to accomplish tasks, personnel strategies, and the effective integration of outside people to aid the small retailer's marketing efforts. All the people of your small retail firm are a part of your marketing mix. Your potential customers know this. And your people may be a major reason why potential customers do or do not trade in your store. You can control your people strategy.

Strategy and Tactics. Your retail marketing strategy is an overall plan by which you take a position in the competitive market. It is composed of two basic parts: (a) determining the target market(s) you will attempt to serve and (b) developing a marketing mix of product, place, price, promotion, and people to serve the target market(s) at a profit. Tactics are the day-to-day adjustments you make in order to make your strategy more effective in the event of changing conditions. Tactics give added flexibility to your marketing program. Tactical adjustments are not changes in the basic marketing strategy. Rather, they are planned-for adjustments that give a fine tuning to the strategy. For example, if your pricing strategy involved selling at competitive prices with a few advertised specials to build store traffic, a tactical adjustment might be to eliminate the advertised specials during a week when business was expected to be exceptionally heavy anyway. The exact form of the tactical adjustment may not be planned too far in advance, but there is an advance plan to make those tactical adjustments that will enhance the overall effectiveness of the planned marketing strategy. In other words, you plan to do the appropriate fine tuning when it becomes desirable to do so.

Strategy itself can be thought of in terms of two levels. The main strategy around which other strategies are formed will be called the *core strategy.* The core strategy is the basic strategy from which all other planning flows. It is based on your differential advantage and is the central focus for

competitive and/or innovative success. Other strategies will be referred to as *supporting strategies.* An analogy may be helpful here. Imagine an old-fashioned, center-pedestal dining-room table. Think of this center pedestal as the core strategy upon which the table top rests. Then, to give added support to the table top, place any number of smaller legs around the periphery of the table. These support legs will aid the center pedestal by giving added strength and stability to the table. Supporting strategies do the same thing for the core strategy. These two levels of strategy will become quite clear as they are used in many of the following chapters. The point is simply that one strategy can be used to reinforce another strategy.

The Eight-Step Process for Planning Your Retail Marketing Strategy. The step-by-step process presented here recognizes that small retailers differ in many ways from large ones when it comes to strategic planning. Our process is a simple and practical one that any small retailer can use without getting involved in complicated, time-consuming, expensive planning techniques. The method recognizes that small retailers are both intelligent and knowledgeable about their own businesses. Thus, what is presented to you here is a skeleton or outline. You must "put the flesh on" to make the outline meaningful for your own small retail firm. No one else can do it for you. Our method is not the only one, but it does work. You can make it work for you.

Our strategy planning method is adapted from Gilmore's "simple, practical method" and can be used for planning your overall marketing strategy or for parts of it such as your product strategy or promotion strategy.[1] The basic tools are a note pad, a conference room, good leadership, and a good management team. If your retail firm is very small, you personally may be both the leadership and the entire management team. That doesn't matter. The method will still work for you. Get your note pad ready. You have many questions to discuss and answer.

Here are the eight steps in planning your retail marketing strategy:

1. Record your current marketing strategy.
2. Identify strategic marketing problems.
3. Divide current strategic marketing problems into core-strategy areas and supporting-strategy areas.
4. Formulate alternative strategies at both core and support levels.
5. Evaluate these alternatives in various combinations.
6. Choose your new marketing strategy.
7. Plan the details for implementing your new marketing strategy.
8. Set performance standards and monitor feedback.

Step 1: Record your current marketing strategy. Don't attempt to short-cut the process at the very beginning (or at any later point) by saying to yourself, "Well, we all know our current marketing strategy, so let's move on to the next step." The odds are that your current marketing strategy isn't written down and is quite fuzzy at best in the minds of your management people. If your strategy is well defined, recording it will be easy. However, for many small retailers the recording step will act as a means of forcing reflection about what the marketing strategy actually is. Ask yourself, "Based upon past marketing actions and activities, how can I best describe our marketing strategy—to the extent that we have had one?" In attempting to honestly answer this question you should

1. Reexamine your company and marketing objectives.
2. Describe your target markets and your success in serving them.
3. Examine the environment in which the past and current marketing strategies operated.
4. Describe the five P's of your current marketing mix.
5. Determine how well the management tasks of planning, implementing, and controlling are being performed.

Once this information (along with numerous information gaps) is down on paper, you have a basis for moving ahead. You have now (perhaps for the very first time) recorded your current marketing strategy to the extent that you have one and to the best of your ability.

Step 2: Identify strategic marketing problems. If the current marketing strategy is less than perfect, one or more strategic marketing problems may exist. Some of these may have surfaced when you were going through step 1. Remember, you are looking for *strategic* rather than *tactical* problems. These could exist in either the core or supporting strategies or both. Ask yourself, "Given the changes that have taken place and that are likely to take place, how valid is our strategy?" You are looking for both weaknesses and unrealized strengths. In doing so, be careful to distinguish between symptoms of problems and the actual problems themselves. Actual problems are often complex and difficult to identify.

If your investigation discloses the existence of strategic marketing problems, you will want to determine and precisely define the elements of these problems. If no strategic marketing problems exist for your retail firm, you are in the enviable position of being able to ask yourself the positive question, "What unrealized opportunities exist?"

Step 3: Divide current strategic marketing problems into core-strategy areas and supporting-strategy areas. Assuming that some strategic marketing problems (or opportunities) do exist, you are now ready to determine whether they are in the core strategy and/or in supporting strategies. A problem in your core strategy will usually be the result of a significant change in either your target markets or the environment. Such problems may call for more complete strategy revisions than do problems found in supporting-strategy areas. For example, if your core strategy was built around a superior store site location as a major differential advantage, what happens to your strategy if some outside factor makes your site location less desirable? Obviously, you need a new core strategy built around a new or adjusted differential advantage.

Problems in supporting-strategy areas will involve less dramatic changes but will require them more frequently. Because the differential advantage remains, their solution may be easier and less costly.

Up to this point you have (a) recorded your current marketing strategy, (b) identified strategic marketing problems, and (c) determined whether such problems are with the core strategy and/or supporting strategies. You now know where you stand. You are in a position to "look at the map" to see where you want to go with your small retail firm.

Step 4: Formulate alternative strategies at both core and support levels. Once the problems have been determined, you can begin the creative process of formulating new alternative marketing strategies. This process considers both core and support levels, even though problems were identified at only one level. This is usually necessary in order to arrive at combinations that are internally consistent.

In this step, restrict yourself only within the broadest of boundaries. That is, consider that anything is possible, given your firm's objectives and resources. Eagerly investigate all alternatives that show promise for success. It is in the next step (not the present one) that you will *evaluate* the alternatives. First, you must gather a list of alternatives.

Alternative strategies are found by actively looking for them. You must look! The number of possible combinations of marketing strategies available to small retailers is almost unlimited. How, then, do you find a few meaningful strategies with so many from which to choose? The process is (a) look for a differential advantage, (b) derive a core strategy from the differential advantage, and then (c) support the core with appropriate supporting strategies. Repeat this process until it is seemingly exhausted, keeping in mind the objectives and target markets. This creative thinking can be quite enjoyable and should also be realistic. See how many alternative strategies you can find to exploit the differential advantage of your small retail firm. Spell out the details of the various alternative strategies at both the core and support levels. You need several good alternative strategies in order to truly evaluate their relative merits in the next step.

Step 5: Evaluate the alternatives in various combinations. In this step you are simply evaluating. You are not yet making a selection. What you want to do here is take a look at both the positive and negative aspects of each alternative. You will be thinking in terms of both core strategy and supporting strategies. Thus, if you had three core strategies called A, B, and C, and each had various supporting strategy combinations, you might have eight alternatives to evaluate: A_1, A_2, A_3, B_4, B_5, C_6, C_7, C_8.

The subscript numbers show that the supporting strategies are likely to be different for each core strategy. In some cases this may not be so.

You are seeking an optimum marketing strategy for a specific retail firm. Some of the questions you should answer with respect to that firm are:

1. What is a realistic sales and profit projection if I follow this strategy?
2. What competition and competitive reaction from other retailers can I expect during and after the implementation of this strategy?
3. What will be the relative effectiveness of alternative strategies for solving the strategic marketing problems identified earlier?
4. To what extent will each strategy impair or enhance the differential advantage of our retail firm?
5. To what extent will each proposed alternative strategy create new problems (or minimize the creation of new problems) in both marketing and nonmarketing areas of our small retail firm?

Step 6: Choose your new marketing strategy. Your new marketing strategy will be a combination of a core strategy and its supporting strategies. The strategy you select is likely to reflect some important subjective elements unique to your small retail firm. For this reason, it is most unlikely that any two retailers will choose identical strategies.

Selecting a retail marketing strategy is an art rather than a science. Any one of many possible strategies could be successful for a small retailer. The one best strategy for a particular small retailer will depend on unique factors. Hence, it is almost impossible for anyone else but you to plan your marketing strategy. If you are going to be involved in the active implementation of your marketing program, you should also play the leadership role in choosing the strategy.

Because there may be several good marketing strategies by which your retail business could succeed, you may want to select a back-up strategy. This back-up strategy would be used only if a major flaw developed in the primary strategy and the flaw could not be corrected by tactical adjustments. An example of such a flaw would be a sudden move by a major competitor (for example, discontinue trading stamps or close a nearby store) that could not have been anticipated. Since much hard work went into the formulation of your back-up strategy, it should be fairly reliable.

Step 7: Plan the details for implementing your new marketing strategy. Up to this point you have been concentrating on *what* it is you are going to do. Now you spell out in detail exactly *how, when, where,* and by *whom* it is going to get done. Although these details may have been implicitly covered in previous steps, you should now explicitly consider the details and plan for results. Items to be covered here are the specific assignment of tasks, scheduling and sequencing, locating outside assistance, planning sources of supply, and the like.

Step 8: Set performance standards and monitor feedback. Your marketing strategy is directed toward the accomplishment of specific objectives. In what ways and to what extent are these objectives being accomplished? You do not actually answer these questions at this point, but you do plan the criteria by which you can later measure the degree of success. The measurement itself comes in the control phase of the PIC management process (see Chapter 12). In the present step you say to yourself, "These are the specific criteria against which we will later judge our performance." Such a statement at this time gives you a standard of performance to use and prevents you from later drawing up performance criteria that make your retail firm "look good" regardless of actual performance.

The second part of this final step is for you to *constantly* be asking, "How are we doing?" You need such continuous feedback for determining what tactical adjustments are warranted to improve strategy implementation and to improve strategy planning for the future.

The eight-step process outlined above is for planning the overall retail marketing strategy. The same eight-step process will be used in future chapters to formulate retail product strategy, place strategy, price strategy, promotion strategy, and people strategy. After you have gone through the strategy planning process for all five P's, you will be able to use this outline in your small retail business.

Filling in the outline takes much hard work. Results will probably be in direct proportion to the effort expended. If you don't plan your own retail marketing strategy, no one will. In effect you then have no strategy. Success, in the absence of a strategy for success, is not likely.

How to Integrate Your Strategy into an Overall Retail Marketing Program

Marketing programs result from integrating the marketing strategy plans for *all* the five P's of the retail marketing mix for *all* the target markets served by your small retail firm. Ideally such a program should be in written form. The time horizon may be one year, or both longer and shorter programs may be used. You should design (following the outline of this book) a set of forms tailored to your business that will make it easy for you to write out your marketing program. Or you may prefer to simply follow the same broad outline each time

you plan your strategy. Whatever format is used, be sure to write out the entire marketing program. This will help you integrate all the separate strategies into an overall program and will give you a document to refer to periodically. Parts of the program will also be communicated to other people in your firm. In attempting to reach the ideal marketing program, you will make some trade-offs among marketing-mix elements and among target markets served in order to reach the profit objectives.

How to Implement Your Retail Marketing Program

You implement your retail marketing program by implementing each and every part of that program to the full extent of the plans you have made. In the implementation phase of the PIC management process, the planned strategies are implemented as adjusted from time to time by marketing tactics. Implementation is accomplished by *organizing* and *directing* work tasks to be performed in cooperation with other people. Briefly, your marketing programs will be implemented by organizing, directing, and tactical adjustments. These are discussed in Chapter 12.

How to Control Your Retail Marketing Program

The retail marketing control process (of the PIC management process) asks the question: in terms of the five controllable variables or five P's of the retail marketing program and the target markets to which this marketing effort was directed, how can we minimize the gaps between planned and actual performance? Control is a continuous process rather than a one-time action. The control process operates at various levels within the marketing system—from the total marketing program down to operational controls, such as reducing merchandise shortages or measuring the effectiveness of a specific advertisement.

In planning for marketing control, you determine (a) exactly what aspects and levels of marketing strategy, tactics, and operations are to be controlled and (b) what standards are to be used against which actual performance will be measured. After planning for control has taken place, the steps in the control process are as follows:

1. Gathering information by measuring actual performance.
2. Management appraisal of performance in terms of deviations from predetermined standards.
3. Making decisions and taking corrective actions.

The Result Is Success

When you follow this PIC management process, injecting into the outline your experience and knowledge of your line of retail trade, the result is **SUCCESS.** Your small retail business will produce customer satisfaction at a profit.

Now that you are a successful small retailer (or at least have a plan for achieving success), be sure to give the appearance of success. Don't overdo it. Don't brag. Make sure you don't offend people. But do let them know that you and your small retail business are successful. Most people, including your customers and employees, would much rather be associated with a success than with a failure.

3

How to Define
Your Target Market

Target Markets for Small Retailers

If you are a small retailer located in a metropolitan area of one million people, how large is your market? Probably your market is but a small fraction of the metropolitan-area population. A retail market is composed of (a) people who have needs with (b) purchasing power in the form of money or credit and (c) the willingness to buy. As a target marketer, you specialize by serving some specific needs for a well-defined homogeneous group of target market customers. You'll make some sales to people who are not a part of your target market, but your marketing program is focused on doing an excellent job of serving some specific needs of those customers you have defined to be your target market.

Defining your target market is one of the most important decisions you can make. It is based upon your differential advantage. It matches your differential advantage with a market opportunity where that advantage can be put to good use in satisfying the needs of customers at a profit. By properly defining your target market, you have taken the first step toward implementing the customer-oriented marketing concept. Figure 2-1 (page 11) pictures the target market as a pentagon (labeled *C* for customer) at the center of our model of retail marketing management. Around this target market customer you will build your retail marketing mix.

What segments of the total market can most advantageously be served by small retailers? Small retailers often select such segments as the following as their target customers:

1. Customers whose needs cannot be filled by big business because the characteristics of the market limit the availability of econo-

mies of scale. Examples of such markets are the geographically isolated small town and the market for customized goods and services.

2. Customers whose demand fluctuates seasonally or by some other short cycle. Examples are tourism, recreation, holiday markets, and the sale of seasonally produced products by small retailers.

3. Customer's needs that can be filled without the expenditure of large lump sums of capital. In other words, small retailers do best in those markets where growth is possible with small increments of capital on a pay-as-you-go or a borrow-as-you-go basis.

4. Customers who can be attracted and kept via strong customer loyalty. For example, customers who can be obtained by inexpensive word-of-mouth advertising from present satisfied customers are attractive targets for small retailers.

5. Customers who have a favorable attitude toward small business. For example, one small retailer may patronize another whenever possible.

6. Customers with a strong group identity. This is especially true if the small retailer is a well-known member of a group.

7. Customers whose buying habits or patterns are incompatible with the methods and business practices of big retailers. An example is the customer who purchases at the convenience food store because he requires more locational or time convenience than is offered by the supermarket.

8. Customers who place a high value on the advice and expertise of a specialist. Small camera shops, hobby shops, and sporting goods specialty stores cater to such customers.

9. Customers whose needs require a product (a combination of goods and services) in which the proportion of goods is low and the proportion of services is high. Many small retail service firms provide both technical and personal services to this market.

10. Customers requiring special services. The small pizza parlor that provides "free" delivery serves such customers.

11. Customers who seek products that are perishable (from either a physical or fashion viewpoint). Small retail bakeries and high-fashion apparel shops are examples.

12. Customers who can be served at a lower cost by a small retailer. Low overhead and flexibility of operations sometimes give small retailers a cost advantage over larger competitors, who may experience diseconomies of scale that more than offset their economies of scale.

13. Customers who can be effectively appealed to without large expenditures for mass-media advertising. Many small retailers reach target customers via personal selling, good location, and the innovative use of "minor" advertising media such as specialty advertising.

14. Customers who place a high value on their personal relationship with the people of the small retail business. What tavern, local restaurant, or ice cream shop could succeed without an owner/manager and employees who were in rapport with the customers? The image of the business is the image of its people.

15. Customers may also favor small retailers for external reasons. For example, in many localities the liquor retailing laws tend to restrict the number of establishments under a single ownership.

These fifteen situations describe markets that tend to favor small retailers. Although the list is far from complete, most small retailers will be able to identify their success and that of other small retailers with one or more of these market situations. Analyze your present target market in terms of this list. Then add to or otherwise modify the list to reflect the customer needs and situations that account for your success. By the time you have completed this book you will

recognize that your target markets are related to the interaction of your differential advantage with (a) inherent market characteristics, (b) consumer behavior, (c) your marketing mix, and/or (d) external environmental variables.

The Market Segmentation Process for Small Retailers

The definition of your target market is a subjective process. It is an art rather than a science. This process, which many successful retailers use to define their target markets, is known as *market segmentation.* In the next few paragraphs you will be given some ideas with which you can conceptually define your target market. The next section of this chapter offers suggestions for making your market definition operational by actually locating your target market customers.

The market segmentation process divides the heterogeneous total market into smaller groups of customers that have rather homogeneous characteristics of significance to the retailer. These smaller groups of customers are called *market segments.* A market segment that you decide to serve becomes a target market for your retail business.

An analogy may help explain the idea of market segmentation. Imagine for a moment a large container filled with mixed nuts, the kind people eat at parties. Included are peanuts, cashews, filberts, pecans, walnuts, and those large nuts that no one ever eats known as Brazil nuts. This large container of nuts is similar to the total market. Now, if you wanted to segment the nuts into internally homogeneous groups, you could easily do so. What *segmenting characteristics* could you use? Obviously, you could use *variety* (putting cashews in one pile, peanuts in another, and so on) as a segmenting characteristic. Other characteristics you might use are size, color, nutri-

tional content, taste, density, shape, smell, cost, and so forth, depending on the purpose for which you were doing the separating. Markets are segmented into smaller groups of customers in a similar manner.

In segmenting the total market to define your own market segment, you will first decide which combination (more than one is usually necessary) of segmenting characteristics to use. All store retailers, for example, will use a geographic characteristic to help define the segment that becomes their target market. Segmenting characteristics are also known as *dimensions.* A fairly comprehensive list of segmenting characteristics (of dimensions) of a market is shown in Table 3-1.

The segmenting characteristics shown in Table 3-1 are *demographic* characteristics. Many statistics are available for these demographics from government agencies, trade associations, and other sources. For this reason, such characteristics are often used in the attempt to define a target market. Other types of segmenting may, in fact, be more meaningful to a small retailer, but they will be more difficult to operationalize. *Benefit segmentation* is an example. It suggests that markets should be defined according to the benefits different customers seek. Thus, customers who seek the same benefits (for example, late hours, acceptance of credit cards) are viewed as a market segment without regard to many of the demographic characteristics. Benefit segmentation could be viewed as a form of market segmentation based upon consumer behav-

Table 3–1.
Some Characteristics or Dimensions
By Which to Segment Markets,
With Partial Breakdowns

1. *Sex* Male, female	7. *Family size* 1, 2, 3, 4, 5, more
2. *Age* 0–5 Preschool 6–12 Preteen 13–19 Teenage . . . . Elderly, etc.	8. *Family life cycle* Young single Young married, no children Young married, youngest child preschool Older, no children at home, etc.
3. *Marital status* Single Married Separated Widowed, etc.	9. *Religion* Catholic Protestant Jewish, etc.
4. *Income* Under $5,000 . . . . Over $25,000, etc.	10. *Race* White Black Oriental, etc. 11. *National origin* Irish Italian, etc.
5. *Occupation* Professional Managers Foremen Skilled craftsmen Students Retired, etc.	12. *Social class* Upper-upper Lower-upper Upper-middle Lower-middle Upper-lower Lower-lower
6. *Education* Grade school or less Some high school High school graduate Some college College graduate Professional or graduate school, etc.	13. *Housing* Own or rent Single or multiple unit Time at present residence Seasonal pattern 14. *Geographic* Rural Urban Suburban Driving time

ior. Another creative approach involves *life-style segmentation.* Under this approach, the small retailer segments according to *activities* (such as hobbies, entertainment, membership), *interests* (such as family-centered or job-centered), and *opinions* (on social issues and so on).

From this discussion of market segmentation one may conclude that the process can get quite complex. Indeed it can. But it need not, especially for a small retailer. Two principles you can use to help you in defining your market (and in planning other parts of your marketing program) are

(1) the principle of market simplification for small business and (2) the principle of market dominance for small business.

The principle of *market simplification* for small business simply tells us not to make the problem of market selection (or any other marketing problem) any more complex than necessary. In an attempt to prove their sophistication, small retailers sometimes emulate big retailers. To do so in selecting a target market strategy would be a big mistake for a small retailer. Keep the problem as simple as possible. Strip away the fancy trimmings from the complex techniques of big business in order to clearly identify your alternative market opportunities.

The principle of *market dominance* for small business states that within any given segment that a small retailer has selected as a target market, he should be able to command enough sales (that is, share of market segment) to exercise some degree of market dominance over that segment of the total market. This principle should hold true for your primary target markets but not necessarily for other segments from which you obtain some of your business. This principle poses the question: What is my optimum share of market in any given market segment? You should have enough sales to exercise at least some degree of mar-

ket dominance. Otherwise, you probably should not cater to that market segment, because marketing will be inefficient, turnover will be slow, marketing costs will be excessive, and so on. Here are two market selection strategies that illustrate the principle of market dominance.

1. A small retailer attempts to obtain 5 percent of the total market by obtaining approximately 5 percent of each of twenty market segments.
2. A small retailer attempts to obtain 5 percent of the total market by obtaining approximately 50 percent of two of the twenty market segments.

Clearly, if the characteristics used to segment the market were meaningful, strategy 2 is superior in terms of marketing efficiencies. Remember, however, that you are seeking an optimum share of a given market segment. An optimum is not a maximum. To obtain a maximum (all you can get) will probably cost too much to be profitable.

The two principles work together. They tell you to do your own thing and not to copy your big business competitors. They also tell you that if you selectively define your target market, you will be able to profitably exercise some of the advantages of a big fish in a small pond.

Suggestions for Making Your Target Market Definition Operational

Now you must move from a conceptual definition of a target market to an operational definition by which you can actually locate and/or identify your target market customers. This is a big step. Depending on the characteristics you used to segment and the preciseness with which you wish to locate your target market, you may or may not be able to perform this step without the assistance of an outside marketing researcher. This chapter's appendix gives an example of a small retailer who hired a consultant to help redefine his target market. The consultant used a questionnaire survey, which yielded a number of leads for revising the retailer's marketing strategy.

Many outside sources of assistance are available to the small retailer (or his consultant) for locating the target market. Studies done by similar but noncompetitive retailers are one source. For example, any small health food retailer could benefit from a study done in Atlanta, which gave demographic and life-style characteristics of health food shoppers and nonshoppers.[1] The local city planning office, the Chamber of Commerce, the bureau of business research of a local university, and trade publications and associations are sources of statistical data and other help. The government documents librarian of a nearby university or public library will assist in finding and using U.S. Census data. The Small Business Administration has also published a small booklet called *Practical Business Use of Government Statistics.*

Depending on the characteristics used to segment and the statistics available in your locality, several methods are available for locating your target market. The five-step approach outlined below is a compromise between mere intuition and the hiring of an expert to do the job. In this approach you attempt to solve the market-location problem by using relatively "free" outside sources such as those mentioned above. The five steps (which are explained in greater detail in the article from which they are quoted) are as follows:

1. Define the "typical" customer or client in terms of basic characteristics (e.g., white males, females 30 to 50 years old, etc.).
2. Select one characteristic and, using census or other demographic data, locate and plot those areas under consideration which have relatively high densities of individuals possessing that characteristic.
3. Using the next characteristic, repeat step two. Continue the procedure until all characteristics have been plotted.
4. Locate the overlap areas which contain the highest densities of all characteristics. These constitute the target market.
5. In the event that all high-density areas (i.e., those having the highest income, the largest number of young males, etc.) do not neatly coincide, subjectively weight each characteristic according to its relative importance. For example, a high income might be considered twice as important as the proper age.[2]

These suggestions apply generally to many types of small retailers. Other approaches to operationalizing a target market definition include developing customer lists, developing prospect lists, and using directories. Forecasting sales is another area entirely. A sales forecast should not be prepared until the marketing strategy upon which the forecast is based has been developed.

New and Changing Markets

Change is one thing a small retailer can count on. Because markets are multidimensional, change will usually be taking place in several directions at once. For example, people are entering and leaving the market every day by moving, acquiring new interests, getting married, becoming homeowners, and so forth. As the importance shifts from one market dimension or characteristic to another, the entire market may be regrouped into a different set of market segments. For example, the large number of working wives and the lesser emphasis on family living is restructuring the market for many products such as prepared foods, fast food restaurants, clothing, and leisure products. Alert small retailers can take advantage of such changes by being innovative marketers rather than simply competitive marketers. Here are some examples: (1) A corner druggist inexpensively added a drive-in window to service customers who wished to shop without leaving their cars. (2) A New York woman became a $100-a-day neatness expert by creating the market of organizing the messy lives of executives and others.[3] (3) A Texas carpet retailer, by cooperating with real estate firms, developed as a new residential market those persons who had been trying unsuccessfully to sell their homes for several months.[4]

As a small retailer, you can increase your sales in one or more of the following ways:

1. Sell more of your present products to your current customers.
2. Sell new products to your current customers.
3. Sell your present products to new customers.
4. Sell new products to new customers.

Whatever combination of market strategies you use, try to be innovative and open-minded. Don't accept as a fact what may be merely a myth. For example, regarding the elderly market, are the following statements fact or myth?

1. Most old people are poor people.
2. If older people do indeed have money, they don't spend it.
3. Everyone wants to stay young; ergo, old people relate to young marketing.
4. Old people's buying habits are ingrained and here to stay.

The source from which the above statements were taken demonstrates all four statements to be myths and goes on to cite government statistics showing that households headed by a person fifty-five or older account for purchases of 42 percent of smoking supplies and tobacco other than cigarettes, 41 percent of coffee, 37 percent of all over-the-counter drugs, over 35 percent of lawn and garden products, and nearly 32 percent of paper towels, napkins, and tissues.[5] These statistics point out the importance of getting the facts and doing a creative marketing job. Even among old people new and changing markets can be found. Many small retailers have become successful by serving previously neglected market segments such as the elderly, the low-income, rural, and minority market segments.

Your Sales and Share of the Market

Techniques for estimating market size and share of the market vary by type of retail trade. Information is available to help you make such estimates. For example, the Small Business Administration has a Small Marketers Aid of four pages. In summary form, this source says:

Knowing what his market share is can help the small retailer to see whether his firm is progressing or falling behind. Is the store getting its fair part of the sales made in its area? Or is it missing sales because the owner-manager is not aware of the potential?

To determine his share of a competitive market, such as the used car market or the furniture market, the small retailer needs facts about: (1) the geographical area in which he does business, (2) his competitors, and (3) total sales for his merchandise lines in his area. The Aid also gives examples of sources of readily available information.[6]

Small retailers are interested in what is happening in the local markets in which they operate. Their market segments within these local markets represent their potential and actual customers. For example, a small supermarket operator in rural Minnesota may be interested by national figures showing that people are eating out more and are buying less of their food from supermarkets. However, he will be more than just interested if this same phenomenon is taking place in his rural Minnesota trading area. This local eating-out trend may influence his marketing strategy toward adding a delicatessen or take-out restaurant to his present facility.

The importance of knowing what is going on in your local competitive market is emphasized by Table 3-2. This table shows how various changes in your sales and those of your competitors affect your share of the market.

Consumer Behavior and Consumer Research Small Retailers Can Do

To be a successful retailer you need to understand consumers. This is not an easy task. Psychologists, sociologists, and many others have spent lifetimes attempting to understand human behavior. The behavior of humans as consumers is complex. During the last two decades, colleges have offered courses in consumer behavior, and many good textbooks have been written entirely about consumer behavior.[7] In this chapter we can do little more than stress the importance of consumer behavior to the small retailer.

In their own way, successful small retailers are students of consumer behavior, and most successful retailers are more than willing to admit that they have much to learn about consumers. However, some small retailers say to themselves or to others, "I know my customers." Knowing your customers is certainly a desirable advantage. It is not, however, the same thing as understanding their consumer behavior. In addition to knowing *who* your market is, you should also seek answers to such questions as *when, what, where, how,* and *why* and at the same time build your own philosophy or overall framework for attempting to explain consumer behavior.

The consumers who patronize your retail store also patronize other small retailers and some large retailers as well. The consumer is influenced by both internal and external factors. Internally, his needs, motives, perceptions, and attitudes will influence what he purchases and where he purchases. However, external influences such as family, social class, the culture, and economic factors will also affect his behavior. One way to view the consumer is as a problem solver who is influenced by these many forces as he carries out his purchase strategy for solving his consumer problems. As a problem solver the consumer would

1. Recognize a problem, such as a deficiency in his current ownership of products.
2. Search for information from sources such as advertisements.
3. Evaluate the information from various sources.
4. Make a purchase decision.
5. Make a postpurchase evaluation of the action taken.

Table 3–2.

How Sales Changes (Yours and
Your Competitors') Affect Your Market Share

If your sales . . .	and the combined total sales of all competitors in the market . . .	any change in your sales indicates that . . .
1. Remain the same	Remain the same	You have maintained your share of a constant market.
2. Remain the same	Decrease	You have increased your share of a declining market.
3. Remain the same	Increase	You have lost some of your share of an expanding market.
4. Decrease	Remain the same	You have lost some of your share of a constant market.
5. Decrease	Decrease	There are three possibilities: (a) You have gained market share if your sales-decline percentage was less than the percentage decline for the total market. (b) You have lost market share if your sales-decline percentage was more than the percentage decline for the total market. (c) You have maintained your market share if your sales-decline percentage was the same as the percentage decline for the total market.
6. Decrease	Increase	You have lost more market share than the percentage decline in sales you experienced.
7. Increase	Remain the same	You have gained a larger share of a constant market.
8. Increase	Decrease	You have gained more market share than the percentage increse in sales you experienced.
9. Increase	Increase	There are three possibilities: (a) You have gained market share if your sales-increase percentage was more than the percentage increase for the total market. (b) You have lost market share if your sales-increase percentage was less than the percentage increase for the total market. (c) You have maintained your market share if your sales-increase percentage was the same as the percentage increase for the total market.

We might say that anything you do as a small retailer to better understand consumers is a form of consumer research. Certainly you can read some books or chapters on consumer behavior. Can you conduct meaningful consumer research on your own customers? Yes, you can do some unsophisticated research from which you will derive benefits. Table 3-3 gives an example.

The consumer research suggested in Table 3-3 is fairly basic. The time, talent, and money requirements are well within the capabilities of most small retailers. Where greater resources are available, more sophisticated and comprehensive consumer research is advocated. Whatever the resources, some attempt to understand the consumer will help the small retailer develop a marketing program that will profitably serve his market.

Table 3–3.

Customer Research the Small Retailer Can Do

The following questions should be helpful in jotting down your conclusions about: (1) the kinds of people you are serving, or seeking to serve; (2) what they need, want, and will buy; and (3) how you can serve them best. Talking with two types of customers can be helpful in working out answers to the questions listed below, especially to questions 1 through 6. One type is your best customers. The other is composed of persons whose income, business, social status, or location makes them logical customers even though they are not regular patrons of your firm.

1. When do my customers like to shop?
   _____A.M. to _____P.M.
2. Do my customers like to shop during evening hours? If so, what nights of the week? _____ . What hours?
   _____A.M. to _____P.M.
3. How do my customers like to pay?
   _____ percent, cash
   _____ percent, 30 days credit
   _____ percent, revolving credit
4. What quality of merchandise do my customers usually buy?
   _____ percent, top quality
   _____ percent, moderate quality
   _____ percent, low quality
5. What type of store has most appeal to my customers?
   _____ percent, new and flashy
   _____ percent, conventional, service type
   _____ percent, discount type
6. How do my customers handle service on the mechanical products they have bought?
   _____ do-it-themselves
   _____ use available service and would buy more if it were available

(continued)

7. Who does most of the buying in the homes of my customers?

_____ percent, the man

_____ percent, the woman

_____ percent, they shop together

8. What is the income level of my average customer?

_____ above average

_____ average

_____ below average

9. What is the age level of my average customer?

_____ elderly

_____ middle aged

_____ young and recently married

10. What is the general attitude of my customer toward his community?

_____ proud and helping to develop

_____ settled and satisfied

_____ disturbed and moving out

11. How does my customer react to new and different merchandise or promotional activities?

_____ responds quickly

_____ responds slowly

_____ responds so slowly that I cannot afford to put great effort into it

12. What major changes has my customer made in the last two years?

_____ income increased steadily

_____ income declined

_____ changed shopping habits

Source: Dwayne Laws, *Pleasing Your Boss, The Customer,* Small Marketers Aids No. 114 (Washington, D.C.: Small Business Administration, 1965), pp. 2–3.

AN EMPIRICAL APPROACH TO MARKETING STRATEGY FOR THE SMALL RETAILER

by William L. Trombetta

A crucial, often perplexing marketing problem which—through the years—has turned entire generations of independent retailers into nerve-wracked insomniacs is that of redetermining the target market of a long-established, but very sick, retail enterprise. A business of this type tends to be handicapped by deeply ingrained management ideas and long-established—though possible disastrous—practices. It also lacks the new-firm advantage of being able to start fresh in a scientifically-chosen location with a carefully conceived marketing plan up front.

When a consultant is called in to deal with a situation of this type, he usually takes the sensible precaution of first investigating carefully what can be accomplished in terms of the firm's existing market structure. In this way, he makes certain what can—and cannot—be done with the present set-up before suggesting what may appear to the proprietor to be radical changes. Remember, he is often dealing with a veteran entrepreneur who has been doing business at the same stand for a long time, is (like most of us) a creature of habit, and is keenly aware of the fact that his methods have produced successful results in the past.

The present article deals with a consulting assignment of this general type. Because the problem is both a common

Dr. Trombetta is assistant professor of marketing and public policy in the School of Management at Case Western Reserve University, where he also serves as the Small Business Institute coordinator in the School of Management. He has had seven years of consulting experience in the area of new enterprise development in his capacity as manager of research and development for the Greater Cleveland Growth Corporation, and has published in the *Journal of Marketing* and the *Cleveland State University College of Law Review*.

and ticklish one, it is believed that the simple approach applied by the author in dealing with this specific case may be of interest to others engaged in counseling small businesses.

Background

In this particular case, the author was brought in as a consultant to assist the management of a fast-food operation that at one point in its 15-year history had achieved an annual sales volume of $249,000. In recent years, however, sales had been declining steadily. They had reached the $140,000 level in the previous year and were still trending downward at the time of the author's initial consultation with the owner-manager.

The latter was a seasoned entrepreneur of proven ability. Originally his operation had been affiliated with a national fast-food franchise, but the parent organization had gone bankrupt while his local outlet was still in its infancy. He had made the best of that bad situation by continuing to operate his local unit under the original franchise name and building it into a moderately successful venture, achieving a relatively high sales volume for an independent fast-food outlet.

Misfortune then struck again, this time in the form of environmental changes in the trade area. These changes, over which the entrepreneur had no control, were at least indirectly responsible for his store's downward slide in sales volume. At this point, the author was called in to attempt to analyze the enterprise's market and develop some insights for a marketing strategy.

Procedure

After thoroughly reviewing the firm's existing situation, the author prepared a simple questionnaire (see appendix), designed to be self-administered by the recipient. This form was distributed to 675 of the client's customers over an eight-week period. To induce the latter group to fill out the questionnaire, the offer was made of a free order of french fries and a milkshake for each completed one returned. The number of usuable questionnaires obtained in this way totaled 138—a number judged sufficient for the purpose at hand.

The analysis which followed focused on basic demographics and purchase patterns. Based on conversations with the owner, "frequent users" of the store's fast-food products were characterized as those likely to make purchases at least once a week. "Light users" were characterized as those making purchases no more often than once a month. Based in part on this rough division, a detailed analysis of the store's current market was attempted.

Survey Results

The results of the survey produced the following highlights:

Two-thirds of the store's customers were under 35 years of age, with slightly more than half in the 18-34 age group.

Approximately 6 customers out of 10 were male.

There was a significant amount of duel-employment in the families patronizing the outlet.

More than half of the families represented had one to three children.

Almost three-fourths of the respondents stated that they patronized fast-food outlets at least once a week—possibly a reflection of the dual-employment characteristics and resultant limitations on the time available for food preparation.

The convenience factor showed up strongly among the respondents' "two main reasons" for patronizing the store. For example, "close to home" was cited by 35 per cent, "convenience" by 14 per cent, and "close to work" by 12 percent.

Most of the customers were drawn from the immediate neighborhood. A surprising 33 per cent of the replies indicated that the customer had walked to the store, while nearly half of those who drove to the store reached it in less than 5 minutes.

Customer loyalty was relatively strong. More than 60 per cent of the respondents stated that this particular store got most of their fast-food business.

Implications for Marketing Strategy

Analysis of the survey results yielded a number of useful leads for revamping the marketing strategy of this small business.

First, several of the findings suggested the desirability of stressing the convenience motive heavily in future advertising and promotional efforts. The high proportion of dual-employment among the store's customers, the large proportion living or working in the immediate area, the relatively large number of walk-in customers, and the customers' own recognition of convenience as a primary reason for this patronage all pointed strongly in this direction.

Second, the prevalence of many young, small families among the store's clientele was another useful piece of information. A possible marketing idea based on this fact would be to supplement the store's traditional single-item pricing with a special "package for four" aimed directly at working parents with one or two children.

Third, while perhaps not clearly apparent from the abbreviated summary of findings presented above, the store's customers appeared to fall mainly into two groups. One consisted of persons working or shopping in a nearby shopping area. This group could be appealed to—at least in part—through complimentary, inter-store promotion. For example, a dry cleaner in the shopping area might agree to display an ad and/or promotional coupons for the fast-food outlet if the latter would reciprocate in similar fashion. The store's second major market segment consisted of nearby residents who either walked or drove a few blocks to make their fast-food purchases. This group could be appealed to via flyers and handbills, possibly featuring an introductory offer or other cut-price special. Advertisements in a community newspaper and spot announcements on a local radio station are other possible ways of reaching this group.

Finally, it should be noted that the store attracted a degree of customer loyalty which appeared unusually strong for the highly competitive fast-food business. Its decline in sales had resulted chiefly from exogenous, environmental changes, rather than from poor management or customer dissatisfaction. The immediate problem, therefore, was one of stepping up promotional activities in an effort to get potential customers into the store for the first time.

Concluding Comments

It is no simple task to redetermine the target market for a declining established business—particularly when the latter is located in an area which is undergoing major physical, social, or economic changes. This article describes a simple technique which was used successfully in just such a situation. The final evaluation of the survey's effectiveness in this particular case must await examination of the fast-food outlets future income statements. However, it is believed to have been successful in accurately describing changes in the market structure of this small business and thus providing the basis for appropriate adjustments in its marketing strategy.

APPENDIX

QUESTIONNAIRE

1. Your Sex:
   Total replies: 138
   a) Male: 59%   b) Female: 41%

2. Is the head of this household:
   Total replies: 138
   a) Male: 83%   b) Female: 17%

3. Age of the person filling out this form:
   Total replies: 118
   a) 13-16: 14%   d) 35-49: 18%
   b) 18-25: 32%   e) 50-64: 6%
   c) 25-34: 29%   f) 65 over: 0%

4. Does the male in this household work full-time?
   Total replies: 108
   a) Yes: 87%   b) No: 13%

5. What is the number of children under 18 years of age living in this house?
   Total replies: 138
   a) None: 37%   e) Four: 5%
   b) One: 15%   f) Five: 3%
   c) Two: 26%   g) Six +:   3%
   d) Three: 12%

6. How many automobiles do you have?
   Total replies: 135
   a) None: 14%   c) More: 47%
   b) One: 38%

7. How often do you purchase ready to eat, carry-out fast food for yourself
   or your family?
   Total replies: 138
   a) Once a month to less than once a month: 27%
   b) Once a week or more: 73%

8. How far did you travel to get here?
   Total replies: 137
   a) I walked: 33%   b) I drove: 67%

   If you drove, it took:
   Total replies: 104
   a) Less than 5 minutes: 47%   c) 5 to 15 minutes: 29%
   b) More than 15 minutes: 24%

9. When you stop for the type of fast food, or carry-out food offered by this
   store, do you often buy here or elsewhere?
   Total replies: 138
   a) Almost always here: 31%   c) Mostly elsewhere: 22%
   b) About half the time here: 41%   d) First time here: 6%

10. For the store that does get most of your business for this type or product—
    what are your two main reasons for buying there?
    Total replies: 157
    a) Close to home: 35%   g) A reputable store: 2%
    b) Lower prices: 9%   h) Close to work: 12%
    c) Better quantity & variety   i) Convenience: 14%
       of food: 24%   j) Attractiveness of
    d) Credit available: 1%   store itself: 2%
    e) Easy parking: 0%   k) Ability to do related
    f) Brand name or nationally   shopping: 1%
       known: 0%   l) Other: 0%

11. Is this the one store that gets more of your business for this kind of product?
    Total replies: 138
    a) Yes   62%   b) No: 38%

12. Are the prices charged by this store pretty much the same for other stores
    like this one?
    Total replies: 121
    a) Prices are higher: 9%   c) Prices are lower: 9%
    b) Prices are about the   d) I am not sure: 14%
       same: 68%

13. Where else do you shop for the type of product that you find at this store?
    By number of responses:
    a) MacDonald's   50%   c) Red Barn   7%
    b) Burger King   32%   d) All Others   11%

Note:
1. Due to rounding, percentages may not sum to 100 in all cases.
2. In cases where multiple answers were given, percentages may exceed 100.

4

How to
Deal With Your
Business Environment

What Your Business Environment Is

The environment in which you operate your small retail business is a given over which you have almost no control, at least in the short run. As shown in Figure 2-1, this environment may be viewed in terms of five major variables:

1. Your economic environment.
2. Your competitive environment.
3. Your political and legal environment.
4. Your societal and cultural environment.
5. Your scientific and technological environment.

Large retailers face a similar set of environmental variables. However, small and large retailers tend to be affected differently by the business environment. For example, certain legislation might be viewed as restrictive by one group and protective by the other. Regardless of size, all retailers will find the environment to be outside their control, at least in the short run. How do you deal with this uncontrollable business environment? Basically, what you do is attempt to understand it as well as you can so that you can adapt your marketing strategy accordingly.

Your Economic Environment

Not even the president of the United States seems to be able to control the economic environment of the country. For most small retailers, the economic environment refers to the condition of the local economy; however, national economic conditions do have an impact on local economic conditions. You are interested in your economic environment because (1) it affects the way consumers respond to your marketing mix and (2) it affects your ability to serve your target market customers. Among the economic conditions that may affect both small retailers and their customers are recession, depression, recovery, prosperity, interest rates and availability of money to both retailers and consumers, employment levels, and general consumer expectations and buying intentions.

As a small retailer, what can you do about the economic environment? It is an uncontrollable variable. Since it is beyond your control, you will want to do your best to anticipate what it will be so you can adapt to it. To anticipate what the economic changes will be, you need simply to read what the so-called expert economists predict. However, the experts are not always in agreement. Certainly the newspapers and television newscasts seem to report more bad than good economic news. Some sources of economic information that small retailers should find especially good are (a) the trade press for their specific line of retail trade, (b) the *NFIB Quarterly Economic Report,* and (c) the bureau of business and economic research at the local university. The trade press will report at least once a year how other retailers of your type view the economy and the impact of economic changes on your type of retail trade. The

NFIB Quarterly Economic Report for Small Business, published by the National Federation of Independent Business (150 West Twentieth Avenue, San Mateo, CA 94403), provides a view of the national economy from the perspective of small business.

To get information on the local economy, you should go to local sources such as the bureau of business and economic research of your local university. Also, pay attention to what is happening in your locality. If your economy is agriculturally based, what are the crop plantings and forecasts for harvest? If your economy is based upon the manufacture of certain products, what is the economic outlook for these products? Your customers will perhaps be working overtime if demand for the products they manufacture is high. If your community is a railroad town or a meatpacking town, ask yourself and seek information on what these industries anticipate for your town in the near future. From the information you and other local retailers are able to obtain, you should be able to properly assess the economic environment of your local market area.

Once you have anticipated what the economic condition will be, it is up to you to adapt your retail marketing strategy in light of the expected conditions. Try to go along with the economic trend and to use it to your advantage rather than fighting against it. For example, if you sell building materials, tools, or hobby items and your town's major employer is expected to be on strike for the next few weeks, what should you do? One strategy might be to promote do-it-yourself projects along with extended credit terms. If you are a fabric retailer, you might have a special sale for "currently unemployed women." If the local economy is extremely prosperous, you might attempt to upgrade the quality of merchandise sold to your present customers. What innovative adaptions can you make in your marketing mix to take advantage of changed economic conditions?

Your Competitive Environment

Competition is a way of life among small retailers. In fact, most small retailers actually enjoy and thrive upon a competitive situation. Your competitive environment refers to the nature and intensity of competition by firms that are trying to satisfy the needs of the same target market customers you are serving.

Competition takes many forms in addition to price competition. You compete in all areas (five P's) of your retail marketing mix. Your competitive environment may also include both large and small retailers. You may compete with retailers whose outlets are of the same type as yours, or you may compete with retailers of different types of outlets. For example, a small retail bookstore may compete with a chain bookstore and the book department of a large department store. In addition, for the paperback portion of its market, it may also be competing with supermarkets, chain drug stores, and discount stores. To be successful, this small bookstore will adapt ,to the competitive environment by selecting as target market customers those segments of the market it can serve best. The bookstore retailer will evaluate the attractiveness of different market segments to various competitors as well as to himself. He will also evaluate the relative attractiveness of competitive offerings to each market segment. Then he selects as target markets those segments in which he will have a good chance of achieving the desired sales and profits.

To be successful, you will also adapt your retail marketing mix to meet the changing strengths and weaknesses of your competitors. For example, if a competing retailer discontinues a particular brand of merchandise, what should your reaction be? If you lower your price, what will competition do? If you raise your price, what will they do? What will you do if a competitor raises or lowers a price?

The structure and amount of competition faced by a small retailer are determined to a large extent by the structure and size of the markets being served. Other significant factors are ease of entry and exit, industry structures, and the directness of competition.

The ease with which competitors may enter and exit your line of retailing is something of a two-edged sword. On the one hand, easy entry due to such factors as low capital and skill requirements may have made it easier for you to get your start. On the other hand, it may mean that many other persons will do likewise until the market becomes overcrowded and unprofitable.

Industry structure is described by economists in such terms as pure competition, imperfect competition, oligopoly, and monopoly. To you as a small retailer, a more meaningful description of structure is whether competition is a national chain, a regional chain, other small retailers, or a boutique in a large department store. Other aspects of industry structure of interest to small retailers involve nonretail levels of distribution. For example, what does the trend toward company-owned units mean for retailing areas such as fast foods, where franchisors are "buying back" units from franchisees? Or, how have the energy shortage, subsequent major oil company policies, and legal developments in some states affected the opportunities and competitive environment for independent service station operators?

In considering the directness of competition we recognize that many products can be substituted for others. This is especially true in our affluent society, where much spending is discretionary to satisfy emotional and ego needs rather than to provide for basic physical necessities. The retailer of lawn care products, for example, is in competition with the lawn care service. The travel agent who is attempting to sell winter vacations in Hawaii or the Caribbean is competing for dollars that might be spent for attending a private college or joining a tennis club.

Your competition is everywhere. What do you do about it? To meet your direct competition, at least, you analyze it so you can adapt to it. You cannot control the competitive environment, but you can take it into account when planning your own marketing strategy. Keep an eye on competition, but don't become obsessed with it. Focus your major attention and efforts on running your own business.

Your Political and Legal Environment

Taxes, zoning, licenses, contracts, rules of regulatory agencies—the list goes on and on. Small retailers hardly need to be reminded that they are operating their marketing programs in a political environment. Most of the marketing activities of small retailers are quite visible. For example, a store's being open on Sunday or the nonavailability of an advertised item cannot be kept secret. Federal, state, and local laws in abundance describe in considerable detail what is legal and appropriate conduct for retailers. Besides regulation, governments also provide assistance for small retailers; for most small retailers, however, the political and legal environment is the one that presents the most problems and the one that takes far too much of their time.

Small retailers who are aware of the rules of the game and take appropriate actions will probably be more successful than those who try to ignore the rules. Are small retailers generally aware of what is going on in the political and legal environment? Yes— if we remember that these people are retail merchants and are not attorneys. For example, one study asked owner/managers of small department stores, appliance stores, sporting goods stores, and toy stores several questions about their awareness of the Consumer Product Safety Commission (CPSC). Only 61.5 percent correctly identified the CPSC as a Federal agency.[1]

Small retailers who are franchisees can also have legal problems. One study of contract-based legal problems of franchisees focused on the importance of the four most common legal difficulties. Most important was sharing advertising costs, second was penalties for violation of contract, third was inspection/evaluation by franchisor, and fourth was minimum performance requirements.[2] From this same study, Table 4-1 points out the characteristics of franchisees with and without legal problems; we can see that legal aspects are tied

Table 4-1.

Characteristics of Franchisees
With and Without Legal Problems

Franchisees with Problems	Franchisees without Problems
Are involved in their first business undertaking	Have previous business experience
Do not have the contract reviewed by their own lawyer	Obtain legal counsel to review the franchise agreement
Accept standard contracts without modification	Request modification of standard agreement formats to accommodate individual or local conditions
Generally have problems in other operational areas of the business	Have generally successful, profitable businesses
Accept franchisors' estimates without verification	Conduct an independent market survey
View business as a zero-sum game	Expect to resolve occasional, routine legal disagreements in the normal course of business

Source: James L. Porter and William Renforth, "Franchise Agreements: Spotting the Important Legal Issues," *Journal of Small Business Management,* 16 (October 1978), p. 30. Reprinted with permission.

in with one's general approach to business enterprise.

We will not review here the major retail marketing legislation of the past century. As a small retailer, what you are really interested in are some legal guidelines for your marketing activities. Table 4-2 shows the selling stages, marketing activities, and potential legal problems that may result for small retailers.

Taxes undoubtedly play too large a part in your interaction with the political and legal environment. Your taxes paid to all levels of government are too high. In addition, you must act as a tax-collecting agent for government. In an article reporting the comments of Senator Gaylord Nelson (head of the Senate Small Business Committee), the observation was made that:

Tax rates discriminate against small business. The largest corporations pay only about 25 percent of their income in federal taxes because of loopholes while many medium-sized firms pay more than 50 percent. Thus a small firm attempting to accumulate capital to grow may be paying twice as much as a giant competitor.[3]

The red tape and the paperwork battle are additional costs to small retailers. Despite presidential promises and some attempts to make reforms, the government is smothering small business with excessive paperwork. Some of this paperwork must be done and some is optional. However, it is often difficult to tell which forms and information requests are optional.

Government at all levels is big government. The cost of dealing with your political and legal environment will probably continue to rise. Some suggested ways of controlling (or perhaps even reducing) the cost of the legal environment include (1) insurance to reduce the risk of litigation and settlements, (2) preventing litigation through better legal planning, and (3) com-

Table 4–2.

Potential Legal Problems
In the Selling Process

Selling Stages	Activities	Potential Legal Problems
Presale	Media Advertising	Deceptive advertising Nondisclosure of material facts Deceptive pricing
	Credit practices	Unfair credit practices Deceptive credit representatives
Point-of-sale	Selling practices	Deceptive packaging, labeling Nonavailability of advertised items Oral misrepresentations regarding product/service
	Contracts	Unfair contract terms Unclear contracts Deceptive contract terms Unfair or deceptive lease contracts
Postsale	Product performance	Unreasonable consumer safety hazard Unsatisfactory performance/quality of product
	Service adequacy	Failure to perform delivery Failure to perform refund/exchange Repair problems (guarantees/warranties)
	Credit practices	Unfair or incorrect billing Unfair creditors' remedies Unfair methods of debt collection

Source: James E. Stafford and William A. Staples, "Legal Guidelines for the Marketing Activities of Small Retailers," *Journal of Small Business Management,* 14 (April 1975), p. 16. Reprinted with permission.

pliance with the laws. Some specific suggestions that follow from these three general principles are that you collect accounts receivable yourself, use a CPA rather than an attorney for tax work, determine whether incorporation is advisable, consider putting an attorney on the payroll, consider using paralegal help, avoid litigation, review insurance, use firm personnel (not attorneys) for routine data collection, monitor legal charges, know local legal fee rates, deal directly with counsel, and use all sources available to stay current.[4]

The same government that taxes you to pay the salaries of bureaucrats in such controversial endeavors as OSHA also provides a considerable amount of assistance to small retailers. For example, the Small Business Administration has several management assistance programs such as ACE, SCORE, and SBI, which enlist volunteer executives, retired executives, and college students and professors to provide management assistance to small retailers. Such assistance is usually free. Why not select one of your marketing problems for a trial of one of these services?

What can you do about your political and legal environment? First, know the law. Second, take the trouble to get involved in the political process. You may find that the best way to do this is through a local merchant's association or nationally through a trade association. For example, as a local grocer or package store owner, you may wish to work against a "bottle bill" that would require a deposit on all containers of carbonated beverages. Such a law would raise your cost of doing business. However, you probably serve customers on both sides of the issue. If you are truly against litter and also against higher costs, you must be very careful about how you participate in

such an issue. At the national level, the National Federation of Independent Business is the largest organization representing the interests of the broad spectrum of small business in Washington. In the final analysis, you deal with your political and legal environment by adapting your retail marketing strategy to it. You are a small retailer, not a lawyer.

Your Societal and Cultural Environment

Your societal and cultural environment is reflected most directly in the attitudes and behavior of your potential customers. They think and act in certain ways and they expect small retailers to think and act accordingly. Acceptable societal norms such as customs (both old and new) carry every bit as much weight as do laws in telling a small retailer what is and is not acceptable retailing practice. In fact, they sometimes carry an even greater influence. For example, in a small farming community, there may be no law regarding which evenings retailers are open, but if the merchants have customarily been open on Friday or Saturday night, group action will be necessary to effectively change that custom.

The behavior and attitudes of customers do change. How do some of the following changes affect your retail business? More wives are working outside the home. People are more interested in the quality of life. More people have more leisure time. The importance of discretionary time is increasing in relation to money. Inflation and energy shortages have changed consumption and living patterns. The family is undergoing many structural changes. Lifestyle changes of many other kinds are boosting the sales of such products as convenience foods, athletic equipment for

newly popular sports such as tennis and soccer, health products and services, and small cars. At the same time, these life-style changes reduce the market for some products such as baby food, cloth diapers, flour in 25-pound bags, big cars, and single-family housing.

What are your social responsibilities as a small retailer? Your principal responsibility is to do an outstanding job of satisfying the needs of your customers. This is your economic responsibility and your role in society. Your output is also measured in social terms as well as economic terms. Retailers are the most frequent contacts most people have with the business world. As a socially responsible retailer, you can do your part to convey the benefits of our free-enterprise economic system to your public.

Our society is made up of your customers. Social problems are numerous in this society. Some social issues (such as minority and female employment, pollution, and consumerism) are closely related to your retail business. The question you should ask yourself is not *whether* you will become involved in social issues but *how* you will be involved. Is your social responsibility limited to what is specifically required by the law? Should you sometimes look beyond what is most profitable in the short run?

You do need to be realistic as well as idealistic. Although you cannot afford the luxury of doing nothing, you must be able to afford what you do in the social-responsibility area. Some examples of things you might do that are not expensive are (a) ask suppliers for written explanations of the ecological effects of their products, (b) be active in civic and church organizations, (c) implement your own voluntary policy for hiring women and minorities, and (d) engage in ethical marketing practices.

Consumerism is a term that has been with us for more than a decade. What is consumerism? It is simply an organized attempt on the part of consumers to protect their consumer rights from being infringed upon by practices of business. The rights of consumers are most often quoted from former President Kennedy's Consumer Advisory Council as (a) the right to safety, (b) the right to be informed, (c) the right to choose, and (d) the right to be heard. If all marketers, including small retailers, had adopted and were properly implementing the consumer-oriented marketing concept, consumerism would not exist.

How does consumerism relate to small retailers? Certainly the consumer protection legislation of the past several years has had an impact. However, consumerism has been directed more toward big business. Perhaps the reason is that big business is simply an easier and more economical target for the organized consumer advocates. Small businesses may or may not have been doing a better job of satisfying consumer needs. Even today, consumers do not have to travel to the ghetto to find examples of questionable business practices among small retailers. However, most small retailers are doing a good job, and small retailers do have the advantage of close face-to-face relationships with their customers.

As a small retailer, you must decide whether you are interested primarily in "moving merchandise" or in acting as a "purchasing agent" for your customers. Regardless of how hard you try, you cannot completely satisfy everyone. In fact, some consumers complain unfairly in an attempt to "rip off" the retailer. Most consumers will be fair if they are treated fairly. However, they do regard themselves as the retailer's customers—not the manufacturer's. For example, if a customer buys a toy at your toy store and his child breaks that toy within the next few days, what does your customer do? He doesn't usually write or call the toy manufacturer. Most often, he will return to your store for a replacement or a refund. He is your customer. In the future, he may not buy toys made by that manufacturer, but he will continue to be your customer if you take care of him. And repeat business is profitable business.

What can you do about consumerism? Get involved by learning what the current consumer issues are. Know the specific requirements for your store as a result of legislation on "truth-in-lending," "truth-in-packaging," product safety, "truth-in-advertising," and so on. Take positive steps to educate your customers by explaining details of your products and services, explaining product features, and demonstrating proper and improper product usage. Another positive step you can take is to form a consumer advisory group made up of some of your customers; such a group can periodically advise you from a consumer's perspective about ways to improve your store. You can also take steps to train your sales personnel in all phases of their work. Then continually check up on them to see if they are performing as trained. For example, have a customer bring in a complaint to see if your people properly handle it. Be sure to take advantage of the fact that you are small. Establish a good face-to-face rapport with your customers.

Your societal and cultural environment may involve some unique problems associated with your location or your line of retail trade. For example, a small retailer in a low-income area faces a different set of problems than one in a wealthy resort area. Whatever the environment, become aware of it, adapt to it, and plan your marketing mix accordingly. Also keep in mind that the environment is changing. Social customs do change. The strength of some social forces may, in fact, be overestimated. Be willing to experiment and take some risks. Who would have believed a few years ago that many Cadillac owners of today would be pulling up to the self-service island and pumping their own gasoline?

Your Scientific and Technological Environment

Both business and consumers have traditionally placed a high value on technological change. Technology affects small retailers in the products sold and in the selling process itself. Electronic technology has been a major force for change in retailing for the past few years and will continue to be so. For the most part, big retailers in the mass-merchandising area have invested more in electronic systems than have small retailers. Nevertheless, many small retailers now have either their own small systems or connections with the system of a larger firm such as a supplier. Electronic technology includes such things as computers for information processing and storage; television cable systems for nonstore retailing; point-of-sale (POS) automatic checkouts, which may utilize optical scanners to "read" prices and other information such as a universal product code (UPC); electronic ordering systems with or without automatic reorder; shoplifting detection equipment; and electronic funds transfer. We will not describe electronic technology in retailing in this book.[5]

A gap exists in retailing (and in most fields) between what is technologically feasible and what is practiced. Some things that are possible are too costly. Part of the gap can also be explained by management and employee resistance. For example, a retail clerks' union may resist a technological change that would displace union workers. The most important resistance probably comes from consumers. For example, so-called "automatic" supermarkets have generally failed. Many supermarkets that are currently using automatic checkouts continue to mark the price on the product at added cost. Customers apparently are not yet willing to give up the price mark that they can read, even though the optical scanner doesn't need it. Consumers will probably change, but not overnight. What percentage of the readers of this book pay their bills by telephone rather than by check?

How do you as a small retailer interact with the scientific and technological environment? It does create new markets and new products. For example, the toy store that didn't stock electronic football the first Christmas season it became popular missed many sales. Technology also creates opportunities in how you operate your business. You must decide not what technology *can* do but what it *should* do. To do so, you should fully understand the options open to you. Even though you don't need technical knowledge, you do need to understand the consumers in your target market and the marketing mix and techniques by which you are currently successfully serving them.

How to Deal with Your Environment

The foregoing descriptions of the five areas of your business environment have included some suggestions on how to deal with each one. These concluding remarks will be more general.

How should you deal with your environmental variables? Remember, they are *variables;* they do change. In the short run, at least, they are uncontrollable. They affect your retail marketing mix and the way potential customers respond to that mix. In the short run you must anticipate change and adapt to it. In the long run you can, individually and collectively, have some influence on the environmental variables.

In the short run, your effectiveness in dealing with the environment may be limited to your ability to predict the direction, force, and effects of change. A good sense of timing also helps. Your inherent flexibility as a small retailer will allow you to quickly adapt your marketing strategies and tactics. Your smallness allows the advantage of flexibility to work for you. However, you must use this advantage. It is not automatic. You may also run up against some of your disadvantages as you attempt to adapt. The environment can sometimes deal rather severely with a small, localized retailer.

In the long run, your tools for dealing with the environmental variables also include anticipating and adapting. Here, of course, your adaptations are those involving planning, implementing, and controlling of an entirely new overall marketing strategy. For example, you might relocate your store, add a new product line, add or drop certain customer services, or develop a unique new advertising strategy.

Besides your individual adaptations, you may act collectively with others to influence your environment. Some of the important collective-action groups for you to consider are your state and national trade associations. There is at least one for every line of retailing. Most of these associations provide information exchange through conventions and publications. Some also engage in lobbying and governmental relations activities. A few examples are the National Association of Retail Grocers of the United States, the National Association of Retail Druggists, the National Retail Hardware Association, the National Sporting Goods Association, and the National Retail Merchants Association. If you don't know the association for your line of retailing, ask one of your noncompeting retailers, or ask your local librarian to find it for you. Becoming an active member could greatly benefit your business.

Trade associations perform many functions for their members. Some of the more important services they can provide are:

1. Promoting better accounting and record-keeping methods.
2. Sponsoring industry-wide meetings and developing leadership within the industry.
3. Operating a liaison service between federal agencies, the Congress, the industry, and its individual members. Some trade associa-

tions also provide liaison service for their members with state and local governments.

4. Providing publicity and public relations programs for the industry.

5. Fostering industry-wide technical research.

6. Maintaining a labor relations service within the industry designed to prevent work stoppages and promote industrial harmony.

7. Issuing special information bulletins to their members. These bulletins report on current affairs affecting the industry, on government orders and legislation, and other, similar matters.

8. Gathering statistics for the industry.

9. Publishing specialized data concerning their industries. Many of these relate to such activities as promoting sales, educating the public to possible uses of the industry's products, or attracting qualified individuals into employment within the industry.

10. Offering training courses to employees of member companies.

11. Supplying other services to the industry such as credit reporting services, savings on the purchase of insurance, and varied economic studies.

12. Furnishing the industry with specialized technical advice that few small members, individually, would be able to afford.[6]

5

How to Plan Your Retail Product Strategy

The Total-Product Concept

This product you are marketing to your customers is more than a physical thing. The *total product* is the overall goods/services combination of tangible and intangible features offered by the small retailer to enhance the customer's capacity for satisfaction. Your product offering should differ from that of your competitors, and the ways in which it differs should be important to the customers of your target market. For example, if you operate a small camera shop, ask yourself why people should buy a standard-size roll of Kodak film from you rather than from some discount store. If you can think of several reasons, you are at the same time defining your product offering according to the total-product concept.

Many small retailers believe that they buy products from wholesalers and manufacturers in order to sell them to customers. This is true in terms of a very narrow definition of product—if by *product* we mean simply *goods*. This is a rather restrictive meaning. It is also rather uncreative. The creative small retailer does purchase goods (and services) from suppliers such as manufacturers and wholesalers. However, creative small retailers go beyond this. Rather than simply selling to consumers, they act as purchasing agents for their target market customers. This results in the total-product concept. Marketing-oriented small retailers are not merely selling goods and services: they are engaging in the buying and selling activities of marketing in order to satisfy the needs of target market customers. Customers don't purchase rolls of film. They purchase the fun and excitement of taking pictures, the satisfaction of becoming a successful amateur photographer, the memories that photographs bring back, and so on. Successful small retail marketers recognize the difference and plan their total product accordingly.

Your Goods/Services Mix

Your product is a combination of goods and services. It may be mostly goods or it may be mostly services. Your product is likely to contain at least a small proportion of each. Varying the proportions of goods and services is one way small retailers can attain unique product strategies. In general, small retailers tend to offer products with a lower proportion of goods and a higher proportion of services than do big retailers. This tends to hold for specific kinds of retailers such as druggists and grocers. It is even more evident in the so-called service sector of retailing, which tends to be dominated by small firms. Examples are barber shops, dry cleaners, real estate firms, and repair shops. The bundle of customer services you provide along with your major goods or services is an important variable in your goods/services combination.

Customers will categorize your retail firm according to the product offered. Goods and services in various combinations take on certain characteristics in the minds of customers and in the way they shop. For example, most marketing books have classified goods as convenience goods, shopping goods, and specialty goods. A *convenience good* is one that consumers purchase often and with a minimum of effort. A *shopping good* is one that they purchase only after making comparisons for such factors as suitability, price, quality, and style. A *specialty good* is one for which the consumer has such a strong preference that he or she is willing to make a special

purchase effort. For most consumers, candy bars and cigarettes would be examples of convenience goods. Furniture, appliances, and clothing are often considered to be shopping goods. A rare blend of pipe tobacco might be a specialty good. This classification may also be appropriate for classifying many services as well as goods.

Products (goods/services combinations) could also be classified according to their characteristics. For example, consider the products you offer in terms of the following:

1. Unit value
2. Significance of each individual purchase to the consumer
3. Time and effort spent purchasing by consumers
4. Rate of technological change (including fashion changes)
5. Technical complexity
6. Consumer need for service (before, during, or after the sale)
7. Frequency of purchase
8. Rapidity of consumption
9. Extent of usage (number and variety of consumers and variety of ways in which the product provides utility)[1]

Services (or products that are mostly services) can be classified in several ways such as by type of seller, type of buyer, buying motives, buying practice, product characteristics, and degree of regulation.[2] This is because services are so varied and have many unique characteristics. Some of these characteristics are intangibility, imprecise standards, the participation of the consumer in the performance of some services, the participation of the seller in the consumption of some services, the inability to store certain services, the ease of entry into many service businesses, and an abundance of small firms providing competitive (but differentiated) services to consumers.

For purposes of planning your marketing strategy, the following classification of service providers may be helpful. Service establishments can be described as being either instrumental or expressive:

1. The *instrumental service provider* offers a service that the consumer considers primarily as a means to some further end. The consumer wishes to reduce all the costs of consuming the service, including the money costs of the service and the time and effort of traveling to the provider and consuming the service.

2. The *expressive service provider* offers a service that the consumer considers primarily an end in itself. Relative to the instrumental provider, the consumer is willing to spend more time, money, and other resources in the consumption process.[3]

We would expect an expressive establishment such as a restaurant to provide high-quality food and service, at a high price, perhaps not at the most convenient location, with a decor that would enhance the entire experience of the consumer. On the other hand, an instrumental restaurant would provide a medium-quality meal and service, at a low price, in a convenient location, with a decor that could be quite plain.

For all retailers, regardless of the proportions of goods and services in their product mixes, the *convenience, shopping,* and *specialty* classification seems to be most popular. This classification scheme has been extended to include not only types of goods but also the types of stores from which consumers purchase. By cross-classifying type of goods with type of store, Louis P. Bucklin arrived at nine types of consumer buying behavior:

1. *Convenience store—convenience good:* The consumer, represented by this category, prefers to buy the most readily available brand of product at the most accessible store.

2. *Convenience store—shopping good:* The consumer selects his purchase from among the assortment carried by the most accessible store.

3. *Convenience store—specialty good:* The consumer purchases his favored brand from the most accessible store which has the item in stock.

4. *Shopping store—convenience good:* The consumer is indifferent to the brand of product he buys, but shops among different stores in order to secure better retail service and/or lower retail price.

5. *Shopping store—shopping good:* The consumer makes comparisons among both retail-controlled factors and factors associated with the product (brand).

6. *Shopping store—specialty good:* The consumer has a strong preference with respect to the brand of the product, but shops among a number of stores in order to secure the best retail service and/or price for this brand.

7. *Specialty store—convenience good:* The consumer prefers to trade at a specific store, but is indifferent to the brand of product purchased.

8. *Specialty store—shopping good:* The consumer prefers to trade at a certain store, but is uncertain as to which product he wishes to buy and examines the store's assortment for the best purchase.

9. *Specialty store—specialty good:* The consumer has both a preference for a particular store and a specific brand.[4]

How do your target customers classify your retail store and the goods/services combinations you offer for sale? The effectiveness of your product strategy and your overall marketing strategy will depend not only on the actual goods/services mix, but also on how well this mix is communicated to the target customers. Product image is discussed later in this chapter.

Your Merchandise Assortment

Having the right merchandise in your store is very important. It must be in season, the right model, the right style, the right size, the right color, the right fabric, the right brand, and so on. Proper buying combined with a good merchandise budgeting and control system will help insure that you are *right* on all these points. Many successful small retailers are greatly assisted in the buying function by membership in buying groups such as voluntaries, cooperatives, and resident buying offices. Such organizations also frequently offer standardized merchandise budgeting and control systems designed for a specific line of retail trade. If such outside assistance is available to you, take advantage of it. Learn the meaning and importance of the elements of the system and try to fully understand how any deviations you make from the system will affect your product assortment and your profits.

Some small, independent retailers do not use a formalized merchandising system and are successful in spite of it. A simple system that is used is better than an elaborate one that is ignored.

Because buying and merchandise management needs and systems vary considerably by type of retailer and because a meaningful discussion of such systems would necessarily be quite detailed and lengthy, this book does not cover the topics except in a limited way.[5] Our brief discussion asks you to consider the following strategic merchandise assortment questions:

1. What product lines are you going to carry?
2. What items or products within these lines will you carry?
3. How much width will you have?
4. How much depth will you have?
5. How much consistency will you have?
6. How will you use tools such as stock turnover and the stock-to-sales ratio to help you plan your assortment?
7. How does the 80/20 principle apply?
8. How can you effectively use scrambled merchandising to help your sales and profits?
9. How can you create customer interest and a differential advantage by the merchandise you offer?

Product Lines Carried: Width, Depth, and Consistency. The first five questions above are closely tied together. They will be discussed as a unit here, and you should consider them simultaneously as you formulate your product mix.

A *product line* is a group of products that are closely related in some way such as their use, the kind of need satisfied, the type of store in which they are usually sold, or the type of customer. Three examples of product lines are hand garden tools, luggage, and frozen vegetables. Your product-market matching strategy will suggest to you the number of lines to carry, the price and quality range of merchandise within these lines, the lines that will be considered major lines, the complementary or minor lines that should be carried, and so on. Space limitations and the lack of funds for investment in inventories may be major limitations to an expanded product offering.

Once your basic identity is decided in terms of the product lines you will carry, you must then decide what criteria or boundaries are to be established for guiding day-to-day decisions on whether a specific item does or does not belong in your product mix. For example, if you decide that your shoe store should include jogging shoes as a product line, you are faced with additional questions such as how much selection, how many brands, in what sizes, in what price ranges, and whether for both men and women.

To determine whether or not a specific item or product fits the product mix, many successful small retailers think in terms of three basic dimensions. These are merchandise width, depth, and consistency.

Width refers to how many different product lines are found within the store. Thus a store that carried only athletic shoes would have a narrower product line than one that carried dress shoes, casual shoes, athletic shoes, boots, work shoes, overshoes, purses, slippers, shoe polish, and hosiery.

Depth refers to the average number of items offered by the store within each product line carried. Stores that specialize in narrow product lines often tend to concentrate on depth of assortment. Thus, we might expect to find a great depth of assortment in the store that carries only athletic shoes. However, many different sports do exist, and each seems to require its own special shoe; therefore, depth may be greater for the more popular sports such as tennis, running, and golf than for such sports as boxing.

Consistency, the third dimension of the retail product mix, refers to how closely the product lines are related in terms of consumer purchasing habits and end use. Both shoe stores described above have a high degree of consistency in their product mixes. Likewise, a racquet shop that sold all types of products having to do with tennis and racquet ball (racquets, balls, shoes, shorts, warm-up suits, bags, and so on) would have a high degree of product consistency. A low degree of consistency is found where scrambled merchandising occurs, as described later in this chapter.

Your pattern of width, depth, and consistency will change over time as the needs of your market change or as you aim to serve different target markets. Such changes involve major strategy shifts. For the interim, strategy guidelines on width, depth, and consistency can be used to determine whether and how individual products fit into your product mix.

Using Stock Turnover and the Stock-to-Sales Ratio. The rate at which merchandise turns over has an impact on your merchandise assortment—and ultimately on your profits. Turnover (or rate of stock turn) and the stock-to-sales ratio are two tools for planning a balanced stock.

The rate of *stockturn* is the number of times during a given period (usually a year) that the average amount of inventory is sold. It can be calculated for a single item, a group of items, a product line, a department, or for the entire store. As a profit

Table 5-1.

Three Methods for Calculating Stockturn

On the basis of cost	
Beginning inventory at cost	$100,000
+ Ending inventory at cost	140,000
= Sum, which divided *by* 2	$240,000
= Average inventory at cost	$120,000
which divided *into* a Cost of Goods Sold of	$480,000
= STOCKTURN of	**4** times
	per period
On the basis of retail selling price	
Beginning inventory at retail	$150,000
+ Ending inventory at retail	210,000
= Sum, which divided *by* 2	$360,000
= Average inventory at retail	$180,000
which divided *into* a Net sales of	$720,000
= STOCKTURN of	**4** times
	per period
On the basis of units	
Beginning inventory in units	5,000
+ Ending inventory in units	7,000
= Sum, which divided *by* 2	12,000
= Average inventory in units	6,000
which divided *into* Net sales in units of	24,000
= STOCKTURN of	**4** times
	per period

planning tool, stockturn can be useful in both the merchandising and store-layout decision areas. It is the combination of gross margin and stockturn that leads to profits.

You should calculate stockturn on the basis of cost, retail selling price, or in units, depending on your method of inventory. The three should not be confused, and the average inventory should be representative of the period under consideration. Table 5-1 shows the three methods of calculation. Higher profits may or may not result from increased stockturn, depending on how the increase is achieved. High stockturn does have some advantages such as keeping merchandise new and fresh, reducing in-ventory carrying costs such as interest and insurance, and reducing the need for markdowns. On the other hand, too high a stockturn can bring disadvantages such as lost sales due to out-of-stocks, higher mer-chandise costs from hand-to-mouth buying and the loss of quantity discounts, and in-creased handling cost from a high fre-quency of small orders from suppliers. The right stockturn varies by the type of mer-chandise and the overall product and mar-keting strategy you use.

The stock-to-sales ratio is the beginning inventory at retail selling price divided by sales for the period (usually a month). Be-cause these ratios are figured on a monthly basis, they provide guidelines on how large a stock you should maintain to meet customer demands for a given month for any line of merchandise. By comparing your own past ratios or typical industry ratios (adjusted for your locality), you can estimate ideal stock levels.

The 80/20 Principle. The so-called 80/20 principle or 80/20 rule is a way of thinking that can be useful to small retailers. It can be used for evaluating, adding, or dropping products and product lines. As applied to product strategy, the principle states: 80 percent of the products (or product lines) account for only 20 percent of the sales; or conversely, 20 percent of the products account for 80 percent of the sales. The 80/20 distribution is found in many aspects of retail marketing. If you are going to use the 80/20 principle effectively, you must have a pretty good idea of what your ideal product mix should be. Is 70/30 (30/70) closer to the ideal? Or, is 75/50 (50/75) the ideal? If a more balanced distribution is desired, you would seek to add products (or product lines) with exceptional sales promise to those 20 percent that now account for 80 percent of your sales. Your intended result would be a flatter or more even distribution so that 25 or 30 percent of your products would now account for 80 percent of your sales, and the total volume of sales would be expanded. Likewise, you could use a reverse strategy to achieve a more balanced distribution by dropping some of the products (or product lines) from those 80 percent that now account for only 20 percent of your sales.

A word of caution: you must pay close attention to the consequences of implementing such a program. Will the adjusted offering meet the needs of your target market customers? Increased efficiency is not an end in itself. In fact, the target market for many small retailers is composed of customers whose needs were ignored in an 80/20-type distribution-cost analysis of large retailers. Be sure to keep the preferences and needs of your customers as your first priority. Some products simply must be carried in order to support the sales and profits from other products.

How to Make Scrambled Merchandising Work for You. Scrambled merchandising is a product strategy that involves the offering of many unrelated product lines. For example, many supermarkets, in addition to groceries, meats, produce, and dairy products also offer a limited selection of toys, hardware, house plants, health and beauty aids, small appliances, underwear, hosiery, magazines, and rental equipment. Because many customers are interested in one-stop shopping, they will purchase such items at the supermarket even though the selection of items may be more limited within each product line. Supermarkets and other retailers have adopted scrambled merchandising in an attempt to earn greater gross margins and ultimately more net profits.

If you are considering some experimentation with scrambled merchandising, consider the following suggestions. First, make certain that the added line or lines of products will be compatible with the desired image of your store. Second, look for product lines that will not divert your time and effort from your main product. Look for products that need little or no extra marketing effort. Look for seasonal or "one-shot" items. Will the item create some interest and excitement as well as some added sales and profits? For the scrambled items, limit both your width and depth of assortment to the best-selling items. If brand names are important to the customer, be sure that the brand (rather than several brands) you carry is an acceptable one—but perhaps not the most popular one if you can make more profits on another acceptable brand. Consider the use of a rack jobber as a source of supply. Also, consider purchasing experimental items on a consignment basis or on a guaranteed-sale basis. Finally, be quick to discontinue a scrambled-merchandise item or line that does not work out well.

Creating Interest. One reason why some stores are "just plain dull" and other stores are exciting is the merchandise they offer. Not all consumers get excited about the same things. In fact some people almost never get excited about anything. However, the success of the "pet rock" and similar fads does suggest that many people are constantly on the lookout for something new and different. Most consumers, even those who don't especially enjoy shopping, can probably think of at least one store that they really enjoy visiting. The merchandise carried by that store is sometimes the reason. Perhaps it is the completeness of the selection or the fact that the store always displays the latest fashions. A reputation for being one of the first stores to stock new products can be quite important. If your store is viewed by customers as a good place to shop for an unusual gift, the gift sales can be quite profitable throughout the year.

Sometimes you may wish to stock certain items to create interest and excitement even though such items may not sell too well. For example, the Neiman Marcus department store is noted for its unusual holiday gift catalog, which offers such items as a chocolate Monopoly set. A small tropical fish shop capitalized on the excitement of the movie *Jaws* by stocking a miniature shark. Keep abreast of what is going on in the world of entertainment, sports, and fashion. You will then be prepared to associate your products with some of the new and exciting things your customers encounter on television and elsewhere.

Your Customer Services Mix

Your customer services mix is an important part of your total product offering. It comprises those services that accompany the physical product or principal service to make up your total product offering. Some common examples of customer services are credit, delivery, returns and adjustments, parking facilities, and extended store hours. A rather comprehensive list is given in Table 5-2. Such a list could be used to compare your customer services mix to potential customer services you might wish to consider.

What are the important strategy questions you face regarding customer services? You will want to (1) consider criteria to be used for determining the customer services mix, (2) determine whether you or some other agency will actually perform each service, (3) establish the role or the importance customer service will play in your product strategy, and (4) make provision for change.

Customer Services Criteria. What your target market customers expect is your most important criterion in determining your customer services offering. For example, if they expect credit and/or "free" delivery, make these services available. In fact, do more than make them available. Go out of your way to promote these services to your

Table 5–2.

A Sampling of Customer Services
Offered by Small Retailers

Adjustments	Layout and appearance
Advertising	Lessons
Air-conditioning	Lighting
Alterations	Location convenience
Auditorium	Lockers and checkrooms
Baby strollers	Merchandise information
Bottle returns	Message service
Bridal registry	Money orders and traveler's
Bulletin boards	checks
Carry-out to car	Music
Check cashing	Notary public
Cleanliness	Paging service
C.O.D. orders	Parking
Cooking schools	Party counseling
Coupon redemption	Personal shopping service
Craft classes	Play rooms or areas
Credit	Postal services
Customer complaints	Repair service
Delivery	Returns and allowances
Display	Rest rooms and lounges
Door man or automatic door	Shopping carts
Drinking fountain	Special orders
Express checkout lanes	Telephone calls out free
Fashion shows	Telephone ordering
Gift certificates	Testing before buying
Guarantees	Trade-ins
Hours	Trading stamps
Installation	Unit pricing
Interior decorating service	Utility bill payment agency
Layaways	Wrapping

Source: Adapted from William H. Brannen, *Successful Marketing for Your Small Business* (Englewood Cliffs, N.J.: Prentice-Hall, Inc., 1978), p. 174. Reprinted with permission of the publisher.

customers just as you would promote merchandise to them. Don't try to skimp on providing the desired services. Such false economizing may lose you some customers to a retailer who is generously providing the wanted services with a smile. On the other hand, make sure your customers (at least a significant number of them) do really want the customer services you are providing.

Other determinants of your customer services offering are store type, location, competition, and overall marketing strategy. Full-service department stores offer many services, whereas discount stores offer fewer services and somewhat lower prices. Most supermarkets don't offer credit and delivery, but most furniture stores and florists do. Suburban merchants offer free parking, but downtown merchants often do not. If competitors are offering a customer service, it may be a necessary defensive strategy to match it even though costs may rise. Sometimes the reverse of the foregoing statements may be true and may provide a key to success for a small retailer. It all depends on your overall marketing strategy, your product strategy, and the way a particular customer service can be used to make such strategies most effective.

Who Performs Services? Who should participate in the performance of customer services? You can offer many services without actually performing them yourself. Credit, for example, can be provided by a bank credit-card system such as Visa or Master Charge. Or a supplier of merchandise may offer consumer credit through the small retailers who sell its products. Delivery can be provided by employing your own people and equipment or by several types of outside delivery services. Repair and installation are examples of other services you may elect to perform yourself or have provided to your customers via an outside provider. From the point of view of the customer, the source of the customer service is less important than his or her satisfaction with the total product (including the service). Remember, if the customer is *your* customer, *you* are responsible for that satisfaction.

Importance of Customer Services. The importance of customer services in your product strategy may vary by such factors as store type. However, small retailers of all types often find it advantageous to stress customer services. *Even in a self-service store, you still need service!* You can readily see the truth of this statement by matching the list of services in Table 5-2 against any self-service store with which you are familiar.

Customer services are important to customers. Besides the prices they pay for products, customers incur other costs of engaging in purchasing activity: (1) monetary costs such as transportation and parking fees, (2) time and effort costs such as waiting in a checkout line, and (3) psychological costs such as those associated with an encounter of an unfriendly sales person. Many customer services may be viewed as a positive step on the part of the small retailer to reduce in some way, or to compensate for, the three kinds of costs incurred by the consumer. What costs do your customers incur to do business with you and what customer services do you provide for them as an incentive to keep coming back?

Your customer services mix will change over time. Customer services have life cycles similar to product life cycles; the same stages of introduction, growth, maturity, and decline can be noted. The life cycles of different services vary considerably in length. A differential advantage may result from being an innovator in the customer services area. Adopting certain customer services such as trading stamps at an early stage certainly has a greater promotional value than waiting until they are on the way out.

Customer services are a major form of nonprice competition for small retailers. The intensity of such competition tends to vary greatly, and you as a small retailer have many strategies from which to choose. For example, you could be a follower, offering only those customer services offered by direct competitors. Most customer services are not difficult to duplicate. However, a total customer services mix might not be so easily imitated by a competitor—or at least not as effectively. Your store might have a strategy of offering essentially the same services but performing them to a higher standard. Or you may offer rather limited customer services but create an effective image by actively promoting them.

As a small retailer, you may be able to design some specific customer services for some rather small target markets. Here is an example: A small supermarket in an older neighborhood, where large homes had been divided into apartments, served a market that included numerous elderly persons. Many of these people did not drive. The owner did not want to get into the delivery business, but he did want to increase his business among the elderly segment. He therefore devised a plan whereby his store would give a free ride home to customers after they selected their groceries and other products. The owner's van was used to provide this service, which was available only on the afternoons when business was normally slow. At a very low cost this "free taxi" service resulted in increased business and increased order size among elderly shoppers who used it. Best of all, the large chain-store competitor in the market area was not in a position to duplicate this service.

Customer Services: Who Pays? Critics sometimes charge that customer services are forced upon consumers. Added customer services are often accompanied by somewhat higher prices. Equity questions arise for the small retailer who is offering "free" customer services. "Free" usually means that the cost is hidden in the price of the product. Not all customers want and use the same customer services. Who should pay? Should the cash customer pay the same price as the credit customer? Should some services such as delivery be "free" or for a specific charge?

Each small retailer must be careful in answering such questions. A total systems perspective would formulate the fundamental question as follows: How does the offering of this customer service affect our total-product offering for each of the target markets we serve?

Product Strategy Affects Your Image

Your image is what people think you are. It depends on product, place, price, promotion, and people—that is, your entire marketing mix. You have an image (positive or negative) regardless of whether you planned one or not. Different people—customers, potential customers, competitors, emloyees, suppliers, and yourself—may have different images of your small retail business. What customers and potential customers think about your store is probably most important. This is your customer image. It is strongly influenced by the products, brands, and services you offer.

Because reality and your product image may not necessarily be the same, you may wish to do some research to see what customers think of your product offering. What they think is really more important

than what you think or what some objective third party might say. For example, even if a testing laboratory says product A is superior to product B, this finding is of little importance if your customers think the opposite.

Positioning your product offering to meet the needs and preferences of your target market customers is the secret. Simply offering the highest possible quality is usually not the answer. Manufacturers attempt to position their products. Large retailers attempt to position (and reposition) their product offerings. You should also position and reposition your product offering so it fits your target market. After evaluating your market and your product, you may try trading up or trading down. Trading up is an attempt to market products of higher status and quality (at least in terms of image) at a higher price. Trading down is the opposite strategy and is probably less often used.

The customer services portion of your product offering has a major impact on your image. For example, consider the packaging you use. Is it a plain brown paper bag? Is it printed? Does it enhance the image you are trying to promote? One tactic small retailers have used successfully to bolster their image of high quality is high-quality packaging. On the other hand, a desirable image can be created by using a completely different approach. For example, a local retail nursery promotes a quality "home-grown" image by cleverly wrapping small starter plants in old newspapers. This also gives customers the impression that costs are being kept low, even though such cost savings may not be passed along to the consumer.

Brands are used by many consumers to identify products. Brands have images, and retail stores often have images that are partially based upon the brands of merchandise carried. As a small retailer, you will want to offer your customers brands that are compatible with your desired image.

Here are three brand strategy options available to small retailers:

1. Sell exclusively under your own brand (private label of the retailer).
2. Sell exclusively manufacturer brands (so-called national or nationally advertised brands).
3. Combine manufacturer and private brands in a desirable proportion.

(Of course, selling unbranded merchandise is a possible alternative for a very limited number of products.)

The small retailer usually is not in an advantageous position to market his own private brand, although there are exceptions. For example, a men's clothing store may put its label on some products, or a tobacco shop may be quite successful with a blend of pipe tobacco carrying the store name. Small retailers often need the consumer confidence attached to the brand names of well-known manufacturers. For example, the image of a small lunch counter may be reinforced by such accessory products as Heinz ketchup or Smucker's jellies.

Small retailers have been able to enjoy some of the benefits of private brands that are owned by such suprafirm organizations as voluntary group wholesalers and cooperative wholesalers. Some of these benefits are the nonavailability of such brands to competitors and the resulting inability of consumers to make direct price comparisons, higher markup percentages, and prices below those of nationally advertised products.

Once you have determined your brand strategy and evaluated how it will affect your image, you are ready to evaluate individual brands to determine which of those available you wish to carry and how strongly you will promote each one.

Your Strategy for Adding New Products (and Dropping Old Ones)

Consumer needs change, manufacturers develop new products, and progressive small retailers are constantly adding new products and dropping old ones. Although manufacturers may face greater risks when offering new products, retailers also take some chances.

First, selling space available to you is

relatively fixed and must return a profit. If such space is occupied by merchandise that isn't moving, profits will not result. Second, you may have to take substantial price reductions (i.e., large markdowns) in order to get rid of a new-product failure. A third and more important risk entailed by new products is that they will prove unsatisfactory for your customers. Complaints, lawsuits, returns, and lost customers may result.

You can reduce your risk in several ways. For example, you might place an initial order of a small quantity to try the product. By prominently displaying and promoting the new item, you can obtain an early indicator of sales success. Or you may have access to reports from buying offices. You may decide to stock only one size (or a few most popular sizes) of the new item. Also, you might have a trial period during which all new items must be evaluated to be reordered. Whatever system you use, it is clear that you do need a system for deciding which new items to give a try. Your space and your dollars are invested in every new product you accept. Experience has shown that small retailers are often more venturesome and less particular in adding new items. They also often carry too many duplicate items and brands, and they are sometimes slow to drop items for which demand has declined substantially.

Some decision criteria that have been used successfully to select new items are suggested by the following questions:

1. Is the product useful to consumers?
2. What will product profitability be in terms of gross margin and actual net profit after expenses are paid?
3. How much promotion and advertising support can be expected from the manufacturer?
4. Does the new product duplicate an existing item, or is it really new?
5. Is the item compatible with present store operations and image?
6. Will the product help to build store traffic?
7. What has been the past experience with this manufacturer; or, if a wholesaler is offering the product of a new manufacturer, what is the reputation of the wholesaler regarding new-product success?
8. Has the item been test-marketed, and what valid test-market results are available and applicable?
9. Are the appearance and the quality of the package satisfactory?
10. Does the expected retail price represent a value to the consumer?

If you were a large retailer, you would have a buying committee to evaluate new items by means of meetings and formal procedures. As a small retailer, you will make your decision on an individual and informal basis. You will therefore want to have a set of decision criteria prepared before the salesmen come knocking on your door to sell you the "greatest thing since . . . ." You can adapt a list such as the ten questions above to fit your particular new-product buying situation. Also, whenever you decide to add a new item, ask yourself: What item do I drop to make room for this one?

Among the reasons for dropping products are inferior quality, excessive complaints or returns, too many repairs, and decreased sales and profits. Because many small retailers are slow to eliminate items from their inventories on a periodic or continuous basis, sometimes they must take rather severe markdowns to get rid of such items. Successful retailers generally agree that taking a sufficient (but not necessarily severe) markdown soon enough is best. Such a timely markdown not only makes it easier to get rid of the item, but it also enables you to use that money and space for items that sell well at the regular markup.

Many successful large retailers have a company policy of simultaneously *trying* to eliminate a duplicate item each time a new item is added. Such a policy could profitably be copied by many small retailers. First, consider items within the same product line or category. Ask yourself: After I make this change, will sales and profits for the line or category be less or greater? At that point, you may wish to consider adding or dropping an entire product line or product category. Or perhaps you'll simply wish to expand or contract your offering in a line or category. However, a final caution is in order: keep in mind the 80/20 principle and be sure never to forget the needs and wants of your target market customers. Whenever you decide to drop an item, ask yourself which item you should add to best serve your customers.

6

How to Plan Your Retail Product Strategy

(*continued*)

Chapter 5 discussed the major areas of retail product strategy. In this chapter you will learn how to formulate your own retail product strategy. First we shall explore the eight-step approach to planning your strategy. Then a comprehensive example will illustrate the use of these eight steps.

An Eight-Step Approach to Planning Your Retail Product Strategy

Because you are a small retailer, you are a target marketer. Target marketing, when used with the principles of market simplification for small business and market dominance for small business, is your core marketing strategy. We call this your *market-product matching strategy*—the matching of your product offering to meet the needs of your target market customers. The exact form of this market-product matching strategy for your retail firm will depend on your company goals and objectives, your marketing goals, the target markets you have selected, your marketing environment, and the differential advantage(s) your firm enjoys.

Within the entire area of product strategy, then, your market-product matching strategy will almost always be your core product strategy and all other product strategies will be supporting strategies.

Let us look now at the step-by-step

method for planning your retail product strategy. The eight steps apply to the broad definition of product:

1. Record your current retail product strategy.
2. Identify your strategic product problems.
3. Divide current strategic product problems into core-strategy and supporting-strategy areas.
4. Formulate alternative product strategies at both the core and support levels.
5. Evaluate these alternatives in various combinations.
6. Choose your new product strategy.
7. Plan the details for implementing your new product strategy.
8. Set performance standards and monitor feedback.

You should be somewhat familiar with this procedure. It is essentially the method described in Chapter 2 for formulating your overall retail marketing strategy. In the present chapter the eight-step method has been adapted to *product* strategy formulation. The tools you will need are the same. They are a note pad, conference room, good leadership, and a good retail management team. You will concentrate now on the product element of your marketing mix, but the process itself will be very similar when you deal with product strategy, place strategy, price strategy, promotion strategy, people strategy, or overall marketing strategy. Essentially, this eight-step process is an outline that you and your managers can use for your retail firm. It lets you direct your marketing efforts toward the marketing goals you have established.

Step 1: Record Your Current Retail Product Strategy. In this first step you are concerned with recording your current product strategy in the broad sense of *product*. So, what exactly do you record? First, you state in very specific terms your core product strategy—that is, your market-product matching strategy. Do this for each of the target markets you serve. Likewise, each of the eight steps in the process applies to each of your target markets. You probably have one or two principal target markets and perhaps another one or two minor targets. For the minor targets, you may decide to take what business comes your way with little or no marketing effort. Or, if such minor markets are seasonal or sporadic, you may do limited planning for them as the opportunities present themselves. In effect, your product strategy may be somewhat similar from one target market to another, but you should have—and record—a separate strategy for each target market served. Such a recording will help you be sure that you are really target marketing by designing a product to meet the needs of each target market.

What do you record in addition to your market-product matching strategy? You record everything else that describes your current retail product strategy. Record the answers to such questions as those raised in Chapter 5 and those listed below.

1. *Core product strategy*
   a. Does our market-product matching strategy serve the needs of our target market customers?
   b. How could we do this better?
   c. Is it compatible with our overall retail marketing strategy, our marketing goals, our company goals?
   d. Is our retail product strategy compatible with the other elements of our marketing mix—place, price, promotion, and people?

e. Is our product strategy internally consistent?

f. If product is a major part of our differential advantage, does this strength match present target markets best?

g. Should we consider selling more products to present target markets, current products to new target markets, new products to current target markets, and/or new products to new target markets?

h. Other questions (to fit your specific situation).

2. *Merchandise assortment and customer services strategy*

a. How many products (goods/services combinations) are we offering each target market?

b. What is our assortment in terms of product width and depth?

c. Is our product mix consistent or do we use some scrambled merchandising?

d. What is our proportion of goods to services?

e. How does our product strategy compare to that of our competitors?

f. Is our product offering well positioned in relation to the market and competition or should repositioning (such as trading up or trading down) be considered?

g. How well do our products compare to industry averages in such performance criteria as stock turnover and gross margin?

h. What are our best and poorest departments, product lines, product categories, etc.?

i. Ask several of the above questions related to the customer services portion only.

j. What is our complete listing of all the customer services we offer? How does this offering differ for each item and in total from the competition?

k. For which customer services do we have a differential advantage?

l. How do customer services affect our image, our costs, etc.?

m. Other questions (to fit your specific situation).

3. *Product strategy over the product life cycle*

a. Are our present products in the introductory, growth, maturity, or decline stage of their life cycle?

b. What innovations have been made to extend the life cycle of our products?

c. Do our target market customers lead, coincide with, or follow the trend?

d. How have we adjusted other elements of our marketing mix (such as place, price, promotion, and people) as our product has moved from one stage to another in the product life cycle?

e. Other questions (to fit your specific situation).

4. *Product feature and identification strategy*

a. Do we emphasize nationally advertised brands or private-label merchandise?

b. How many quality levels do we carry?

c. Do we emphasize bottom, middle, and/or top of the lines?

d. What role does packaging play?

e. In what ways do we go beyond the manufacturers' warranty?

f. How do our services for such items as installation and repairs compare to our competitors'?

g. Do target market customers identify our store name with certain brands?

h. How much do we know about our product image?

i. Is this image what we want it to be?

j. Other questions (to fit your specific situation).

5. *New product strategy*

a. Do we have a strategy for new products?

b. Does our new product strategy also include customer services?

c. Who is in charge of our new product strategy?

d. How do we find out what new products our target market customers want and need?

e. Do we have a list of set criteria for new-product evaluation?

f. Other questions (to fit your specific situation).

Be honest and as nearly complete as possible in describing your current product strategy. "Tell it like it is!" Once this has been accomplished, you have an information base for moving on to the next step.

Step 2: Identify Your Strategic Product Problems. Unless your current product strategy is perfect, you have some product problems (or opportunities) with which to deal. Some of these product problems may have been indicated in step 1 when you were answering the questions. You should now attempt to specifically identify these strategic problems (not all product problems will be strategic) and define them in operational terms. Your strategic product problems may exist in the core (market-product matching strategy) and/or in any of the supporting product strategy areas. Also, remember that you are looking for *strategic* rather than tactical product problems. Strategic product problems will often relate very directly to place, price, promotion, and/or people strategies because your product strategy is not formed in a vacuum; it is an integral part of your retail marketing mix.

Problems are not the same thing as symptoms of problems. So be certain that what you are identifying is the real problem rather than simply a surface symptom that some product problem does exist. Use the broad definition of product to correctly identify problems. Don't ignore the customer services portion of your product offering. In this step you are attempting to identify all important product problems. Many of these are current problems that could not have been anticipated the last time you reviewed your product strategy.

If your investigation uncovers no serious product problems, ask next what opportunities exist that could be realized by changes in your product strategy. Of course, such changes should not adversely affect the soundness of the present product strategy.

Step 3: Divide Current Strategic Product Problems into Core-Strategy Areas and Supporting-Strategy Areas. This should be fairly easy. We have already stated that the single core-strategy area of your product strategy is most likely your market-product matching strategy. In other words, you determine simultaneously what product(s) you market and to whom you market them. This simultaneous determination means that as a target marketer you are matching market and product. However, markets (and products) do change; when they do, your core product strategy must change. This change will probably be a shift of emphasis in the way you apply your target marketing strategy. For example, your target markets may be redefined along different dimensions. Problems in the core product strategy tend to occur less often than problems in supporting areas; when they do occur, however, the impact may be substantial.

Most product strategy problems are in the supporting-strategy areas. In the list on pages 65–67, note that potential problems in the supporting-strategy area were classified under such headings as merchandise assortment and customer services strategy, product life cycle, product feature and identification strategy, and new-product strategy. This is not an exhaustive list. In step 2 above you have presumably identified those areas that are important to you; if so, then step 3 is somewhat clerical. However, you should not neglect supporting strategies because they help insure the success of the core strategy.

Now that you have (a) recorded your current product strategy, (b) identified strategic product problems, and (c) determined which are core and which are supporting, you are ready to plan for the future. Where do you go from here? What are the options? Where do you want to go?

Step 4: Formulate Alternative Product Strategies at Both the Core and Support Levels. You now begin the innovative process of creating new product strategies. This does not necessarily mean new products, although, in the broad sense, the product offering may be new. The planning of new strategies may take place at both the core and support levels even though problems were identified at only one level. In this step, do not limit your thinking. Product strategies work in combination with each other, in combination with the overall marketing strategy, and in combination with place, price, promotion, and people. In this step you are seeking alternative product strategies; in the next step you will evaluate them.

You find alternative product strategies by looking for them. Where do you look? Here are a few suggestions.

Analyze the product strategies of new retailers. Often, new retailers (whether they are franchises, subsidiaries of large chains, or independent small retailers) will base their new business on some new product strategy. Visit their stores. Talk to their managers. See for yourself exactly how well the new strategy is working for them. Then

ask yourself whether or not such a product strategy will be appropriate for your target market(s). Or perhaps ask how such a product strategy could be adapted to meet the needs of your target market(s).

A second source of product strategy alternatives is the trade press. Trade publications for your type of retail business publish numerous "success stories" of how different retailers succeed in various aspects of the business. Many of these stories may suggest new product strategies for you to consider.

A third source of such ideas is meetings. Your trade group probably has at least one national and one state or regional exposition/meeting. Go to these. Besides being a good place to have fun, such meetings bring together other small retailers with problems similar to yours, as well as product and equipment suppliers. These retailers and suppliers may suggest alternative solutions to your problems.

Other sources of product strategy alternatives are your regular suppliers, your customers (who supply information via want slips, suggestions boxes, and the like), results of marketing research done by you or by suppliers, and changes in the environment (such as legislation).

You can probably add some specific sources to the list above. Successful product strategy ideas seldom remain secret for long. This is true of most successful ideas. As you gather ideas for formulating your alternative product strategies, you will notice that many of them involve more than the area of product (core and support) strategy. They involve the interaction of product with the other parts of your marketing strategy. List *all* the alternatives.

Step 5: Evaluate These Alternatives in Various Combinations. You are now ready to evaluate the product strategy alternatives listed in step 4. In this step you are merely evaluating; you are not yet selecting a specific alternative. Evaluate each alternative and meaningful combination of alternative product strategies in terms of your goals and resources. Consider the potential sales and profits of each, the competitive reactions you might expect, the effectiveness of alternative product strategies in solving current problems identified in step 2 above, effects upon other areas of your marketing mix, and so on.

Each manager on your marketing team may have his own criteria for evaluating product strategy alternatives. To receive maximum input and benefit, you might wish to make up a master list of criteria before the actual evaluation discussion begins. The weighting of individual criteria by individual managers need not be standardized, but some general understanding of the relative importance of each criterion is helpful. If you discuss core strategies first and then discuss alternative supporting strategies, your discussion should be followed by a consideration of various combinations of core and supporting product strategies.

Step 6: Choose Your New Product Strategy. You should now be ready to make a decision. Your product strategy choice is one that you plan to live with for quite some time—probably a year or longer. The new product strategy will be a combination of a core strategy (perhaps the same one you have had) and its supporting strategies. Some parts of your supporting product strategies are likely to be new. The implementation of your new product strategy may require frequent tactical adjustments to get it in "fine tuning."

The new product strategy you select will be the combination that you have decided is best for your retail business at the present time. It need not resemble the strategy of your competitors. Usually your new product strategy will not depart radically from your old one. If a radical departure is involved, it should be based upon good information concerning your target market and should take into account your differential advantage and your goals. You may also wish to select a back-up product strategy. However, you should not plan to go to the back-up unless your primary product strategy proves to be unworkable after it has been given a fair chance and has been adjusted by the appropriate marketing tactics.

Step 7: Plan the Details for Implementing Your New Product Strategy. Your new product strategy results in a new product offering to your market. Implementing it will require that many details be taken care of. In this step you are planning all the plannable details of exactly how your new product strategy is to be implemented. How, when, where, and by whom are certain things going to be done? Any details of implementation that you do not specify in this stage will probably not get done, or at best will be done inefficiently or ineffectively. If you want the product strategy to be in reality what you have decided that it should be, you must spell out the details of implementation. Otherwise, lower-level operating personnel will make up their own rules as they go along.

Step 8: Set Performance Standards and Monitor Feedback. This is a planning step rather than the actual control process itself. You are asking for both quantitative and qualitative criteria to be used later in determining how and to what extent the specific objectives of your product strategy have been accomplished. The actual application of these criteria will come later during the control phase of management. In the present step you are defining what your criteria will be for measuring successful implementation of the planned product strategy.

The second portion of this final step is to plan for constant feedback from the market. With such feedback, you will be able to make your product strategy more effective. The exact form and sophistication of such

feedback will vary, but even the smallest retailer should provide for it.

The eight-step outline above is a format by which you can plan your product strategy. Filling in this outline involves much hard work. You may be tempted to say, "We know what our product strategy is—so let's get on with the business of selling." Such "common-sense" planning tends to yield a "me too" kind of retail store limited by a narrow definition of product.

A Comprehensive Illustration of the Eight Steps in Planning Retail Product Strategy

To illustrate the eight-step planning procedure we'll use a convenience food store called Ed's Quick Market (a fictitious name). Ed's small store is located in a suburb. It is surrounded by apartments on one side and single-family houses on the other. This new area is served by a nearby shopping center containing two major supermarket chains.

Because Ed is a small retailer, his product offering strongly emphasizes the customer services he offers. Ed is a single-store operator but does have long-range hopes of eventually operating several convenience food stores. He and his wife, Mary, are the present management team—and a large part of the store's labor force. They also receive management advice and assistance from their voluntary group wholesaler, a trade association, and other noncompeting convenience food store operators.

The goals, target market(s), marketing environment, and differential advantage for Ed's Quick Market are as follows:

1. *Goals:* For the near future, Ed and Mary are seeking sales and profit growth at the pres-

ent location. A 15 percent sales growth (includes higher prices due to inflation) this year is expected to result in a 20 to 25 percent profit growth. They plan to stay in the same business and serve the same target market.

2. *Target market:* Their target is the residents of the area who are within walking or short-time driving distance to the store. By definition, they choose *not* to serve the same needs as the two nearby chain supermarkets. Extended store hours, convenience, personal and friendly service, and fast purchase time are used to segment the market.

3. *Marketing environment:* The economy is very favorable locally. Residents have high income and enjoy discretionary spending power. The trading area has a large number of working wives, mostly middle-class residents, both families and singles, a greater-than-average mobility into and out from the area, a young-to-middle-age distribution, and a modern life style with emphasis on leisure-time activities.

4. *Differential advantage:* The site location of the store is very advantageous. Other assets are experienced management, time and place convenience to the customer, excellent

physical facilities, and the good image of an established business.

We are ready for the eight-step process of planning product strategy for Ed's Quick Market. Because our example is hypothetical, you will have to make some reasonable assumptions about Ed's overall marketing strategy as well as the strategy in the areas of place, price, promotion, and people.

Step 1: Record Your Current Product Strategy. Ed and Mary know their current product strategy even though it is not written down. They decide this is a good time to put it on paper. This will also let them see if they agree on what the current product strategy is.

They agree that their core strategy for matching market and product is to serve the convenience needs of the people of the immediate area with acceptable goods and a high level of service. They are target marketing toward those people of the immediate area (specifically defined geographically) and realize that they will also get some passer-by traffic from people living outside the area. Their emphasis is on filling convenience needs rather than weekly grocery shopping needs. They are offering convenience and service at a slightly higher price. Target customers are willing to pay for the convenience of not having to enter the shopping center and large supermarket for a few items. Customers demand quality but will accept some substitutes and less-advertised brands. Some passer-by customers are slightly different, but this portion of the business is too small to call for a separate product strategy. Ed and Mary note that they really don't know how well they are serving the target market (or how large a share they are serving). Perhaps some feedback is needed. They have the only

convenience food store in the area, but they compete with many other types of retailers.

Ed and Mary used the list on pages 65–67 as an outline for recording their current supporting product strategies. Their notes were quite lengthy and will not be duplicated here. One thing they did was to describe their entire goods assortment. They also used the list as a checklist for recording the customer services they offered. One item they discussed at length was their store image. They thought it was a good one, but they decided they weren't sure what image the store did have in the minds of customers and potential customers. They also noted that the new products were added from time to time and old products were dropped. They weren't sure that their trial-and-error method for adding and dropping products was as good as it might be.

Step 2: Identify Your Strategic Product Problems. While going through step 1, Ed and Mary made some notes in the margin regarding some items that might involve strategic product problems:

1. Need more feedback from market on market share and how satisfied customers are.
2. Check merchandise assortment—especially for duplicate items.
3. Check customer services mix for cost, usage, and comparison to convenience stores in other areas.
4. Need better definition of desired image and more information on actual image.
5. Need better new-product evaluation method.

They identified several other problems but decided that they were not of the strategic variety—or they were a part of one of the five strategic product problems already identified.

Next, Ed and Mary decided to examine each of the five problem areas more closely to determine (a) how to better define each problem in operational terms and (b) whether they were dealing with the real problem or merely a symptom of a problem not yet truly defined. They also decided to take a positive approach by seeking to identify new opportunities as well as problems. They were currently doing a good business and earning a nice profit, so most of their problems and opportunities focused on how to do a better job.

Regarding problem area 1, they noted that they knew many of their customers by name but knew very little about them. Could census data help? Did the local newspaper have consumer preference data for the area? What differences, if any, existed between current customers and potential customers who did not patronize the store? Could more products be sold to present customers? Ed and Mary decided they could use much more information about the target market and how well their total product offering was meeting its needs. They realized, however, that such information costs both time and money to get. Some compromise would have to be made between the costs and benefits of further information.

The merchandise assortment area, especially that of duplicate items, seemed to be a constant problem. It also tied in closely with the need for a better method of new-product evaluation. They reasoned that a part of this problem might be due to buying from too many suppliers. This problem area definitely required more attention. Did the problem derive from the merchandise assortment strategy or from the implementation of that strategy?

After discussing and investigating possible problems in the customer services mix, Ed and Mary decided that strategic problems did not exist here. If there was a problem, it was simply the age-old one of covering the costs of the services offered.

The image problem area included product strategy as well as all other elements of the marketing mix. Ed and Mary decided their first effort should be to find out what image of the store was in the minds of present customers. From that point, a more comprehensive plan could be formed to determine the product image, place image, price image, promotion image, and people image, which all combined to form the overall image of the store. What should that overall image be? This would take some thought, information, and time.

Step 3: Divide Current Strategic Product Problems into Core-Strategy Areas and Supporting-Strategy Areas. Ed and Mary thought their core product strategy was fairly sound. After all, business was good; they must be doing a few things right. If there was any problem in their core strategy of market-product matching, it was simply finding more market information so they could do a better job. Only with additional information could they tell whether a serious problem (or opportunity) existed in the core strategy. All other strategic product problems identified by Ed and Mary in step 2 were in the supporting-strategy area.

Step 4: Formulate Alternative Product Strategies at Both the Core and Support Levels. Ed and Mary looked in several places for alternatives. They checked the competition, the trade publications, their suppliers, and other sources mentioned in step 4 early in this chapter. From these sources they arrived at a lengthy list of possible product strategy alternatives that could be combined in numerous ways at both core and support levels. Most of their alternatives did not deviate substantially from their present product strategy. Here, for example, are some of their alternatives for the new-product area:

1. Expand selling area in order to add more new products.
2. Add products from new product lines but not from present product lines.
3. Create a checklist of criteria for new-product decisions.
4. Add only new products that have proven successful at other convenience food stores.
5. Try to add new products with higher gross margins.
6. Add only new products carried by the major wholesaler.
7. Add new products only after customer requests.
8. Use a fund of $X to experiment with new products on a revolving basis.
9. Periodically eliminate duplicate items.
10. Feature new products in the store's advertising.

Step 5: Evaluate These Alternatives in Various Combinations. In order to make the evaluation stage more meaningful, Ed and Mary decided to first make up a list of criteria by which they would evaluate alternatives and various combinations of alternatives. They listed the criteria in the form of questions to be answered, and they agreed that no specific weights would be used but that each alternative evaluation would be categorized as (a) unacceptable, (b) acceptable, but lacking in some way, (c) acceptable, and (d) very acceptable and showing real promise. Sorting the alternatives in this way, they felt, would allow them to concentrate on the best ones.

They then used the list of criteria to discuss and evaluate the alternative product strategies. For some of the more promising ones they decided to list advantages and disadvantages in terms of their own store, their company goals, their marketing objectives, and their overall retail marketing strategy.

Step 6: Choose Your New Product Strategy. It was now time to make a choice. Ed and Mary were generally satisfied with their core product strategy and decided not to make any changes there. In supporting product strategy areas they did want to make some changes. First, they felt that they could sell more to present customers if they could find room to stock more items—both present and new items. They were not financially in a position to expand the building. So they decided to see whether present space could be used more effectively. This resulted in some minor changes in fixtures and layout, as described in step 7 below. They also decided to create a new method for dealing with new-product additions and old-product deletions. Their objective here was to increase turnover, improve gross margins, and at the same time serve more convenience needs of their present target market customers. A third area of the supporting product strategy on which they decided to concentrate was that of information. Somehow they were going to get and use (at a low cost) more information about their customers and potential customers and about the image of the store.

Ed and Mary realized that the three changes in the product strategy were not major deviations from their current strategy. Rather, they were the designation of areas for improvement. For that improvement to become a reality, someone was going to have to make some additional efforts. There was not much question who the two "someones" were.

Step 7: Plan the Details for Implementing Your New Product Strategy.

Even though both Ed and Mary would be heavily involved in planning and implementing the new product strategy, they realized from their past experience that some outside help was available. For the space-utilization project, their program involved their own analysis of current space utilization, consultation with a layout expert from their major wholesaler (for a small service fee), the "free" consultation of a representative from a fixtures and equipment firm, and a relatively minor expenditure for a few new fixtures and some modification and rearrangement of present ones. The actual carrying out of the plan was to be delayed for two months in order to (a) make certain the plan was sound and (b) permit the change-over to take place during a period when the store would not be so busy.

The development of a method for dealing with product additions and deletions was assigned to Mary. She was to spend a certain number of hours during the next four to six weeks working on the problem. At the end of that time, she and Ed would agree on a plan. In the meantime, they had both agreed to a general moratorium on buying new products. This would give them a chance to "see the forest instead of the trees" insofar as the new-product problem was concerned. Although they might make an exception where it seemed called for, the general rule was to not buy new items during the period. This also would be helpful in creating a somewhat lower stock level when it came time to rearrange the layout. It wouldn't hurt the working-capital situation, either.

Reflecting on the market information and image area, Ed and Mary felt that solving this problem might take more time and expertise than they could personally give. They wanted good results, but they didn't want to spend a fortune. Who does a good job and works cheap? Ed had recently read in the *Journal of Small Business Management* about some university students and professors, who were working with the Small Business Administration on actual business problems of small firms. He wondered whether his firm and problem might qualify for some SBA assistance, and he decided to call them. The wheels were set in motion, and within three weeks Ed and Mary were having an initial interview with a university professor and three graduate students who were going to thoroughly investigate the problem area—at almost no cost to the store.

Step 8: Set Performance Standards and Monitor Feedback.

In this final step, Ed and Mary were planning what performance standards they would use (probably at the end of one year) to measure how well their new product strategy had worked. They were also planning ways to monitor the market on a continuous basis throughout the year.

Some of the items they discussed were the number of out-of-stocks, a want-slip system, total sales, sales by department and product category, stock turnover, stock-to-sales ratio, level of markdowns, customer complaints, returns and allowances, merchandise shortages, gross margins by department and product category, productivity of shelf space, and other operational merchandise controls. They also realized that this step involved much more than merchandise control because their total product was much more than goods. One area was image. They decided to ask the university-SBA team to make recommendations for setting performance standards and monitoring feedback regarding their image.

Performance standards for the product addition-deletion program could include many of the operational controls mentioned above. However, Mary was not satisfied to simply use such measures. She planned to do a separate sales and profitability analysis for all new products during the coming year. She was planning ways to compare them to each other and to their present products and product categories.

Both Ed and Mary knew that all the quantitative controls for all parts of the new product strategy would produce some interesting (and perhaps very revealing) results. However, they knew also that there was a qualitative dimension to their product strategy. In the final analysis they must answer the question: What should the product offering of our store be?

7

How to Plan Your Retail Place Strategy

What Retail Place Strategy Includes

Your customers want to purchase *when* and *where* it is convenient for them. The customer-oriented small retailer tries to satisfy customer needs by having a place strategy that offers the right products at the right time and place. This chapter and the next describe how to plan a place strategy that will combine with your product, price, promotion, and people strategies to form a successful overall marketing strategy.

Place strategy involves four major areas of decision: (1) your relationship with your suppliers; (2) your location and site selection; (3) retail store layout and image; (4) sometimes, physical distribution.

Relationships with Your Suppliers

The first area includes such questions as

1. The types of channel-of-distribution systems you may join.
2. Your role as a small retailer in the channel of distribution.
3. How channels of distribution change.

4. The area of franchising from the perspectives of both the franchisor and the franchisee.

In order to provide the goods and services your customers wish to buy, you must establish, maintain, and sometimes sever relationships with a number of suppliers. Although these suppliers may be producers such as farmers or manufacturers, they may also be middlemen such as wholesalers, buying offices, and manufacturers' representatives. The remainder of this chapter gives you a framework for deciding what your relationship with your suppliers should be.

Types of Channel Systems

A channel of distribution (or channel system) includes the producer and the ultimate consumer and all the middlemen who help to market the product. Manufacturers often use more than one channel to market their products. Likewise, a small retailer may be a member of several channel systems by helping to market the products of several manufacturers and by purchasing from several wholesalers. Some alternative channels of distribution are:

1. Manufacturer to consumer.
2. Manufacturer to retailer to consumer.
3. Manufacturer to wholesaler to retailer to consumer.
4. Manufacturer to manufacturer's agent to retailer to consumer.
5. Manufacturer to manufacturer's agent to wholesaler to retailer to consumer.

Note that all the above alternatives except the first include a retailer. Actually, because there are many types of retailers, wholesalers, and other middlemen, there are many more channel alternatives than those listed above. Although the small retailer is usually a channel follower rather than a channel leader, it is important for him to understand how the entire channel system works if he is going to use the marketing concept to satisfy his customers at a profit.

Perhaps you consider yourself to be an independent retailer. Or, you may be affiliated in some way with a larger group or organization. Whatever the case, you have probably dealt on a voluntary or contractual basis with many of the same suppliers and sold many of the same products for several years, and you have probably been involved in several forms of cooperation with other channel members. Instead of acting as totally independent businesses, channel members tend to perform certain marketing functions for one another. In other words, coordinated and integrated channel systems seem to be the rule rather than the exception in today's market. What forms do channel systems take? Today's channels of distribution may be classified as follows:

1. *Traditional* or *conventional* marketing channel systems are "those fragmented networks in which loosely aligned and relatively autonomous manufacturers, wholesalers, and retailers have customarily bargained aggressively with each other, established trade relationships on an individual transaction basis, severed business relationships arbitrarily with impunity, and otherwise behaved independently."[1]

2. *Vertical marketing systems* (*VMS*) can be typed as *corporate systems, contractual systems,* and *administered systems.*

   a. *Corporate systems* are pretty much the same thing as integrated chain store systems. These systems, which account for about 30 percent of all retailing, may get their impetus from a retailer (such as Sears) or a manufacturer (such as Firestone).

b. *Contractual systems* have three subtypes: wholesaler-sponsored *voluntary chains,* retailer *cooperatives,* and *franchising organizations.* Each involves a voluntary contractual integration of retail stores (or service units) with the sources of supply. Contractual systems may account for 35 to 40 percent of all retail trade. Franchising has been extremely popular in recent years. Used throughout the history of the automobile for franchising auto dealers, this method has recently been used to bring entire management systems to retail and service firms in such areas as fast foods, car rentals, movie theaters, and motels.

c. The *administered system* entails the vertical integration of a product line or a classification of merchandise rather than an entire store. This system often involves selected retailers cooperating with a comprehensive marketing program developed by a manufacturer.

In actual practice these types of channel systems are often found in various combinations. For example, the wholesaler who sponsors a voluntary chain may also operate a chain of corporate stores. An important point to remember is that being an "independent" retailer in a traditional channel system is not your only channel alternative. You should consider the advantages of a VMS. The amount of independence you must sacrifice for such advantages as lower cost of merchandise, management assistance, and proven marketing programs varies considerably from one VMS to another.

Your Role in Supplier Relationships

The role of the small retailer is to fully understand the channel system and to cooperate with other channel members. In other words, you should do everything possible to help your vendors and their salespeople help you. The wisdom of such a strategy is easy to see when the "shoe is on the other foot." Consider the following:

The customers you like the best are those who treat you with respect and who buy a great deal from your store. You will go beyond the call of business to please these people and retain them as customers. Casual shoppers receive minimum service and few favors, and those who keep bothering you with returns or complaints of one kind or another often receive scant treatment.[2]

Your suppliers are interested in helping you. It is in their own self-interest to do so.

The more you sell to your customers, the more your suppliers can sell to you. As a small retailer, you do not usually hold much power in the channel of distribution because the market you can deliver is relatively small. There are, however, some exceptions. For example, small furniture retailers usually have more channel control than other small retailers because

1. Small furniture manufacturers hold exhibits at central markets, giving retailers the opportunity to play one manufacturer against another.

2. Consumers are able to store-order buy.

3. Many items lack brand identity.

4. Retailers are granted exclusives.

5. Manufacturers offer cumulative quantity discounts. All these industry practices give bargaining power to the small retailer.

Your role is to be a good follower in the channel of distribution by taking advantage of the help offered by your wholesalers, salespeople, independent resident buying offices, manufacturers, and so on. Although some of their services and programs will not fit your needs, many of them will confer numerous advantages. So examine and evaluate what is offered. Some of the benefits you may gain are summarized below.[3]

Wholesalers offer services such as promotional help, market information, financial aid, accounting systems, management policies and methods, and help with long-range problems. Promotional assistance includes securing items to be featured (usually at a price concession) in the retailers' advertising, providing point-of-purchase promotional materials to help stimulate "impulse" sales, providing showrooms where retailers can send their customers to inspect large assortments of merchandise, and coordinating cooperative advertising programs in which manufacturers pay for a part of the cost of advertising placed by the wholesaler or retailer. Wholesalers provide market information on consumer demand, price levels, supply conditions, and new developments. Financial aid to retailers includes open credit and extended dating for seasonal items. Accounting systems, some of which provide marketing data and comparative expense ratios, are provided by wholesalers directly or by competent accounting firms secured by the wholesaler. Many wholesalers also provide help in day-to-day operations such as employee and public relations and management procedures. They also give long-range help in real estate planning, equity financing and insurance counseling. Some of these benefits are "free" to the retailer; others are at a fee. Even when a payment is involved, you may find that the wholesaler can perform such services better and more economically because the cost is spread over many retailers.

Small retailers who sell items that involve new styles and current models need to know what is going on in the central market cities such as New York and Chicago. For this reason, small (and large) retailers of apparel, home furnishings, and similar merchandise often use the services of a resident buying office. Located in a central market city, a resident buying office helps the retailer by performing such services as the following:

1. Advises on best sources of merchandise.
2. Keeps in continuous contact with current market styles and prices.
3. Buys merchandise when the retailer is unable to come to the central market.
4. Follows up on orders.
5. Handles adjustments for returns and canceled merchandise.
6. Facilitates retailers' buying trips by arranging appointments, providing office facilities, and accompanying him or her to manufacturers' showrooms.
7. Sponsors retailers' meetings, buyers' clinics, and fashion coordinating services.
8. Helps plan promotional activities for special events.
9. Provides regular fashion and merchandising reports.
10. Sometimes provides central buying for private brands.

Of course, the major benefit you receive from other channel members is the ability to offer the right merchandise to your customers. However, the benefits described above help you to do a better job. The amount and the quality of the benefits you receive depend not only on the suppliers from whom you purchase but also on how you relate to them. How can you build and maintain good relationships with your suppliers? Here are some suggestions:

1. *Try to understand your suppliers' salespeople and what motivates them.* Two basic characteristics of successful salespeople are empathy and ambition. Because he is empathetic, the salesperson will look at problems from your perspective and try to help solve your problems. Be prepared to ask the suppliers' salespersons for the kind of help you want. Have some suggestions. Because of his ambition, the salesperson is always striving to accomplish his goals. Although as a small retailer you will probably not be able to present the salesperson with a large order, you may be able to help him fulfill another equally important objective. For example, by building a small special display, you may help the salesperson fulfill his quota on this type of advertisement. The sale of even only a few dozen more items as a result of the display may translate into a large percentage increase in sales. This will permit the salesperson to report to his company that he secured an additional special display that resulted in a large sales increase (in percentages) for an additional retail store. This salesperson may thank you by telling you about a good deal or getting you some scarce product.[4]

2. *Treat suppliers' salespeople with respect.* Don't ignore them. Their time is money, and the time they spend on your small account must be productive. Keep appointments and don't waste their time. Also, don't insult the salesperson, his company, or his merchandise—even if it doesn't suit the needs of your store. Be positive and constructive in whatever objections you feel you must make.

3. *See as many suppliers as is practical but concentrate your purchases with a few.* Seeing a large number of suppliers will enable you to get a feel for the market. You will find out what new products are available. Also, you will probably want to add a new supplier from time to time. In order to maximize your importance as a customer, however, you should concentrate your purchases with a few suppliers. For example, if you spread your annual purchases of, say, $1 million evenly among 50 suppliers, you will be a small account to all your suppliers. However, if you concentrate 80 percent of your purchases (that is $800,000 annually) with three or four suppliers, you will be an important customer to each of them. (You may need to spread out the remainder of your purchases quite a bit in order to get the merchandise mix you desire for your store.)

4. *Build and maintain good relationships with other persons in the supplier companies—not only the salesperson.* Pay your bills on time, take the discounts to which you are entitled (*before* they have expired), accept merchandise as ordered, and be fair in returns and complaints to the suppliers.

There are, of course, many other ways to build and maintain good relationships with your suppliers. Experience has probably taught you some methods of your own. Most of your suppliers really do want good relationships with you and your employees. Both parties can profit greatly from such relationships.

New and Changing Channels of Distribution

Channels of distribution change at all levels. An example at the retail level is the recent growth of specialty stores dealing exclusively in athletic shoes and apparel. This change has caused manufacturers and wholesalers of such products to rethink and redefine their own channels. Should they sell to such outlets and risk losing the goodwill of their present retailers? Should they abandon present retailers for the newer store types? Should they operate their own chains of retail stores? What other options should they consider? The answers are not easy and will vary from firm to firm. Likewise, as a small retailer, you will be affected (and possibly benefited) by changes in the channels of distribution. The two kinds of channel changes you should be aware of are

1. The adding or dropping of an individual source of supply.
2. A basic structural shift in the channel of distribution.

Of course, these two kinds of changes may take place at the same time.

The addition of a new source of supply and/or the dropping of a current supplier may seem insignificant, but for a small retailer such a change may require an entirely new marketing strategy. The small retailer's affiliation with a particular supplier may be an important part of the retailer's differential advantage. Thus, if a coveted supplier decided to drop a competitor in favor of making your store its "authorized dealer," all parts of your marketing program would be affected. For example, you would need to decide which products to discontinue to make room for the new products, what pricing changes (if any) to make, how to promote the new items, how to best train your sales and service personnel, and so on.

A basic structural shift in the channel of distribution is illustrated by the sport shoe and apparel example above. Scrambled merchandising (which was discussed in the product chapter) has also led to some basic channel shifts. For example, health and beauty aids, which were formerly the province of drug stores, are now sold in huge quantities by mass merchandisers such as supermarkets and discount stores. Also, the energy crisis of recent years has forced many retail outlets to close owing to a lack of suppliers (for example, retail gas stations). Other examples of basic channel shifts are the takeover of many franchisee retail outlets by the franchisor, the increase in nonstore retailing by the use of such methods as party plans and catalogs, the increase in the renting rather than outright purchase of products, and the rapid expansion of franchising in some product lines. A basic structural shift in the channel of distribution usually occurs for a combination of reasons. For example, improved technology combined with both the self-service concept and an expanding market of price-conscious consumers to create the self-service dry cleaning industry. The impact on traditional dry cleaners was mixed. Some gained and some lost. The effects of a basic channel shift on your retail business could also be mixed. Such changes may occur not only at the retail level but also with your sources of supply. Sources who can supply you with the right merchandise at competitive prices are an asset for you. Therefore you should not only evaluate your reactions to basic channel shifts, but also ask how such shifts affect the competitive strength of your suppliers.

Change is one thing you can count on. New products, new competitors, and new market opportunities are part of the excitement of retail marketing. By having an overall marketing strategy that looks first to serving the needs of a defined target market, you can profitably participate in change.

Franchising

Most consumers today are well aware of the existence of franchising. Many small retailers have considered the possibilities of becoming a franchisee. Some have done so. A few have become franchisors. Spectacular successes and equally disastrous failures have resulted. The rest of this chapter will discuss the *marketing* aspects of franchising, mostly from the point of view of the small retailer. For a more complete discussion of both the marketing and nonmarketing aspects of franchising, you should consult additional sources.[5]

An idea of the importance of franchising can be gained from the following overview:

Franchising in the United States is growing into a dynamic and mature business activity, increasingly accepted and respected by the public, by all levels of Government, and by other areas of the private sector. Sales growth has been steady, employment is on the rise, and movement into foreign markets by U.S. franchisors has accelerated. Franchising has increasingly become highly attractive to many large corporations as a means of diversification, while franchisees are enjoying a competitive edge over other small business entrepreneurs by their use of tradenames, marketing expertise, acquisition of a distinctive business appearance, standardization of products and services, training, and advertising support from the parent organization.

This major force in the U.S. economy is not merely another industry. It is a way of marketing a product or service, and is being successfully adopted by an ever-widening variety of industries and businesses. The remarkable thing about franchising is that it is probably the only form of business entity that, by its very nature, contributes to the creation of new business units.

Franchise sales of goods and services are expected to reach $299 billion in 1979, an increase of 18 percent over the sales reported for 1977, while the number of establishments will be ap-

proximately 492,000 in 1979, up from 450,800 in 1977. Employment in franchising, including part-time workers and working proprietors, is estimated at 4,150,759 in 1977, a gain of over 9 percent from the 1976 level of 3,792,341.[6]

The importance of franchising is also illustrated by the pie chart shown in Figure 7-1. An estimated 31 percent of all retail sales in 1979 was accounted for by franchising. However, as the pie chart clearly shows, most of these franchised sales were by auto and truck dealers. Gasoline stations also accounted for a good-sized slice. Fast foods were third in sales, and the remaining types of franchisees accounted for only a small fraction of sales.

Franchising businesses may be classified into the following types:

1. Automobile and truck dealers.
2. Automotive products and services.
3. Business aids and services.
4. Campgrounds.
5. Construction, home improvement, maintenance and cleaning services.
6. Convenience stores.
7. Educational products and services.
8. Fast-food restaurants (all types).
9. Gasoline service stations.
10. Hotels and motels.
11. Laundry and drycleaning services.
12. Recreation, entertainment, and travel.
13. Rental services (auto and truck).
14. Rental services (equipment).
15. Retailing (food).
16. Retailing (nonfood).
17. Soft drink bottlers.
18. Miscellaneous.

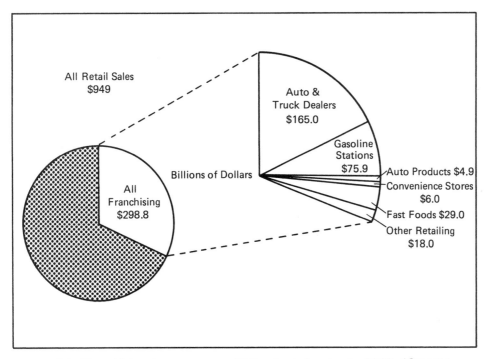

Figure 7-1. Franchising to encompass 31% of retail sales in 1980. (*Source: Franchising in the Economy 1978-1980,* U.S. Department of Commerce)

A drive down any major street in your town or a "walk" through the Yellow Pages of any telephone directory will reveal some of the hundreds of names involved in franchising.

Franchising can also be classified as either (a) traditional or (b) business format. Traditional franchising may be described as follows:

Traditional types of franchising, otherwise known as product and trade name franchising, consist, primarily, of product distribution arrangements in which the franchisee is to some degree identified with a manufacturer's supplies. Typical of this segment are automobile and truck dealers, gasoline service stations, and soft drink bottlers. Together they dominate the franchise field, accounting for almost 77 percent of all franchise sales in 1979.[7]

Business format franchising (which is also referred to in this chapter as the service sponsor-retailer system) has a greater degree of integrated relationships between the franchisor and the franchisee. Business format franchising has been described as follows:

When a franchisor establishes a fully integrated relationship that includes not only product, service, and trademark but also a marketing strategy and plan, operating manuals and standards, quality control, and a communications system that provides for information feed-forward and feed-back, this is known as business format franchising. This form of business is typical of the newer types of franchising that range from fast food restaurants and non-food retailing to lodging, personal and business services, rental services, and real estate services. . . .

Large franchisors continue to dominate business format franchising, with 47 companies accounting for almost half of all sales and for 55 percent of all establishments in 1977. These companies, of which 27 are engaged in automotive products and services, non-food retailing, and fast food restaurants, reported 132,662 outlets with sales of $27 billion.[8]

Another common way of classifying franchising is as follows:

1. Manufacturer-retailer systems.
2. Manufacturer-wholesaler franchises.
3. Wholesaler-retailer franchises.
4. Service sponsor-retailer systems.

Manufacturer-retailer systems have been used for selling cars and trucks, gasoline and related products, and Singer sewing machines. As mentioned above, the auto and truck sales and gasoline service station sales account for a major part (about 80 percent) of all retail franchise sales. In other words, retail franchise sales would be substantially lower without auto and gasoline sales.

Manufacturer-wholesaler franchises are used by the soft drink industry, including such giants as Coca-Cola and Pepsi. The manufacturer sells syrup to the local bottler who processes, bottles, and sells pop to retailers. These many retailers are part of the channel-of-distribution system but they are not part of the franchise system.

Wholesaler-retailer franchises are illustrated by voluntary groups and retail cooperatives. In a voluntary group, the wholesaler owns the warehouse and various affiliated retailers own the retail stores. In the retail cooperatives, the member retailers cooperatively own the warehouse. Voluntary and cooperative chains are common in supermarketing, variety stores, hardware stores, home and auto parts stores, and drug stores. Among the well-known names are Super Valu, I.G.A., Fleming, Red & White, Ben Franklin, Western Auto, Gamble's, Coast-to-Coast, Ace, and True Value. I.G.A. (Independent Grocers Alliance) is an alliance of retail member stores and several separate independently owned warehouses throughout the country. Some large corporate chains such as Walgreen Drugs act as voluntary wholesalers for affiliated stores known as agency stores. Sears and Montgomery Ward franchise agency stores in small towns. These operate mostly as catalog order stores.

Service sponsor-retailer systems are also known as business format franchises, franchising company systems, or idea and service franchises. Service areas include fast food, recreation, campgrounds, entertainment, hotels and motels, travel, business and personal services, and transportation leasing. Some of the familiar names and the corporate franchisors who own them are Burger Chef (General Foods), Burger King (Pillsbury), Pizza Hut (Pepsi), Baskin Robbins (United Fruit), KOA, AAMCO, Holiday Inn, Howard Johnson, Hertz, Manpower, and Putt-Putt.

You may become involved in franchising as either a franchisor or a franchisee. If you have a successful program that can be packaged together for duplication by others, you may become a franchisor. This will allow you to grow very rapidly with a limited amount of your own capital. However, the small retailer more commonly plays the role of franchisee. As a franchisee, the small retailer grants the franchisor some degree of control over his marketing program in return for the proven and successful programs of the franchisor. In particular, the franchised retailer gives up some control over the marketing mix. The franchisor may also determine (to the extent the law permits) the target market to be served by each franchisee. The amount of control held by the franchisor varies from company to company. Whether or not, and with whom you should franchise depends on your goals, your personality, your resources, and industry trends. In the next two sections we will examine the advantages and disadvantages of franchising from the views of both franchisor and franchisee.

Franchising from the Franchisor's Perspective

Successful franchisors make their money from several sources, most of which require the long-term cooperation of successful franchisees. Major sources of revenue include initial franchise fees, royalties, rental of premises, sale or leasing of equipment, sale of supplies, sale of raw materials, sale of franchise products, sale of services such as advertising programs and management assistance, other fees, and the operation of their own retail outlets.

This system offers the franchisor the following major advantages:

1. Franchising offers the opportunity for rapid expansion because investment capital is obtained locally through the franchisees. Franchise fees provide capital to the franchisor; the sale and lease of other items are sources of funds; and at the same time the franchisee is often franchising a large part of the cost of the retail facility.

2. As an owner-operator of the retail unit, the franchisee is often more highly motivated than a hired manager would be. If the franchisor provides good training for the franchisees, good retail management will result.

3. Competitive strength and economies of scale benefit the franchisor (and the franchisee) because the larger franchise organization is operated as an integrated system.

For example, purchasing, advertising, site selection, training, and information gathering can be spread over a large number of outlets.

4. The franchisor avoids many retail operating problems. For example, because the decentralized franchised units are less desirable targets for large labor unions, the franchisor avoids labor relations difficulties. Franchising has been popular in types of retailing that employ large numbers of part-time workers at irregular hours.

Along with these advantages franchisors face two major disadvantages:

1. Franchisors have less control over the channel of distribution. In fact, as we discussed in Chapter 4, conflict between the franchisor and franchisees may even result in legal problems. Franchisees must be convinced through persuasion rather than management edict.

2. The franchisor may make fewer profits than he would if all retail units were owned and operated as a corporate chain. Many franchisors do, in fact, also operate retail units. Figures indicate that company-owned retail units produce higher sales and profits than do franchised retail units. However, these higher sales and profits are often the result of choice locations and the "buying back" of high-volume, profitable units.

How can the franchisor minimize these disadvantages? One method is to choose good franchisees. In the past, franchisors have made the mistake of selecting innovative franchisees rather than day-to-day operational conformists. Franchisors should select franchisees on the basis of credit and financial standing, personal management of operations, past work experience, personality (the ability to meet the public and win respect), health, and educational background.[9] Although different types of businesses may require slightly different qualifications, most franchisors agree on the qualities noted in the following paragraph:

Franchisors in five different kinds of franchise operations, Fast Foods, Automotive, Other Retail, Route, and Labor, agree that the ideal franchisee should be young and married. They are inclined to agree that the husband-wife team is desirable. Perhaps the most important requirement, however, is that the prospective franchisee be financially sound, preferably having considerable savings beyond his franchise expenses. Some college education, or college degree, is favored, with high-school graduation being the minimum acceptable level. Previous experience operating any business is helpful. Personality requirements are relatively simple: franchisors want an energetic, cheerful, cooperative individual. Thinking ability, communication skills, and prior knowledge of equipment are not vitally important.[10]

Franchising from the Franchisee's Persepective

The franchisee may receive the following benefits from franchising:

1. Management training in proven operating methods when the franchise is acquired, and on a continuing basis.
2. Assistance from experienced experts for site selection, inventory control, record keeping, legal needs, and marketing research.
3. Financial assistance.
4. A proven operating system for doing business.
5. An established brand name with proven customer appeal, which will identify the retail franchise outlet.
6. The buying power of the franchisor, which may (if savings are shared) result in lower purchasing price for franchisees.
7. A "turnkey" facility, ready to do business.
8. Large-scale promotional techniques such as professional television commercial productions and "national" promotions.

At the same time the franchisee gains these benefits, he also takes on the following disadvantages:

1. The franchisee may pay fees and a portion of the profits or sales to the franchisor.
2. The franchisee has less control over marketing programs and other aspects of the business and, in fact, sometimes "buys" the complete marketing program of the franchisor.
3. The franchisee may have no guarantee that his retail business will continue; the franchisor may fail or exercise his "buy-back" option, or the franchise may be arbitrarily terminated.
4. The franchisor may require the franchisee to complete many reports and conform to rigid requirements.
5. The marketing program of the franchisor may not be workable in some localities. For example, a resort-area franchise outlet depending on seasonal business may have

special marketing problems and opportunities.

6. Unsatisfactory performance (or a lack of performance) on the part of the franchisor may make the franchise worthless. For example, management training programs may turn out to have little or no value.

The above lists of advantages and disadvantages are by no means complete. However, they do suggest some of the things to check into if you are considering becoming a franchisor or franchisee. If you are interested in learning more about franchising check your local library and write to the International Franchise Association, and contact your nearest field office of the Small Business Administration. The address of the International Franchise Association is 1025 Connecticut Avenue, N.W., Washington, D.C. 20030. If you are evaluating an individual franchise opportunity, the SBA publication, *Franchise Index/Profile,* would be a good place to begin.[11]

Future Outlook for Franchising

What about the future? Are all the good retail franchise opportunities gone? Probably not, but for some lines of retailing, such as fast foods, good locations are much harder to find. *Franchising in the Economy 1977–1979* reports the following trends and outlook:

1. There has been an increase both in the formation of franchisee advisory councils and franchisee associations and in franchisee participation in them.

2. Multiunit franchisees are increasing in number and importance.

3. Because the average person now eats seven meals each week away from home, competition between grocery outlets and fast-food chains bears watching.

4. The newest franchising area is real estate. In 1975 only 3808 franchised real estate offices existed; by the end of 1979 this number had increased to approximately 22,000.[12] The rapidity with which the franchising concept can redefine the competitive structure is amazing!

8

How to Plan Your Retail Place Strategy

(*continued*)

The previous chapter discussed your relationships with your suppliers. This chapter will cover your strategies for (a) location and site selection, (b) retail store layout and image, (c) physical distribution, and (d) formulating your place strategy.

Your Location and Site Selection Strategy

Do you know of any retail firm that sells inferior and sometimes stale products, offers little service, charges slightly higher than average prices, advertises infrequently and ineffectively, and hires incompetent and discourteous sales personnel, but nonetheless does an apparently successful business? If so, the chances are that the business is cashing in one an excellent location. The author is familiar with more than one such firm located near university campuses. Conversely, a retailer who does an excellent job of everything but is handicapped by an extremely poor location may find success very difficult to achieve. A good location is of the utmost importance to your retailing success.

Meaning and Importance. There is a big difference between having a retail location and having a **strategy** for retail location. Your chances of securing the best retail location(s) are greater if you have a good location strategy. Your retail location strategy and decisions that follow may be considered on three levels: (1) the selection of a market area such as a town or city, (2) the selection of a type of location such as the downtown central business district or a planned regional shopping center, and (3) the selection of a specific site. The term *location* is used to refer to any of the three levels. The term *site* is translated into *site type* when referring to the second level; *site* itself usually refers to the third level. The term *site location* encompasses all three levels. Thus, we refer to the overall area of retail store site and location strategy as site-location strategy.

The importance of site-location strategy to small retailers is emphasized by the following comments:

1. Although a good location may be a major factor in the success of many retailers, it is almost impossible for even the best SB (small business) retailer to succeed in a bad location.

2. The advantages of a good location (levels 1 and 2) can be negated by a bad site (level 3).

3. Good site-location decisions must be made continuously (or periodically) because the environment of a retail store does not remain static. It changes constantly by either getting better or worse.

4. Every time the retailer (even the successful one) renews a lease, he has made a location decision.

5. A good retail site is a major complement to but not a substitute for good merchandising strategy.

6. Because the store retailer operates from a fixed site location, he must be conveniently located for the customer to come to him.

7. Site selection is one of the most important factors in the success of SB retailers.[1]

The importance of site location to the small retailer is further illustrated by examining the trade-offs between an ideal location and other elements of the retail marketing mix. Although a good location will probably call for a fairly high rent, the suitability of a particular location is not always indicated by price. Each business has different requirements. For example, the numerous gasoline service stations that have been abandoned in recent years because of the energy crisis have converted to new uses with mixed results. Some continue to remain empty; some have had several unsuccessful tenants; and others have been successfully converted to the retailing of donuts, auto equipment, auto audio equipment, and so on.

Although some common principles may exist, each line of business does seem to have its own specific requirements with respect to site (level 3). Regardless of these differences, however, all types of small retailers should formulate a site-location strategy. Many small retailers mistakenly skip the strategy planning in favor of getting the front door open as soon as possible so they can start ringing up sales. They simply seek an available site or find a vacant building without asking themselves why the building is unoccupied. Is it because the previous tenant (as well as several others before him) was not successful at the site? Might there be something wrong with the site?

In forming your site-location strategy, you should consider the trade-off between location and other elements of your marketing mix. Will a better location enable you to charge higher prices in order to cover your higher rent? Will a better location mean lower costs for media advertising? Some successful retailers say that the cost of such items as advertising and promotion is inversely proportional to the quality of a location, as shown in Table 8-1.

Table 8–1.

The Inverse Relationship
Between Site-Location Quality
And Amount of Promotion Expense

If your site location is:	Then your promotion expense will be:
1. Worst	1. Most
2. Worse	2. Much more than average
3. Bad	3. More than average
4. Average	4. Average
5. Good	5. Less than average
6. Better	6. Much less than average
7. Best	7. Least

Making the correct site-location decision is especially important because of its relative irreversibility. It is much more difficult to change than some other elements of your marketing mix. However, although leases and fixtures represent long-term commitments, changes can always be made at a cost. In fact, if a serious site-location error has been made (and implemented), it may be better to pay the cost of getting out of a bad location than to live with that mistake for several years. Once in a great while a retailer will get "bailed out" from a poor site-location decision through what can only be called "dumb luck." Consider the following case:

Spatial position as a differential advantage is illustrated by the following example. A druggist had a location adjacent to a college campus, but on a thoroughfare infrequently used. The residential area tapped by the converging roads consisted of a mere 200 families. Consequently, the druggist had an extremely precarious existence until the university built a 1500-unit dormitory across the street from his store. He then enjoyed a brisk and profitable business from all the students living in the dormitory—not through his own foresight, of course, but because of his unique location.[2]

The example also illustrates how the uniqueness of a site can represent a differential advantage—and one that cannot be duplicated by competition simply because two stores cannot occupy the same space at the same time. Marketing strategies are successfully built on differential advantages.

Planning Your Site-Location Strategy. Because a unique site can represent such a powerful differential advantage, you will want to do some planning in order to acquire one. The eight-step process used throughout this book can be adapted to plan your retail site-location strategy. Apply the process to the three levels mentioned earlier (market area, site type, and specific site). To help you in this process, the three levels are discussed in the pages that follow.

Another source of assistance you may wish to use at this point is your trade association. Research on site locations has been done for many years. For example, the National Retail Hardware Association publishes through its research foundation a 124-page book called *How to Evaluate Hardware Store Locations.*[3] The supermarket industry and shopping center planners have also been very active in site-location research. However, much of this research has been oriented toward large, multiunit operations and would be misleading or of limited value to the small, single-store operator. Also, the techniques used (such as space/sales share, analog, gravity models, and regression) are sometimes quite complex. If you are going to use such techniques in solving your site-location problems, you should consider hiring an experienced consultant. Before you do this, however, plan your own strategy for site location; then use the consultant to help you operationalize your strategy.

Whether you use a consultant or not, your site-location strategy should be formulated **before** you analyze any specific sites, because your strategy plan will provide the criteria by which to evaluate each site. At this point a basic difference between small and large retailers emerges. Small retailers may skip level 1 entirely. In other words, the small retailer may select a market area (town or city) on the basis of such nonbusiness criteria as climate (for reasons of health) or present family location. Perhaps this isn't the way it "should" be done, but this is a reality of small business. No matter what the size of your business, however, you will find a strategy plan (preferably written) to be of great help in deciding whether to acquire additional site(s), increase the store size at a present site, remodel, move to a new site, terminate or abandon a site, place a site in a new type of location (for example, a shopping center), place a site in a new market area, or carry out some combination of the above.

Analysis using the eight-step process takes place on three levels: (1) market area, (2) type, and (3) site.

Level 1: The Market Area. As mentioned above, some small retailers skip this step by limiting the market area to their home town or city. Limiting the market area in this way may sometimes be a wise choice because it provides the opportunity to operate in familiar surroundings. On the other hand, it excludes many possibly more lucrative opportunities. Even if you have already decided to locate in your home town, don't neglect to analyze the important market-area factors as they apply to your retail business.

The market-area factors of concern to small retailers can be divided into two types: market and environmental. Market factors, which were discussed in Chapter 3, include population and population trends, trading-area size, purchasing power and its distribution, and buying habits. Environmental factors, which were discussed in Chapter 4, include economic considerations such as character of industry, progressiveness of community, and nature and intensity of competition as indicated by store saturation, state and local legislation, and other factors of special interest (such as the presence of a college, a tourist attraction, or an outdoor recreation facility). Finally, the small retailer may have some individual preferences regarding market-area factors. For example, many small retailers prefer the competitive structure (as well as the way of life) offered by a small town.

An example of a company whose site was chosen by paying close attention to market-area factors is Waterbed City, a Florida retailer. The young managers of this firm used site-location research as an important key to their aggressive expansion. *Industry Magazine* reported:

Keith and Michael explain that they carefully research site selections. First, Florida State

Transportation Department statistics are studied, an effort which determined that the Coral Gables store would be passed by 36,000 cars each day. Waterbed City outlets are planned ten to twenty miles apart, each having "high visibility and lots of square footage," observes Michael.

Management also keeps a keen eye on demographics. The 1970 U.S. Census registered a 37 percent increase in Florida over the previous decade, the biggest spurt of any state in the nation. Mid-decade Commerce Department surveys peg Florida's population at 8.2 million; Dade and Broward Counties combined numbered 2.2 million residents.

Florida leads Southeastern states in per capita income, rated in 1975 by the Commerce Department at $5,638, though the region lags behind national figures. And per capita income statistics in Waterbed City territory have traditionally outdistanced state averages.[4]

Level 2: Type Alternatives and Factors. The real question to be answered in level 2 is not whether you personally prefer a regional shopping center to a strip development. The real question is what types of customer traffic (automobile, public transportation, and pedestrian) generation can be expected due to the location type you select? In level 2, you are dealing not with a specific site; you are considering a site-type. For example, you may ask how the traffic expectation or trading-area coverage would change if you located your retail store in a large regional shopping center rather than in a neighborhood business district. Each location type offers different advantages and disadvantages for different retail store types.

Retail type alternatives are usually classified according to descriptive or structural criteria. A typical list might include the following types:

1. *Free-standing locations,* where a retail store is adjacent to no other retailer and therefore depends on its own pulling power and promotion to attract customers.

   a. *Neighborhood stores* located in a residential neighborhood and serving that small trading area.

   b. *Highway stores* located along highways (and intersections of interstate highways) and attracting customers from considerable distances.

2. *Business-associated locations,* where a group of retail stores offers a variety of merchandise lines, works together to attract customers to the area, but also competes against each other for these customers. This type of location can be further classified as either unplanned (or at least not centrally planned) or planned (that is, centrally planned) shopping centers. Each retailer in the *unplanned* center presumably plans for his location on an individual basis.

   a. *Unplanned locations*

      1. *Downtown or central-business-district (CBD) stores* usually have a trade area that varies according to the size of the town or city and the nature of the surrounding area.

      2. *Periphery or edge-of-downtown stores* have lower rents, rely on traffic generated by the downtown, and may sometimes offer parking facilities.

      3. *Neighborhood-business-district stores* are small clusters of retail businesses serving the neighborhood trading area.

      4. *Secondary-business-district stores* were the predecessors of the planned shopping centers, composed of an unplanned cluster of stores (perhaps around a larger store) located on a major intersection of a city.

      5. *Highway-business-district stores* or business strings are adjacent retail businesses strung out along a major highway to form an unplanned shopping area dependent on automobile traffic.

   b. *Planned shopping centers*

      1. *Regional shopping centers* are the largest planned shopping centers; often

they are anchored by two or more major department stores, have enclosed malls, serve a large trading area, and have high rents. In effect, they are "new downtowns" with free parking.

2. *Community shopping centers* are anchored by a junior department store or branch of a major department store and one or two supermarkets. They serve both the convenience goods and shopping goods needs of a section of a large city or several smaller towns.

3. *Neighborhood shopping centers* usually have a supermarket, variety store, drug store, and a few other stores selling convenience goods to the residents of the neighborhood.

The suitability of a particular location type depends on the kind of retail store being considered. For example, a large supermarket unit of a very successful supermarket chain failed in a very successful large regional shopping center, probably because potential customers were unwilling to fight the shopping-center traffic each week in order to do their weekly grocery shopping. Conversely, four department stores are doing extremely well at that same regional center. As a small retailer, you will evaluate location types somewhat differently than would a large retailer.

Market factors should determine your site-location type. Ask yourself where (in terms of type) your target market customers prefer to shop. The location type you select will limit the size of the market area your store will serve. For example, a small store located in a regional shopping center may draw (with the help of the rest of the center) customers from 40 or more miles away, whereas a store of the same size in a neighborhood business district will be pretty much limited to that neighborhood. However, this does not necessarily mean that one store will do more business or make more money than the other.

All stores—even those that sell similar goods and services or constitute different branches or units of department and chain stores—cater to different target markets. For example, the downtown main bank and its various drive-in suburban locations serve different market segments. Supermarkets seek locations both in shopping centers and as free-standing units. Automobile dealers seem to locate in close proximity to other automobile dealers. Success does not seem to be restricted to any single type of location. However, the selections of a target market and of a location type are closely related. Your marketing strategy should take account of this interdependence.

Three examples of the interdependence of target market and location type are provided by the waterbed retailing industry.

Example 1. Waterbrothers, Inc., a manufacturer and distributor of a variety of waterbed and related products with two retail outlets in Buffalo, leased 3000 of the 21,000 square feet in a Taft Furniture store. Waterbrothers manages and operates "The Waterbed Store" at Taft with its own personnel. This leasing arrangement is an attempt to sell waterbeds in a conventional furniture store. The synergetic effect suggests that both the sale of waterbeds and conventional furniture would benefit from the increased customer traffic.[5]

Example 2. New Sleep, a Salt Lake City waterbed retailer, has as its target market the middle-class family. The owner explains that the professional image of the firm (which comprises four stores) and the area's traditional Mormon family value system make family marketing a good idea.

Often one family member will buy a waterbed and then other family members will follow suit. To insure that New Sleep stores are noticed, traffic surveys are taken and sites that 25,000 cars pass per day are selected.[6]

Example 3. A Cincinnati waterbed retailer has two locations designed to attract two distinct target markets. These are described as follows:

The Waterbed Store has two outlets, each with a different look. The new branch, featuring the contemporary, opened on June 11 of this year, in the University of Cincinnati Village. At the original location, in the Mt. Adams district, the funky prevails. The two stores have deliberately distinct looks to capture the market adjacent to their areas. Mt. Adams is high on a hill over looking the downtown Cincinnati area, frequented by tourists. The entire neighborhood of older buildings, some renovated and some not, contains unique shops with diverse items ranging from functional Swedish imported tube furniture to secondhand odds and ends. Italian pizza bakes next to a well-recommended French restaurant. The area is interspersed with wine, crafts baskets, plants, and rocks, all jumbled together on the narrow hilly streets. . . . The new Vine Street store in the U. district . . . is frequented by younger couples and customers from the professional ranks.[7]

The classification of consumer goods and retail stores into convenience, shopping, and specialty types may give you some clues in selecting a location type (see Chapter 4 for a discussion). Rental rates, availability, restrictions, and your own preferences may also affect your choice. Because of the increasing importance of planned shopping centers, let us discuss some of the factors a small retailer might consider in deciding whether or not to select this type of location.

Many shopping center developers and landlords treat small retailers differently than they do major chains and department stores. As a shopping center tenant (especially in regional and community centers), the small retailer does not have the same advantages and disadvantages as the larger retailers. Although shopping center developers and landlords look for successful retailers of all sizes, 60 to 70 percent of the floor space of many shopping centers is occupied by large chains and department stores. A proven successful small retailer may have a fair chance of securing a good shopping center site, but the new (first-store) small retailer is definitely at a disadvantage. Lease-guarantee insurance, available directly and indirectly through the Small Business Administration, may be purchased by the small retailer to make him a less risky tenant. Although it may not always be desirable or feasible, the SBA also offers financial and other assistance for developing shopping centers composed of small retailers.

Some advantages offered by shopping centers are customer traffic, professional management, parking, image, and balanced tenancy. On the other hand, the total cost of occupancy (which includes the costs of finishing the space into a completed store, basic rent, percentage-of-sales rent, maintenance for malls and parking lots, utilities, tax increases, joint promotions and merchants' association) is high. It may also be difficult for the small retailer to project a distinct image or atmosphere in a large center. It is not easy to keep from getting lost in the crowd. Finally, not all shopping centers are created equal. Some are better than others. In some markets, shopping centers have been overbuilt. Population and traffic patterns change.

In other words, once you have made the

decision to use the shopping center type of location, you must devote your energies to choosing the best one(s). This brings us to the discussion of how to select a specific site.

Level 3: Site and Site Factors. Traffic counts, checklists, census data, customer spotting by license plates, and expert advice are available as aids in the actual selection process. Before beginning this process, however, you should formulate a strategy that defines the criteria by which you will judge each site. For example, if your strategy calls for plenty of easy parking, many sites will be automatically eliminated. If you plan to stay open until late in the evening, certain shopping center sites will be unsuitable. Eight criteria to be considered are listed by Nelson:[8]

1. *Adequacy of present trading-area potential:* How much total business volume can be expected (by all sellers of your type) from the people within the trading area of the site?
2. *Accessibility of site to trading area:* Can potential customers, whether *generative* (generated by the store itself), *shared* (resulting from the generative powers of its neighbors), or *suscipient* (in the area for nonshopping purposes), be easily and conveniently served by the site?
3. *Growth potential:* Is the site in a trading area of growing population and income?
4. *Business interception:* Is the site on the major routes to other retailers of products of the same types?
5. *Cumulative attraction:* Do competing and complementary stores share business with the site, thus attracting more customers?
6. *Compatibility:* Do businesses adjacent to the site help each other by interchanging customers?
7. *Minimizing of competitive hazard:* Have you taken into consideration the location, char-

acter, size, and type of present and potential competitors, and does the site minimize such competitive hazards?
8. *Site economics:* In terms of cost versus productivity, what is the efficiency of the site regarding such physical factors as size, shape, topography, and facilities?

Questions such as these will help you understand and define your site requirements. When the actual process of locating your site begins, however, you may run into some very practical kinds of problems. For example, the desired site may not be available, it may not be on the preferred side of the street (sunny side and going-home side are preferred by many retailers), or its positive features may be offset by some disadvantages (for example, it may be near vacant buildings or dead traffic spots). It would be wise to find out the recent success-failure history of the site.

If you are selecting a site within a shopping center (especially a large one), you face additional challenges. Some factors to consider are the effects of center design and nonretail facilities on your site, the importance of corner influence, and whether the center is open late hours and Sundays. Also, in many centers, convenience goods stores and shopping goods stores are grouped separately. This works best because consumer purchasing patterns and parking needs vary for the two types of goods.

Some common shopping center designs are (1) the strip, which may be straight, "L" shaped, or "U" shaped; (2) the mall, which may be open or covered; and (3) the hub or cluster. Each design offers different advantages. For example, the strip offers better visibility from the road, while the cluster offers closer proximity to a major department store.

Corner influence is the value added to a

site because it is located at the intersection of two streets. Corner influence may be quite important in an unplanned business district. It may also have some value for small shopping centers. (Keep in mind, however, that we are referring to whether the shopping center itself is located at an intersection, and not whether a site within it is buried in a corner.) For a large shopping center, corner influence often is negligible.

Although customer interchange between retail facilities and those that are nonretail (such as country branch offices, professional offices, and theaters) is rather low, many retailers welcome nonretail facilities in a center as long as they don't cause parking problems.

Finally, stores that are open when the rest of the center is closed should be located at the front of the center for good visibility and to minimize costs for lighting and security.

What about service retailers? Is a site-location strategy important to them? If your product is primarily a service rather than goods, your location is still very important to your customers. Although a reputation for high-quality workmanship may attract customers despite a poor location, business would be even better at a good location. Even for services that are delivered to the customer in his home (for example, home repairs, plumbing, lawn service, and decorating service) potential customers are inclined to do business with firms that are conveniently located. The site-location problems of service retailers are similar in most respects to those of other retailers.

An example of a retailer who successfully expanded into three stores at adjacent sites was reported in *Sporting Goods Business,* the national news magazine of the sporting goods industry.[9] Nestar's Sporting Goods, Inc., was a full-line sporting goods store selling popularly priced merchandise in an 11,000-square-foot store. It continues to sell such items to price-conscious customers. However, on each side of the original store, the Nestar family now operates a specialty store. One is a 5000-square-foot camping store called Wilderness Travel Outfitters. It carries specialized equipment and employs experienced campers as sales personnel. The value of its inventory has increased from an original $30,000 to $200,000, which it turns 2½ to 3 times a year at a 40 percent markup. The other store is a 3000-square-foot ski shop called the Warming Hut. By operating as three separate stores, the Nestars have been able to maintain three distinct images and at the same time enhance the value of their original site.

Your Strategy for Retail Store Layout and Image

We now turn our discussion of place strategy to the subject of store design. The layout, physical appearance, and image that your retail store projects to potential customers comprise a major portion of your place strategy. Rather than describe the actual mechanics of exterior design and interior layout patterns (such as "grids" and "free flows"), we will discuss here the *issues* you should consider in your layout strategy. Once your strategy has been determined, you can use the advice of experts in store design and equipment to achieve your strategic layout objectives.

Retail store layout requires a *definite plan* by which equipment, fixtures, merchandise displays, selling and sales-supporting areas, and other facilities are properly arranged. The specific form of the layout should be determined by its function or purpose. To please the customers, layout should minimize the time and effort needed to locate merchandise, provide the right atmosphere, and take into account buying habits and preferences. These objectives may have to be compromised, however, because the small retailer must also keep expenses (such as labor and shoplifting) to a minimum. For example, a big influence on layout and the selection of store fixtures in recent years has been the switch from service-type selling to self-selection (also called simplified selling) and self-service.

The following layout strategy topics are adapted from the "nine basic layout ideas that retail managers should remember when they make layout decisions":[10]

1. Value in space.
2. Customer traffic flow.
3. Impulse goods versus demand goods.
4. Related merchandise departments.
5. Good-looking and action-related merchandise.
6. High-gross-margin and high-sales-volume departments.
7. Seasonal departments.
8. Store image.
9. Other considerations.

Using Your Valuable Space. Good management of your retail space can help make you a more successful retailer. Space is a limited and valuable resource. Often the more valuable space is reserved for selling activities. Space for receiving, storage, offices, employee lounges, workrooms, and so on will occupy space not suited for selling. Our discussion will be limited primarily to selling space under the assumption that you have already determined what space is necessary for nonselling activities.

Your space-allocation decisions may be thought of in terms of how much and which selling space will be used for each (1) department, (2) product group or category within a department, and (3) individual item. Which of these three levels concerns you most (or at all) depends upon such factors as number of stores owned, total store size, number of departments per store, whether you are planning self-service versus self-selection, and the use of space to create store image. For example, a few very small retailers may find their personal experience and close knowledge of customer preferences to be the best guide for space allocation. However, most small (and larger) retailers will rely on measures of selling-space productivity such as sales per square foot. These measures may help them draw up a model stock plan or basic stock list. Because the appropriate calculations vary by type of retailer, we will concentrate below on some underlying principles of space management. Your trade magazines will give methods for calculating space productivity and comparable figures for retailers of your type.

Self-service retail stores such as supermarkets have led the field in space management methods. However, space management is still an art rather than a science. Our knowledge of the effects of changing shelf-space allocation is fragmentary. Trial-and-error methods and experiments by retailers and academic researchers have been performed on only a limited number of products. The generalizations that can be made from such studies are also limited.

Many space-allocation studies are based upon the concept of space elasticity. This is the ratio of relative change in unit sales to relative change in shelf space. The following space-allocation principles seem to hold generally true:[11]

1. The impact of shelf space on unit sales differs among products. Although the relationship is not clearly understood, once a product has received a threshold level of exposure, staple goods are probably less responsive to increases in exposure than are so-called impulse items.
2. Space elasticity (ratio of relative change in sales to relative change in shelf space) *tends* to be higher for private labels and packer-label brands than for "national" or manufacturer brands.
3. Space changes *tend* to have greater sales effects in product categories having many brands than in those having fewer brands.
4. Space changes *tend* to have greater sales effects (that is, greater space elasticity) for faster-selling items than for slower-selling items.
5. Regular-size (or best-selling size) items *tend* to have more space elasticity.
6. Changes on shelves close to eye level have a greater impact on sales than changes on shelves above or below eye level. However, within any given shelf level, sales tend to be affected equally by like changes in amount of shelf space.

Remember that these six principles are generalizations. Factors unique to your store and your merchandising techniques will determine how applicable they are for you.

As a small retailer you may be particularly interested in what happens to sales as shelf space is redistributed among competing brands in a product category. For example, will giving more space to brand X pizza mix at the expense of brand Y pizza mix increase your total sales and profits for the pizza-mix product category? If so, you should probably make such a change (unless brand Y has other advantages). Thus by looking at the total sales and profits for all pizza mixes, you can manage your space better. Also, by comparing all pizza-mix sales and profits to those of other product categories, you may decide to expand (or reduce) the space devoted to the pizza-mix category.

One method many large retailers have used in recent years to boost sales per square foot of floor space is to make better use of vertical space. Large department stores such as J. C. Penney's have remodeled stores with fixtures that display merchandise better and at the same time make better use of vertical space. Pamida Discount Stores (formerly Gibson's) were pioneers in using tall shelving. Beating high rents by wise use of vertical space is a tricky business, especially if you want to avoid a cluttered look. Some small retailers have successfully used vertical space by building balconies and alcoves. Others have used narrower fixtures that display more products even though they must be restocked more frequently. One very small retailer with whom the author consulted was able to increase his behind-the-counter display area quite substantially by building very inexpensive pegboard racks to the ceiling. These racks were also out of the reach of potential shoplifters. Visit some small stores in your area to get ideas on how to stretch your available space.

Customer Traffic Flow. All the stadium seats are not on the 50-yard line. Likewise, not all selling space is equal in value. The crucial variable is the amount of customer traffic flow. Layout both affects and is affected by customer traffic flow. Customer traffic within your store is similar to auto traffic within a city. Location of merchandise within your store should take advantage of potential customer traffic patterns in the same way your store location takes advantage of auto traffic patterns. The big difference is that within the store you have more control over the traffic. Within limits, you can lead customers wherever you want them. You are the traffic cop.

Your purpose in controlling customer traffic is to direct as many customers as possible past as much merchandise as possible in order to increase the total opportunities for purchasing. One way to accomplish this is to place merchandise items (or departments) that are natural traffic generators in remote areas of the store. Customers are thus forced to pass through other departments where they are exposed to other items. (If you use such a strategy, be careful not to inconvenience your customers too much or they may go to a competitor.) So-called impulse items are almost always placed at high-traffic locations such as at ends of aisles and near check-out counters. Supermarket shoppers have a definite tendency to shop the perimeter of the store. Perimeter aisles receive nearly twice the customer traffic as interior aisles. In departmentalized stores, space along main aisles receives more traffic. Elevators, escalators, and stairways are all traffic movers that affect space values.

Many of the above statements refer mainly to self-service and self-selection stores. For specialty shops operating with a high degree of sales assistance and service, customer traffic patterns are of less importance. For example, an exclusive women's clothing store whose customers are always accompanied by a salesperson does not need to regulate customer traffic patterns in the same way as a supermarket.

Some retailers and authors advocate the practice of dividing the total store area into a grid and assigning "rents" to various sections. For example, because customers have a natural tendency to turn to the right when entering a store, the right front portion would be assigned a higher "rent" than an equal amount of space in the rear of the store. Although such a practice may be useful, you should keep in mind that because layout and customer traffic flow interact (that is, each can affect the other), cause and effect are not always clear. You may also wish to chart the actual traffic patterns before making any changes in your layout.

Remodeling and expansion provide special opportunities for getting more value from your space and changing the flows of customer traffic. Two examples of successful expansion are given below.

Example 1. Baldwin's Biz Mart installed a $35,000 glass elevator in Kirksville, Missouri (population 17,000) to speed customers up to its new second floor retail athletic goods department. Because the elevator is unique in this rural area, many people come into the store just because they want to ride the elevator.[12]

Example 2. People's Sporting Goods of Cheyenne, Wyoming, was surrounded on both sides at its present downtown site. In order to add a new department called The Locker Room, it expanded downward. The key to success for this basement department was the decoration of its entrance with a brilliantly lit mural done by a local artist. Painted against a predominantly white background, the mural is dedicated to the past, present, and future athletes of Cheyenne. The entrance stairway to the lower level is also a full seven feet wide. The Locker Room, which inventories 4000 pairs of athletic shoes, is attractively decorated with wooden displays and authentic locker doors. Needless to say, business has been going up since People's expanded down.[13]

Figure 8-1. People's Sporting Goods, showing entrance to lower level. (Photo courtesy of George Kaufman)

Impulse Goods Versus Demand Goods. Your store probably sells both impulse goods and demand goods. Demand goods are those that customers are already planning to buy when they enter the store. You can therefore place them in somewhat less accessible locations. Goods bought on "impulse" are not so easily described. The following four types of impulse buying take place:

1. *Pure impulse buying* is truly unplanned and probably accounts for a very small portion of so-called impulse buying.
2. *Reminder impulse buying* occurs when a customer sees an item in the store and is reminded of a need and a previous decision to buy.
3. *Suggestive impulse buying* occurs when a customer sees a product for the first time while in the store and rationally visualizes a need without previous product knowledge.

4. *Planned impulse buying* occurs when the customer enters the store with some specific purchase(s) in mind but also with the intention of making some additional purchase(s) depending on appeals such as special prices and coupon offers.[14]

The increase in impulse buying reflects the fact that customers are doing more of their purchase planning at the store rather than at home. In a sense, your store and its layout have become a life-size visual shopping list. Almost any item could be bought on impulse by some consumers. However, the following nine factors are associated with more ease of customer buying and can be used as criteria for identifying impulse items (these nine are broad guides, because no impulse items exist *per se*):

1. Low price.
2. Marginal need for the item.

3. Mass advertising.
4. Self-service.
5. Mass distribution.
6. Prominent store display.
7. Short product life.
8. Small size or light weight.
9. Ease of storage.[15]

Related Merchandise Departments. If you place complementary items in adjacent locations, sales will probably increase. If merchandise is departmentalized, related product groupings within each department are often displayed together. You can do this on a permanent basis, such as in a boutique, or use a temporary special display. Even though this method involves duplicate display, the results can be a sizable increase in sales. Another idea is to locate departments with different seasonal patterns adjacent to each other. Such a seasonal exchange of selling space provides for greater use of selling area and more total store sales.

Good-Looking and Action-Related Merchandise. Some kinds of merchandise have more display appeal than others. For example, fresh fruits and vegetables have more display appeal than canned or frozen fruits and vegetables, a sports car has more display appeal than auto parts, and fashion items have more display appeal than staples. In both self-service and self-selection merchandising, your displays must attract customers without the help of a salesperson. The right fixtures can be a big asset. Fixtures should display the merchandise to its best advantage but should not distract the customer's attention from the merchandise (because they themselves are not for sale). In addition to the right fixtures, such things as regular rotation of all stock, the

proper placing of price tags, good lighting, fully stocked shelves, and overall cleanliness can help to sell merchandise. A good way to find ways of making the merchandise in your store look better is to visit several other stores (both those that sell merchandise of your type and those that don't). Notice which things you find appealing and which things you don't.

Manufacturers offer help to small retailers by providing good packaging and point-of-purchase displays that are usually both good-looking and action-related. Look for some the next time you are in a supermarket, drug store, or variety store. A good example is Tic Tacs, a fruit- or mint-flavored candy packaged in a small plastic container and usually displayed in an attractive case near the cash register. At this high-traffic location customers pay about 25 cents for a half-ounce package. That's $8 per pound.

High-Gross-Margin and High-Sales-Volume Departments. Some products and departments have higher gross margins than others. Small products with high unit values (for example, jewelry) carry high margins and are thus able to pay the "rents" for good selling space. Another factor to be considered in layout decisions, however, is the rate of stock turnover. Stock turnover, also known as rate of stockturn, is the number of times during a given period (usually a year) that the average amount of inventory is sold. Three methods for calculating stockturn were given in Table 5-1.

Stockturn can be a useful tool for both layout and merchandising decisions. It is the combination of *both* gross margin and stockturn that leads to profits. Although increased stockturn may or may not increase profits (depending on how the increase is achieved), it does offer other advantages such as reduced storage costs, lower inventory investment, fewer markdowns, and fresher merchandise.

Seasonal Departments. Flexible layouts are becoming quite popular in many types of retail stores. What was new merchandise at the beginning of the season becomes clearance merchandise before the end of the season. Space used for expanded toy and gift displays may later be used for spring items such as lawn and garden products. Layout and customer traffic patterns are affected by the season of the year.

Other time variations such as hour of day or day of week (or month) can also affect your layout. For example, portable displays may at times replace portable checkouts. If you take advantage of such flexibility in your layout, your space will work harder for you.

Store Image. Your store image is affected by nearly everything you do. Layout is an important part of store image. The image your store is attempting to project should be apparent to customers when (or even before) they enter. Projecting the image that is right for your target market customers will make them feel welcome and comfortable. At the same time, it will discourage persons who are not part of your target market from coming in to shop. At first this may sound like a disadvantage. However, you can't be all things to all people. Keeping people who are not part of your target market from shopping at your store will save you much time and cost in terms of wasted sales time, returned merchandise, and complaints.

Layout is but one of the elements of interior design used to create the desired store image. Also used are color, light, texture, music, and anything else that appeals to the human senses. The Locker Room example cited above demonstrates this. Another example is provided by the Seattle hi-fi retailer who goes after the quality target market:

The decor of these stores (each one is approximately 3500 sq. ft.) says a lot about the type of customer that Magnolia Hi-Fi attracts. Tweten says, "We're not at all the type of warehouse operation with the equipment stacked up in boxes." The stores are designed with a quiet and very relaxed elegance. The exteriors are a classic white block with a black inlay around the entrance, which is also decorated with rock gardens and plants. The carpeted, nicely paneled interiors are broken up into a number of smaller, intimate rooms, complete with easy chairs and ashtrays, and featuring differing specialties—from car radios to home hi-fi systems to Video Beam TV projectors. The small, relatively enclosed spaces reduce the sounds from other systems being tried out and more closely approximate the living situation in which the customer will ultimately be listening to his hi-fi. No big vacuum-like spaces in this store.[16]

A final example of an unusual layout that helps create store image is provided by a La Canada, California, sporting goods store that is built around a sixteen-foot-high concrete and reinforced-steel mountain. Mr. Olberz, the store's owner, says he built the rock to give the store class and to identify the store as the place to buy mountain and rock climbing equipment. Built by a plasterer and painted by an artist, the rock includes all the basic rock formations found in California such as jam cracks, chimneys, and overhangs. Yes, customers actually do climb on the rock, and it is used for teaching climbing techniques.[17]

Other Considerations. The other considerations that will affect your layout depend on the type of retail business you are in. For example, if you carry large or bulky items, they should be placed for easy stocking and carry-out. Items requiring extensive stock reserves may be displayed near the reserve stock areas. Also, the limitations imposed by your building may dictate certain layout alternatives.

Physical Distribution

Most small retailers are involved in physical-distribution activities such as transporting, storing, materials handling, inventory management, and order processing. For some, however, it plays a larger role than for others. Consider, for example, the photograph processing service whose retail stores are small buildings in the parking lots of shopping centers. By guaranteeing one-day service or no charge to its customers, this service retailer is competing on the basis of speed. A less obvious example is the drug store that usually has the hard-to-get prescriptions without the delay entailed in receiving supplies from the wholesaler. Both of these retailers are competing by superior physical-distribution management.

Our limited discussion of physical distribution is intended to point out that the distribution of products and services to your customers (and from your suppliers to you) is a part of place strategy. To some extent you can control it and use it as a part of your marketing mix. Physical distribution involves not only serving but creating the demand for your products and services. In other words, you can attract and serve some customers by the mere fact that you perform some physical activities in such a way that these customers are better served. Give some thought to how you might use physical distribution as a part of your place strategy.

How to Formulate Your Retail Place Strategy

This chapter and the previous one have discussed the topics you should consider in formulating your retail place strategy. In order to devise a strategy uniquely suited to your target market and retail marketing mix, use the eight-step process outlined in this book.

Now that you have defined your target market (Chapter 3), considered your business environment (Chapter 4), planned your retail product strategy (Chapters 5 and 6), and planned your retail place strategy (Chapters 7 and 8), you are ready to consider the third P of your retail marketing mix: pricing strategy.

9

How to Plan Your Retail Price Strategy

Pricing is an art. It is mastered through practice and a desire for continued improvement. Although both large and small retailers have some discretion in setting the prices of their goods and services, surprisingly few have well-defined price strategies. This is not as it should be. Remember that pricing is one of the five elements or P's of your retail marketing mix. Even retailers who do put some thought and planning into pricing may consider this to be part of the financial process rather than of the marketing mix.

Why is pricing surrounded by so much neglect and confusion? One reason is that retailers find price theory hard to put into actual practice. Most retailers have fallen into the routine of using some type of cost-plus formula pricing for similar groups of products. Such formula pricing is easy to

use and usually works fairly well, especially for retailers who understand what is behind the average markups and why one market percentage rather than another is being used. Most of the theoretical basis of pricing is supplied from ouside the retailing field by economists. For example, a pamphlet from the SBA advises the small marketer as follows:

The "best" price for a product is not necessarily the price that will sell the most units. Nor is it always the price that will bring in the greatest number of sales dollars. Rather the "best" price is one that will maximize the profits of the company.

The "best" selling price should be cost oriented and market oriented. It should be high enough to cover your costs and help you make a profit. It should also be low enough to attract customers and build sales volume.[1]

Although this advice may seem too general, it does outline the principles by which to maximize profits and is certainly more helpful than the equivalent but more technical advice that your best price is that at which marginal cost equals marginal revenue.

Our Scope of Coverage. This chapter and the next discuss practical pricing topics of interest to small retailers. Coverage is necessarily less than complete. The economic analysis of price, geographic pricing practices, and most of the legal aspects of pricing are not discussed. Although these topics are not unimportant, they are beyond the perspective of small retailing. For example, owing to their size, small retailers are not often challenged on legal aspects of pricing. Some small retailers (such as auto dealers and gasoline service station operators) must conform to specific price laws but other retailers have much freedom. For most small retailers, state and local laws and customs are usually more important than federal laws. The Consumer Goods Pricing Act of 1975, which became effective in March, 1976, ended all interstate use of "fair trade" pricing or resale price maintenance.[2] The legal death of "fair trade" removed one of the federal laws that for many years directly affected the pricing strategies of many small retailers.

In this chapter we will cover price and pricing objectives, the importance of pricing, your price image, how to figure your markups, and how to use markdowns and other adjustments in your pricing strategy. The next chapter covers the eight-step process for formulating your pricing strategy, pricing problems of special interest to small retailers, and the pricing of services. A practical pricing checklist is included as an appendix in Chapter 10.

What Is Price?

Price is the amount of money paid to you by your customer for some product. It is the agreed-upon monetary value of a product in a market transaction. However, every transaction also involves some other kinds of costs. From the customer's perspective, the cost of an item is measured not only by its price (although this certainly plays a large part) but by the amount of time and energy that must be spent in acquiring it. For example, a customer may be willing to pay a higher *price* at the convenience food store in order to avoid the higher *cost* (but perhaps lower price) at a crowded super-market during a busy period.

From the small retailer's perspective, price is both an element of the retail marketing mix and, as the only income-generating element, is a rather direct determinant of profitability. Unit price multiplied by the volume of units sold equals total revenue. Unit price multiplied by units sold, less costs, equals profits. Also, because it is a means of cultivating your market, price sometimes determines the quantity you sell. Strategic questions in pricing are how much, in what form, when, with what discounts, and so on.

Your Pricing Objectives

To effectively use price as one of the elements of your retail marketing mix, you should formulate some rather specific pricing objectives. These objectives should be consistent with your overall marketing and company objectives. Which pricing objectives will be appropriate for your retail firm will depend on such factors as your target market, your differential advantage, your environment, and the rest of your strategy. The following list suggests some general pricing objectives that may be tailored to fit your specific requirements:

1. Maximize long-run profits.
2. Maximize short-run profits.
3. Desensitize customers to price.
4. Maintain loyalty of suppliers and get their sales support.
5. Enhance image of the store and its offerings.
6. Be regarded as "fair" by customers.
7. Create interest and excitement about an item.
8. Be considered trustworthy and reliable by rivals.
9. Help in the sale of weak items in the store.
10. Discourage others from cutting prices.
11. Make a product "visible."
12. Build traffic.[3]

After you have determined a list of pricing objectives appropriate for your store, try to determine the importance and priority of each price objective so that when objectives come into conflict with each other, you will have a basis for making decisions.

The pricing objectives of large and small retailers often differ. Consider, for example, the area of profitability. Big retailers should perhaps aim for satisfactory or level profits over time, but small retailers would be wiser to try for profit maximization (usually in both the short and long run). Small retailers whose profits do not attract much public attention and who have successfully carved out desirable target markets are in a good position to try for profit maximization. Other small retailers may seek a target return such as a return on sales, investment, or time spent. For example, the operators of a small family-run store may seek a fixed dollar amount of profit to cover their living expenses. Most of the pricing objectives listed above treat price in terms of its role in your retail marketing mix rather than in terms of the profit that results from a successful mix.

The Importance of Pricing

Many small retailers think that consumers are extremely interested in price. In fact, retailers have much more price knowledge and are much more price-conscious than most consumers. This is not to say that pricing should not be an important part of your marketing strategy. But it does mean that in forming your pricing strategy, you should try to assess the importance of price to your target market customers. It is probably fairly important that your prices be within some acceptable range; however, some of the other elements of your marketing mix may be of greater importance.

Table 9-1.

Importance of Patronage Factors
As Perceived by Both
Retail Pharmacists and Consumers

Patronage Factors	Rank Given by Consumers	Rank Given by Pharmacists
Free delivery	1	10
Waiting time	2	5
Charge accounts	3	6
Variety of merchandise	4	8
After-hours service	5	9
Location	6	2
Records for taxes and insurance	7	7
Pleasant atmosphere	8	4
Price	9	3
Skilled pharmacist	10	1

An example of how retailers sometimes attribute more importance to price than do their customers is provided by a study in Alabama of retail pharmacists and their customers.[4] (The results of this Auburn University study are shown in Table 9-1.) Although pharmacists ranked price as the third most important reason why customers patronized their stores, the customers ranked price as ninth (next to last) in importance. It is also interesting that being a "skilled pharmacist" was ranked first by the pharmacists and last by the customers. Perhaps this suggests that both "price" and "skilled pharmacist" are assumed by customers to be pretty much the same from one drug store to the next.

The importance of price to the consumer (and therefore to the retailer) depends on the consumer and the situation. Many of us will shop the specials at the supermarket and then spend money "like water" when on vacation. Generalizations are proven by their exceptions. Consider how the following generalizations apply to your store and customers:

1. Consumers do not have a high level of knowledge concerning the exact prices of products. Most consumers have an idea of price range but not exact price. This applies to both frequently and infrequently purchased products.

2. Some consumers are more price-conscious than others. For example, high-income consumers are often less price-conscious than low-income consumers. However, for some items, such as groceries, noticeable exceptions may be found.

3. Consumers with the best knowledge of prices tend to be male, older, single, and of higher income. (So if you are selling to rich, elderly bachelors, your marketing mix should probably emphasize price and value.)

4. Price is more important to the "discount" shopper.

5. The size of the purchase often influences how price-conscious the consumer will be.

6. Who pays for the product (for example, the

individual consumer or the company expense account) influences how price-conscious the consumer will be.

7. Private-label consumers tend to have a somewhat better knowledge of prices than do national-brand purchasers.
8. Consumers often use price as an indicator of quality.
9. Because consumers often find it difficult to judge individual prices, they use their overall price image of the retail store as a guide.

The relative importance of pricing in your retail marketing mix is ultimately determined by the importance of price to your target market customers. Their response is what counts. Economists ignore the role of nonprice competition and therefore tend to overstate the role of price. In fact, consumers are probably less concerned with actually getting the lowest possible prices than with proving to themselves and others that they are "smart buyers." In other words, people enjoy finding a bargain not so much because of the few dollars they save, but because it proves them to be shrewd. (How many people do you know who didn't "get a good deal" on the last car they bought?) This perception of oneself (even if it is faulty) is quite important. Most consumers in fact know very little about prices. Therefore, the *price image* of a product may be as important, if not more important, than the actual price. Large retailers, such as Sears, have for many years followed a pricing strategy of charging very low prices on a selected 100 or 200 key items that have good customer visibility. The low price image created by these items sets the tone for the price image of the store as a whole. Nonvisible items may carry somewhat higher prices (but care should be taken to treat the customers fairly—they are not fools).

Your Price Image

Does store X have low prices or merely a low price image? Are prices actually higher at store Y or is that merely the impression given by the plush decor? What is your price image? What *should* it be?

Price image both affects and is affected by your overall store image. Your price image is the message about your pricing that has been communicated to your present and potential customers. It is what they think about pricing, regardless of what the actual facts may be. The price image is communicated by several means. Your advertising and other promotion methods are one of the major ways of doing this. For example, the size of type used in the ad, the amount of space given to quoting prices versus white space or descriptive text, and the theme of your newspaper advertisements all help to communicate your price image. Likewise, your products, your place strategy, your actual prices, and your people strategy all help to convey your price image to customers and potential customers. A store that desires a low price image should, for example, (a) carry some lower-quality, lower-priced items, (b) be located in an average or less-than-average location rather than in a mall of exclusive shops, (c) have low prices on many visible items, (d) promote price rather than high style or quality, and (e) employ salespeople who are oriented to low-priced merchandising.

Whatever your price image, it should be

compatible with the target market you are attempting to serve. The right price image will attract the right customers to your store. At the same time, the "wrong customers" will know immediately that your store is not for them. The advertising and window displays of many women's clothing stores illustrate this strategy; high prices are charged to create an image of high fashion.

Our culture has developed some rather subtle methods for conveying price image. Consider, for example, the price advertising used by supermarkets. Most supermarkets attempt to create a low-price image. However, a careful examination of advertisements and actual prices shows that (a) some supermarkets put considerable effort into conveying an image of high quality whereas others do not, (b) actual prices vary considerably depending on whether the merchandising emphasis is on national or private brands, foods or nonfoods, and so on, and (c) different types of customers have different price images of the various supermarkets. It seems that within the broad range of "low" prices expected by most customers, a supermarket is able to create its own distinct price image.

A few examples of successful use of price image are worth examining:

Example 1. Renner's Sports Center of Jamesburg, New Jersey, has achieved a 10 to 15 percent annual increase in archery sales by making sure archery customers get results with their hunting or target shooting. The store's owner thinks the archery industry has placed too much emphasis on price. His belief is that customers don't become interested in a sport because of the price of equipment.[5]

Example 2. The Bike Shop is a store in Omaha from which my family has purchased seven high-quality bicycles of various sizes and shapes over the past few years. All were sold at the full price suggested by the manufacturer. I was recently in the Bike Shop to buy a replacement tire for my son, who seems to "burn a lot of rubber." The price was $7.50, which included "free" installment of the tire on the wheel. I actually installed the tire myself, but I realized immediately that this "free" service (which was included in the price) was most compatible with the full-service, full-price image of the store.

Example 3. A local tire retailer and a local toy retailer use a price appeal in their advertising messages that goes something like this:

At _____ we have the lowest prices in town. Come in and see. Compare prices. If our prices are not already lower than anyone's advertised prices for similar items, bring in their advertisement within three days and we'll beat their price by an additional 2 percent.

This is certainly an attempt to create a low-price image. However, neither of the above stores charges very low prices. In fact, one of them charges prices that are quite high when compared to competition. But who compares? Only marketing professors and a very few other people. The ethics of such pricing practices may be seriously questioned.

How to Figure Your Markups

As we noted earlier, many retailers use their cost plus a markup to determine their selling price. Markup (also called markon) can be a very useful tool for formula pricing, especially if you understand what is behind it. Our explanation below is short and easy to understand. Many retailing books give more detailed explanations.[6]

Markup is the difference between your cost for a product and the selling price. Unlike gross margin or gross profit, which reflect the actual results of markdowns, shortages, spoilage, and so on, markup is used as a planning concept. It can also be described as the amount added to the cost in order to determine the selling price.

Markup is a basic pricing tool used in retailing. An understanding of markup is essential to successful merchandising. Although markup tables, markup wheels, and computers may be available to shortcut the computations, it is important to understand what is behind the computations. Markup percentages and stock turnover are often inversely related. That is, the higher the markup percentage, the lower the rate of stock turnover; and conversely, the lower the markup percentage, the higher the rate of stock turnover. *Stock turnover* (also called *turnover* or *stockturn*) is defined as the number of times during a given period (usually a year) that the average inventory is sold. The stock turnover calculation (which can be made at cost, selling price, or in units) was discussed in Chapter 5. Its link with markup in determining total dollar gross profit is most important. Simply stated, the more units of product you sell at a stated markup, the greater will be total dollar markup. If more units of product are sold at an even higher markup, the total dollar markup will be even greater.

In our discussion we will use the following symbols or abbreviations:

C = cost
SP = selling price
MU = markup

% = percent or percentage
$ = dollar(s)
> = greater than

As we stated above, by definition

$$\$MU = \$SP - \$C$$

This equation can be stated in two other forms by moving the equivalent positions around:

$$\$C = \$SP - \$MU$$

and

$$\$SP = \$C + \$MU$$

Calculating Markups on Selling Price and Cost. Markups are frequently stated in percentages. That is, the $\$MU$ is stated as a proportion or percentage of another quantity such as $\$C$ or $\$SP$. Although MU may be expressed as a percentage of either C or SP, it is customary and conventional to express MU as a percentage of SP unless specifically stated otherwise. However, not everyone follows this convention.

It is sometimes desirable to convert % MU on C to an equivalent value expressed as % MU on SP. Conversely, it is sometimes desirable to convert % MU on SP to an equivalent value expressed as % MU on C. As mentioned above, such conversions can be performed by using tables, wheels, and computers. Conversions can also be made using the following formulas. The choice of formula depends on which items are known and which item (only one) is unknown.

To obtain % MU on SP, use any one of the following three formulas (depending on which quantities are known):

By definition: $\% \; MU \text{ on } SP = \dfrac{\$MU}{\$SP}$

By substitution: % *MU* on *SP* =

$$\frac{\$MU}{\$C + \$MU}$$

In percentages: % *MU* on *SP* =

$$\frac{\% \ MU \ \text{on} \ C}{100\% + \% \ MU \ \text{on} \ C}$$

The first equation expresses $MU as a proportion or percent of $SP. In other words, $MU is divided by $SP. The second equation makes a substitution in the denominator (we saw earlier that $SP = $C + $MU). The third equation (which is analogous in its structural format to the second equation) is used if your known quantities are in percentages, and it converts a % *MU* on *C* to a % *MU* on *SP*. In all three equations, the answer will appear as a fraction or a decimal. The percent form is attained by multiplying the answer by (100%/1). For example, 1/3 = .333 = 33⅓ percent.

To obtain % *MU* on *C*, use any one of the following three formulas (depending on which quantities are known):

By definition: % *MU* on $C = \dfrac{\$MU}{\$C}$

By substitution: % *MU* on *C* =

$$\frac{\$MU}{\$SP - \$MU}$$

In percentages: % *MU* on *C* =

$$\frac{\%MU \ \text{on} \ SP}{100\% - \% \ MU \ \text{on} \ SP}$$

As with our previous set of equations, the first equation above simply expresses $MU as a proportion or percent of $C. The second equation makes a substitution in the denominator (we saw earlier that $C = $SP − $MU). The third equation (which is analogous in its structural format to the second equation) is used if your known quantities are in percentages, and it converts a % *MU* on *SP* to a % *MU* on *C*. In all three equations the answer will appear as a fraction or

decimal. The percent form is attained by multiplying the answer by (100%/1). For example, 1/3 = .333 = 33⅓ percent.

Try a few simple problems. In numbers 2 and 3, put your answers in the blanks.

1. If a retailer buys a product for 50 cents and sells it for 75 cents, what is:
   a. $MU   a. 75¢ − 50¢ = A. 25¢ ___
   b. % *MU* on *C*   b. 25¢ ÷ 50¢ = B. 50% ___
   c. % *MU* on *SP*   c. 25¢ ÷ 75¢ = C. 33⅓% ___

2. If a retailer buys a product for 42¢ and sells is for 69¢, what is:
   a. $MU   a. _____ ¢
   b. % *MU* on *C*   b. _____ %
   c. % *MU* on *SP*   c. _____ %

3. What are the equivalents for the following percentages?

% *MU on C*	% *MU on SP*
a. 100%	_____ %
b. 43%	_____
c. _____ %	25%
d. _____ %	36%

You may check the reasonableness (but not the absolute correctness) of your answers by remembering the following simple rules:

1. % *MU* on *C* can be > 100 percent.
2. % *MU* on *SP* can*not* be > 100 percent.
3. % *MU* on *C* is > equivalent % *MU* on *SP*.

The Danger of Confusing Bases. Percentages cannot be taken to the bank or used to pay expenses. These require real dollars. However, you do calculate your profits and business expenses as a percentage of net sales. This is the basic reason for the custom of calculating markups as a percentage of selling price. Many retailers think in terms of markup on cost. This is because they know their cost from their invoices. They must then add some markup to arrive at their selling price. An alternate formula you may wish to use to arrive at your retail selling price is:

$$\$SP = \frac{\$C}{100\% - \text{desired } \% \ MU \text{ on } SP}$$

Thus, if your dollar cost was $5 and your desired percentage markup on selling price was 33⅓ percent, you would calculate your selling price as follows:

$$\$SP = \frac{\$5}{100\% - 33\frac{1}{3}\%}$$

$$\$SP = \frac{\$5}{66\frac{2}{3}\%}$$

$$\$SP = \frac{\$5}{.66\frac{2}{3}}$$

$$\$SP = \$7.50$$

Use whatever formula you find easy to use, but be sure not to confuse a percentage markup based on cost with a percentage markup based on selling price. They are not figured on the same base. It's like trying to add apples and oranges. The following example illustrates the danger of confusing bases. Suppose a sharp salesman tries to sell you a new item by claiming it has a 50 percent markup. (He doesn't say whether the 50 percent is based on cost or selling price.) You know that a 50 percent markup on cost equals a 33⅓ percent markup on selling price. If that is the markup he is talking about, you will probably lose money, because to cover your expenses and make a profit you need at least 35 to 40 percent markup on selling price. However, if the salesman is talking about a 50 percent markup on selling price (equal to a 100 percent markup on cost) you can probably make money on the item if you sell it.

Tables of Equivalent Markups. Rather than use the above formula, some retailers prefer to use tables that show the equivalent markup percentages based on cost or selling price. Table 9-2 lists some widely used equivalents in fraction and percentage form. Note that the numerator of all fractions is 1 and that for equivalent percentages, the denominator of the fraction is always 1 greater for *SP* than for *C*. This is because *SP* is greater than *C*.

The contents of Table 9-2 can be restated as follows:

1. Doubling the cost results in a 50 percent markup on selling price.
2. Cost plus 1/2 of cost equals a 33⅓ percent markup on selling price.
3. Cost plus 1/3 of cost equals a 25 percent markup on selling price.
4. Cost plus 1/4 of cost equals a 20 percent markup on selling price.
5. Cost plus 1/5 of cost equals a 16⅔ percent markup on selling price.

Table 9-2 can also be restated in this way:

1. A 100 percent markup on cost equals a 50 percent markup on selling price.
2. A 50 percent markup on cost equals a 33⅓ percent markup on selling price.
3. A 33⅓ percent markup on cost equals a 25 percent markup on selling price.
4. A 25 percent markup on cost equals a 20 percent markup on selling price.
5. A 20 percent markup on cost equals a 16⅔ percent markup on selling price.

The Effects of Averaging. The above markup calculations may be used to price individual items, product categories, or entire departments or stores. When more than one item and markup percentage are involved, an average markup is calculated. This is a weighted (rather than simple) average in which the amount of merchandise

Table 9–2.
Equivalent Percentages and Fractions
For Markup on Cost and Markup on Selling Price

Equivalents on C		Equivalents on SP	
%	Fraction	Fraction	%
100%	1/1	1/2	50%
50%	1/2	1/3	33⅓%
33⅓%	1/3	1/4	25%
25%	1/4	1/5	20%
20%	1/5	1/6	16⅔%

sold is multiplied by the markup percentage for each item. For example, if a department sells item A at a 50 percent markup on selling price and item B at a 30 percent markup on selling price, the average markup for the department is *not* 40 percent unless exactly equal dollar amounts of A and B were sold. If $5000 of A were sold and $10,000 of B were sold, the total dollar sales for the department would be $15,000. The total dollar markup for the department would be $5500 ($2500 from product A plus $3000 from product B). This amount is 37 percent of the $15,000 sales of the department. Thus, the average markup on selling price for the department is 37 percent even though neither product was sold at this exact markup.

When markups are averaged together in this way, the sales of one product can affect the markup of an entire department. Suppose that bananas account for 20 percent of the sales volume of your product department and are sold at cost, while the other 80 percent of your sales volume is sold for a 35 percent markup on selling price (exclude shrink in the example). Because the bananas yield no profits, your departmental markup will be not 35 percent, but rather 28 percent. Because bananas are a high-volume item, selling them at cost has reduced your departmental markup a full 7 percent of selling price. If, on the other hand, you had sold an item such as peppers at cost, the reduction in markup would have been much less. For example, if peppers account for 5 percent of department sales volume, selling them at cost rather than at the 35 percent markup would reduce the departmental markup to 33¼ percent. It turns out that the markup percentage lost by selling bananas at cost (7 percent) is about the same as that lost by selling peppers at cost (1¾ percent) *and* selling bananas at a 10 (rather than at 35) percent markup (5 percent). Which is the better merchandising idea depends on other factors.

How to Use Markdowns and Other Price Adjustments

As we noted earlier, markup is a tool for planning prices and profits. The small retailer knows that all products will not be sold at their initial markup. Some items will receive added markups or upward price adjustments, while others will receive markdowns, downward adjustments, and employee discounts, or fall victim to shoplifters. All deviations from the planned markup result in a corresponding variation in gross margin (also called maintained markup). Many successful retailers actually plan for a certain amount of deviation. However, in order to maintain balanced stocks and to promote the store, markdowns should be carefully scheduled and sufficiently large. A book that covers all phases in the use of markdowns suggests the following:

1. Broken assortments should be reduced while the merchandise is current and in demand.

2. Seasonable merchandise should be marked down before the close of the selling season, as the demand lessens.

3. Staple merchandise should be reduced as soon as the control records indicate an overstocked condition, or when the merchandise takes on a "beat" or "shopworn" look.

4. Opportunities to promote the sale of marked-down merchandise exist in every phase of a season—preseason, early season, peak season, and postseason.

5. Not all items of a range need to be marked down if only some of the colors and sizes are slow sellers. Only those colors and sizes that are slow sellers should receive markdown consideration.

6. Markdowns taken when sales are in an upward swing afford greater opportunities for sales.

7. Markdowns taken during a season will develop sales with greater acceptance than markdowns taken after the season.

An understanding of these considerations, based on the merchandising fundamental that "the first markdown is the cheapest markdown," will make the cash registers ring with a minimum of markdowns and a maximum of profit.[7]

10

How to Plan Your Retail Price Strategy

(*continued*)

This chapter continues the discussion of price as an element of your retail marketing strategy. It will cover how to formulate your own profitable retail pricing strategy using the eight-step strategy formulation process, some practical pricing issues of special interest to small retailers, and pricing for small retail service firms. Finally, the appendix to the chapter will present a pricing checklist for small retailers.

How to Formulate Your Own Profitable Retail Pricing Strategy

Before you set specific prices, you should have a pricing strategy. Such a strategy provides the framework for making pricing decisions. The eight steps in the "how to" of retail price strategy planning are as follows:

1. Record your current retail price strategy.
2. Identify your strategic retail price problems.
3. Divide your current strategic retail price problems into core-strategy areas and supporting-strategy areas.
4. Formulate alternative retail price strategies at both core and support levels.

5. Evaluate the alternatives in various combinations.
6. Choose your new retail price strategy.
7. Plan the details of implementation for your new retail price strategy.
8. Set performance standards and monitor feedback.

These eight steps are similar to those used in previous chapters but have been adapted to fit the price element of your retail marketing mix. As before, this simple and practical method of planning your pricing strategy requires only a meeting room, pad and paper, and some leadership and initiative. Since your price strategy is a part of your overall marketing strategy, we will assume that you have already (a) defined your overall company and marketing objectives in specific terms, (b) defined your target market, (c) discovered your differential advantage, (d) properly assessed your retail marketing environment, and (e) made at least some tentative decisions regarding products, place, promotion, and people. Your pricing strategy is not formulated in a vacuum. It both affects and is affected by the rest of your retail marketing strategy. However, here we will concentrate on price. The outline that follows will give you as much direction as possible, but when it comes down to formulating your price strategy for your particular retail business, it's up to you to do a good job.

Step 1: Record Your Current Retail Price Strategy. For each target market you serve, you should have a current pricing strategy. If you do have one, however, the chances are good that it is quite vague and rather incomplete. General statements such as "being competitive on price," "pricing to offer the consumer a good value," or "pricing to maximize profits in the long run" are not much help to you at this point. What you need are some concise statements of exactly what your store is currently doing in making its pricing decisions, and why. For example, your core pricing strategy may currently be to follow the leader in your market area. The *why* may be that (a) you think you have no other choice, (b) you haven't taken the trouble to investigate any alternatives, (c) this core strategy has worked very well, or (d) you really don't know why.

For many small retailers (and some that are not so small) an attempt to record the current pricing strategy will yield the conclusion that pricing is done by formula and that formula is used in the absence of a pricing strategy. For example, cost-plus seems to be a very common method for determining retail prices. The cost-plus method is not necessarily applied in the absence of a pricing strategy, but often it is. Cost-plus means that you determine your cost (total cost or some other cost figure) and then set selling price by adding a markup. Calculations for doing so were given in the previous chapter. It is a simple and direct method for setting retail prices, but unless the decision on *how much markup* should be added is based on a realistic pricing strategy, such "formula" pricing can be quite misleading. Setting retail prices and having a retail pricing strategy are *not* the same thing. However, you must begin somewhere, so begin by recording exactly what you have been doing and why you have been doing it. So, record everything that describes your current pricing strategy. Using this record as a base, you are now ready to move on to the next step.

Step 2: Identify Your Strategic Retail Price Problems. If your current pricing strategy is not perfect, some strategic (as well as tactical) pricing problems may exist. Finding and properly identifying pricing problems (and opportunities) is the second step. You should be cautious to distinguish between problems and symptoms of problems. For example, if a customer complains that the price is "too high," is that what she really means? Or is price here a focus for sales resistance due to a number of factors? Strategic pricing problems may exist either in the core (that is, related to the differential advantage) or in supporting price strategies.

How do you seek out and find strategic

pricing problems? Some problems may have surfaced in step 1 above. You can find others by actively looking for them. The list of pricing objectives given early in the previous chapter may suggest pricing problems. The amount of profits you are making does not necessarily indicate the existence or the absence of a strategic pricing problem. Profits are a result, not a cause—and they are the result of many factors besides price. So, if profits are up or down, price may or may not be the cause. But price always bears looking at. Some indications of the existence of pricing problems are

a. Changes in dollar or unit sales.
b. A shift in the proportion of sales among the different price lines carried.
c. Changes in competitors' price strategies.
d. Changes in the amount of sales made at less than regular prices.
e. Changes in costs and expenses of doing business.
f. Lost sales actually due to pricing policies.
g. Customer complaints about prices and price policies.

Symptoms do help to point out problems. Evaluate these symptoms and use them.

In effect, you should search everywhere to find potential pricing problems. However, you should be sure to confine the search to those target markets that you are actually serving or planning to serve. Our principle of market simplification says that you should avoid imitating the pricing practices of big retailers, many of whom serve several target markets or perhaps target markets different from yours. As a small retailer, you are involved with one (or, at most, a few) target markets. This is to your advantage. Try to identify strategic pricing problems that deal only with your target market.

Step 3: Divide Your Current Strategic Retail Price Problems into Core-Strategy Areas and Supporting-Strategy Areas. Here you determine whether the price problems are core or supporting. For example, if your core strategy was built around a differential advantage, such as very high-quality products at equally high prices, a decision to add a new product or a new brand will present you with the question: Can we duplicate our high-quality and high-price core strategy, or do we lack the differential advantage with the new product or brand? Perhaps the high quality of the new product would not be easily recognized by customers. Perhaps we should not add the new product or brand. Perhaps an entirely new core marketing strategy is appropriate for the new product, requiring a new role for price in the retail marketing mix.

Price strategy questions that you will often consider to be *core* questions are:

a. How important a role price will play in your overall marketing strategy.
b. The price relationships among the related products you sell.
c. How you react to various forms of price competition from rivals.
d. When over a period of time you should make a basic shift in your overall basic pricing approach.

Core pricing strategy questions are those which deal very directly with your differential advantage. Your core price strategy (taken together with your core strategies for product, place, promotion, and people) is a main pillar of your overall marketing strategy. Your supporting price strategies are those that support either the core price strategy or some other core (or supporting) strategy.

Both core and supporting price strategy

areas require your time and attention. Even though supporting strategy areas are not as important as the core ones, this does not mean that they are unimportant. Good planning and execution in support areas may make a big difference in the success of your firm. In addition, problems probably occur more frequently in supporting- rather than in core-strategy areas. Therefore, you have more opportunities to excel in the supporting area.

Up to now you have (a) recorded your current retail price strategy, (b) identified your strategic pricing problems, and (c) divided these price problems into core and support areas. That is, you have analyzed your past and present performance with the price element. Upon this base you can now begin to plan for the future.

Step 4: Formulate Alternative Retail Price Strategies at Both Core and Support Levels. Some of the alternative pricing strategies you may wish to consider are briefly discussed below. These may be used in various combinations. Competitive strengths and weaknesses and the objectives of small retailers make some price strategies more or less attractive for small retailers than they would be for large ones. Other strategies seem to be equally attractive for both small and large retailers. The alternative pricing strategies are (a) price-level strategies, (b) product-line pricing, (c) stability pricing strategies, (d) psychological pricing strategies, (e) discriminatory pricing strategies, and (f) other areas of pricing strategy.

Price-level strategies are used by most small retailers. They involve the setting of prices at, above, or below the price level of target market competitors. You should always make the comparison within a single target market. Selling at different prices in different target markets involves another consideration of price strategy. Extreme cases of price-level strategy are skimming and penetration. These terms usually apply to the pricing of new products in relation to costs, desired market share, and potential competition. Such strategies are usually set by the manufacturer of the product, but they affect and are carried out by retailers. Therefore, small retailers should be aware of the price-level strategies of the manufacturers they represent.

Skimming combines relatively high prices (sometimes, all the traffic will bear) with heavy promotion in the early stages of the product life cycle. Over time, price is gradually lowered to attract additional segments of the market and meet competition. *Penetration* pricing sets new-product prices at slightly above costs in the hope of achieving a substantial market share in the early stages of the product life cycle. Penetration attempts to discourage competitive entry by other producers. Skimming and penetration are two extremes. You could also select a middle ground. Many small retailers tend to favor a skimming strategy because profit margins are usually better even though unit sales may be less. Skimming provides immediate dollars, which can be used for further promotion and/or taken as short-term profits.

Whether you should price at, above, or below the level of competition depends on such factors as costs, location, store hours, price sensitivity of customers, competitive reaction, and services offered. In effect you should seek the price-level strategy that is compatible with your target market, your environment, and your other marketing strategies. If you are going to price substantially above or below the level of competition, be sure that your target market customers can easily discover the reasons why.

Product-line pricing strategies are a way of taking account of both costs and demand differences in the various products making up a total product line. For example, prices for the "stripped-down" model, the "standard" model, and the "deluxe" model are established with a definite relationship to one another. Manufacturers often suggest product-line prices for retailers, but retailers usually have quite a bit of freedom in following such suggestions. Also, retailers can determine which part(s) of the line to emphasize. Products aimed at the same target market should bear meaningful price relationships to each other. This helps retail salespeople "trade up" the customers.

Regarding product-line pricing, one pricing expert noted that special attention should be given the "end items"—the lowest- and highest-priced items in a line. The lowest-priced item in a line affects sales greatly, because it is most frequently remembered by consumers and is often used as a basis of price and quality comparison. This price expert says:

For these two reasons, and possibly there are others, reductions in the price of the lowest-priced item in a company's line are likely to have a highly stimulating effect on sales. Similarly, increases in that price are likely to reduce sales far more than would increases in the price of in-between items.[1]

A term that is sometimes confused with product-line pricing (the pricing of a complete product line) is the somewhat different strategy of *price lining*. Price lining is the practice of selecting a few desirable retail selling prices for the products in a line. The store buyer then buys products to sell at those chosen pricing points. Manufacturers

also vary quantity and quality in order to sell at selected retail pricing points while allowing certain markups to retailers. For example, cookies may be packaged to be retailed on a "mix or match" basis at a selling price of three bags for $1. If costs increase, the size of the bag will decrease.

Stability pricing strategies once relied heavily on the so-called "fair trade" laws. Other forms of resale price maintenance designed to keep prices relatively stable are used by many marketers. These include limiting the number of retailers, consignment selling to maintain price and title in the hands of the supplier until the retailer has sold the goods to the consumer, cooperative promotional programs that limit participation to those retailers following "suggested retail prices," preticketing of merchandise, and extensive price advertising by manufacturers. Practices such as price notification of upcoming price changes and guarantees against price declines are given to retailers (and sometimes to consumers) to lessen the impact of price changes. Many of the methods of stabilizing prices are controlled by suppliers rather than retailers, but the retailers must participate to make such strategies effective.

Psychological pricing strategies are the several ways in which the expression of a price uses the principles of psychology. For example many retailers believe $1.98 is a much better price than $2. This is called *odd pricing*. Among the forms of psychological pricing strategy are the following:

a. *Prestige pricing:* The consumer assumes that a high price means high quality.
b. *Leader pricing:* A well-known and widely used low-priced product is given a "special" price to get customers into the store. If sold

at less than cost, it may be called a "loss leader."

c. *Bait pricing:* An advertised low price is used to get the customer into the store where salespeople attempt to switch the customer to profitable merchandise.

d. *Odd-even pricing:* Prices end in certain numbers, such as $1.98 or $39.95. At one time the odd price was also believed to be a means of discouraging cashier theft.

e. *Customary pricing:* Price is kept stable at one level over a long period—for example, the ancient 5-cent candy bar or the 10-cent comic book. Inflation has made customary pricing obsolete.

f. *Multiple-unit pricing:* Several units of an item are offered at a single price, such as three for 89 cents. Interestingly enough, even though 3 for 89 cents is more than 29 cents each, you will probably sell more of many products by pricing them at 3 for 89 cents. Can your cashiers handle multiple-unit pricing?

Discriminatory pricing strategies involve the variability in the prices charged similar buyers for similar products under similar conditions. Discriminatory pricing is usually favored by those customers who are discriminated *for* and opposed by those who are discriminated *against.* As a small retailer, you should ask yourself: Do our customers and potential customers know that our pricing strategy is to discriminate among customers? Under a *variable-price* policy, different prices are charged to some customers for the exact same product, at a given time, for comparable quantities and conditions of sale even though other customers did not receive this "different" price. On the other hand, a *single-price* policy is the practice of charging all customers the same price regardless of the size of their purchase or the conditions of sale. In between the extremes of variable-price and

one-price policies is the *nonvariable-price* policy, which does allow for different prices but only because of differences in size of purchase and conditions of sale. Nonvariable prices are uniformly administered and generally known about by classes of customers.[2]

Price discrimination takes many forms at the retail level and it is usually legal. A single-price policy works best in self-service stores and in large retail stores such as department stores where price bargaining between salespersons and customers would be very difficult to administer. Variable and nonvariable pricing can both be used in small retail stores. Many customers even expect to bargain on certain types of purchases. For example, some stores such as retail paint stores follow a standard practice of charging shelf price but giving a discount of 10 percent or more to steady customers and to almost anyone else who is knowledgeable enough to ask for the discount. Small retailers, marketing students, and many other people don't pay "list" price for their new cars, but some people do. Is this price discrimination?

Other pricing strategies are available to small retailers. *Unit pricing*, which shows the price per unit of weight or measure, can be used to influence consumers to buy larger sizes and brands with better markups. Some small retailers will use a strategy of *leasing* (or leasing with the lease payments applicable to purchase) rather than outright sale. Price will vary accordingly.

Although we have briefly discussed the main pricing strategy alternatives, the number of possible combinations is great. How can you evaluate each alternative and combination of alternatives as they apply to your small retail store?

Step 5: Evaluate the Alternatives in Various Combinations. You should now evaluate the pricing strategy alternatives generated in the previous step. Remember that you are merely evaluating alternatives; you are not yet selecting an alternative. Each alternative strategy and several meaningful combinations of alternatives should be evaluated in terms of your company goals and resources, marketing objectives, and price objectives. The effectiveness of alternative pricing strategies in helping to solve the current pricing problems identified in step 2 above should be considered. Pricing affects various parties such as your suppliers, your consumers, your competitors, and others. You should ask: What will be the desirable and undesirable effects of each pricing strategy alternative on each of these parties? You should also remember that what you are evaluating is alternative pricing strategies and not alternative prices. You and your managers should have some agreement among yourselves as to what criteria are to be used, and the relative importance of each, in evaluating the pricing strategy alternatives. Such agreement is essential, because price is such a nebulous element of the marketing mix.

Step 6: Choose Your New Retail Price Strategy. The time has now arrived for you to choose your new pricing strategy. It will be a combination of core and supporting price strategies, consistent with the rest of your marketing mix. Although its implementation will be adjusted on occasion by tactical moves, your basic pricing strategy should be chosen to last for some time. It will probably reflect your subjective value judgments and those of your managers. In many ways it will be probably identical to your previous pricing strategy.

Step 7: Plan the Details of Implementation for Your New Retail Price Strategy. How, when, where, and by whom is your new price strategy to be implemented? You now *plan* all the details so that the actual implementation will be smooth. Any details you fail to specify now will probably be neglected in the implementation. Things for you to consider here are timing, discount schedules, markdown rates and dates, cost calculations, projected sales estimates, the gathering and using of price information, and the assignment of specific tasks. For example, if your new pricing strategy calls for a semiannual 10 percent off regular price sale, are your cash registers and sales personnel capable of handling this? If certain customers such as schools, clubs, and churches get special discounts, do the salespeople know how to handle this? And do they know how to handle returns of merchandise sold at less than regular price? In this step you need to plan some down-to-earth details for making your new price strategy work. You should give special attention to areas where your strategy has been changed.

Step 8: Set Performance Standards and Monitor Feedback. In this step you set the criteria by which you will later evaluate your success in accomplishing your pricing, marketing, and company objectives. Thus you *plan* what the standards will be rather than actually use them, and you *plan* how feedback will be monitored rather than actually monitor the feedback.

Execution and control of the pricing strategy you have formulated will succeed only to the extent that the pricing strategy is sound and is a solid element in an overall sound marketing strategy. The planning phase is essential for successful execution and control. A "me too" pricing strategy or a lack of any pricing strategy at all is a neglect of one of the important five tools of the retail marketing mix. Setting prices and making other pricing decisions is meaningful only within the framework of a pricing strategy. You must determine your own price strategy. No one else can do it for you.

Some Practical Pricing Issues of Special Interest to Small Retailers

The pricing issues we look at next are probably also discussed in some of the trade journals you read. These pricing issues are (a) price cutting and price wars, (b) pricing during inflation, (c) how to make price changes, (d) price bargaining and group discounts, and (e) the importance of retail credit.

Price Cutting and Price Wars. Although small retailers are "competitive" on prices, they usually prefer to compete on a non-price basis. This is also true of large retailers. Retailers wish to exercise control over the setting of prices rather than have the forces of the marketplace do so. By "gentlemen's agreements" or simply by observing each other's pricing behavior, many retail competitors end up with similar prices. Is this competition or collusion?

Experience suggests that price collusion among small retailers is not uncommon. It has different social implications than would collusion among large firms because small retailers, both individually and collectively, do not exert much market power. For this reason and because enforcement would be nearly impossible, price collusion is rarely a legal concern among small retailers. For example, one small grocer can tell the small grocer on the next corner that he is raising milk prices 2 cents a half gallon to adjust for an increase in his wholesale cost from the dairy. Or, more likely, the driver of the dairy truck will act as the messenger. In any

event, before a day has gone by, both grocers will again have the same price (probably 2 cents higher) on milk. Are they competitive, or were they in collusion to raise the price of milk? The answer is probably "yes" to both of these questions. One observer stresses the necessity for price collusion among small retailers in the following terms:

The reason for such collusions is easy to understand. In most instances, the small businessman views his market as inelastic; there is only so much volume that can be done in the territory and lowering price does not increase it sufficiently to offset the loss of margin. So the businessman feels very strongly that he must protect the price structure for the goods he sells. He knows price cutting quickly leads to losses. Thus the price cutter becomes a hated foe. One must understand the strong emotions underlying this matter for they are not to be taken lightly. The businessman's entire life and the welfare of his family are tied up in his business. If it goes under, he is ruined. His life is a shambles.[3]

Price cutting as a marketing strategy (not the same thing as a temporary price reduction) is not often used by most small retailers. Most of them simply do not have the necessary financial resources to give them the staying power to survive a potential price war. Price cuts will be matched by large competitors if the cuts have been successful in drawing customer attention and business away from competitors. Therefore, small retailers are likely to "stay in line" in markets where they compete against large rivals. Price wars are more likely to take place where rivals are pretty much the same size. However, a small retailer may be forced to participate in a price war started by other firms.

What are your alternatives to getting involved in a downward spiral of prices that becomes a price war? You could close for a couple of weeks and then try to get your customers back. That would be tough. You could participate in the price war by matching but not undercutting prices. That will probably lose you some money. You can ignore the price war and let the competing rivals have the price-sensitive business. That will cost you some sales volume. Or you can attempt to end the price war by making carefully chosen public statements and by identifying the causes of the price war. Among the possible causes could be oversupply of a product, entry of a new retailer, actions of a supplier such as a bakery or dairy, or the desire of a competitor to increase market share. Whatever the reason, remember that price wars are sometimes fatal for small retailers.

Pricing during Inflation. Inflation increases your costs and the value of your inventory while at the same time it decreases the value of the profits you earn. And, with progressive income taxes, you get to keep a smaller percentage of your higher profits—if you are lucky enough to earn higher profits. When and how you raise your prices during inflation has important marketing and profit implications.

For small retailers, inflation means more funds are needed to support the same amount of physical inventory and a higher replacement cost for inventory. Inventory appreciation may show up as paper profits, depending on the inventory valuation method being used. Inflation means that pricing deserves more attention from the small retailer. The general rule is to take all price increases as soon as possible and to take the increases on all existing inventory as well as on incoming merchandise. Today's special sale price is yesterday's regular price. Consumers are urged to buy now before anticipated price increases go into effect. Your own buying practices can help you profit from a price increase. For example, a small retailer is told by his wholesaler that cigarette prices will go up 10 cents a carton next week. Knowing that cigarettes don't stay fresh forever and not having an excess of working capital, the retailer decides to buy a three-week supply this week in advance of the price increase. He sells this week's supply at the old price. Next week and the following week he makes an extra 10 cents on each carton sold. Hopefully, the new retail price of cigarettes will be more than 10 cents higher than the old price. If it is not, the percentage markup on cigarettes will decline even though the dollar markup stays the same.

How to Make Price Changes. On the college campus where I teach, the vending machine company has raised its prices (usually a nickel) every year for the past three years. Why haven't the students staged a vending machine boycott? Although I'm certain that at least a few students (and faculty members) have kicked a few vending machines, there hasn't been a boycott. The reason is that the price increases were timed to occur during the break between the end of spring semester and the beginning of summer session. Very few students were around to notice the price increase, and by the beginning of fall semester, new and returning students did not know what the old price had been.

Timing of price increases is important for all types of small retailers. The general rule is to take price increases as soon as possible. However, some times are better than others. Timing of price changes by small retailers is especially important for fashion and season merchandise. Too early a markdown amounts to a price-cutting strategy. Too late a markdown is almost totally ineffective. The amount of the markdown is also important. In general, total dollar markdowns will be less if you take a substantial markdown the first time, thus eliminating the need for additional markdowns. Added markups should always be taken as soon as possible on the assumption that, if an added markup is in order, the conditions that call for that added markup may not last forever.

Publicity, or sometimes the lack of it, and the form of the announcement of a price change can affect the outcome. For example, having a special sale just before a price increase goes into effect may increase sales and "soften the blow" to customers. At times, such as when a small increase is to be made or when a quiet price cut is desired, publicity will be avoided.

Should you change the product rather than the price? Probably not. Lowering the quality or decreasing the quantity of the product your customers are buying should not be done without some experimentation to see how well the changes will be accepted.

Price Bargaining and Group Discounts. Should a small retailer such as a furniture store, a drug store, a clothing store, or an auto parts store have so much price flexibility that very few customers pay the marked price and almost all customers get a dis-

count, the size of which depends upon their individual bargaining skill? Should bargaining for discounts be done on a group basis? A major employer, a student organization, a union, or some other organization representing a large group of consumers may contact a group of retailers who agree to give discounts to individual consumers belonging to the organization. A look at the participating retailers in these discount schemes reveals that most are small. In fact, large retailers are noticeably absent. Large retailers lack the flexibility to administer such programs, even if the programs could be made consistent with their merchandising methods and one-price image. Small retailers do have such flexibility. Whether or not they should use it here is another question.

The key factor in using either individual or group discounts is whether enough additional business results. At the same time, you want to keep the loyalty of customers not receiving the discount. One way is to attempt relative secrecy. Another way is to be open but very selective as to which individuals and groups receive publicity about the discounts. A third method may be to give some kind of a deal to all customers and make them all think they got the best deal. Whatever method you use, you should maintain rather tight control over the administration of the program and always take care to give at least the appearance of being fair to everyone.

Price bargaining, if properly done, gives your customers an opportunity to participate with you in the setting of prices. Participation can be a very important tool for building customer loyalty.

The Importance of Retail Credit. Your customers pay for the products they buy from you. The price is important, but how and when they pay the price is also important to them. Some customers live on credit by spending money they haven't yet earned. Others who can afford to pay cash find credit to be more convenient for certain purchases. If the goods and services you sell have a sufficient markup to support it, you should probably grant credit. (Groceries, for example, are sold on a low markup, and prices would have to be raised substantially to sell groceries on credit.) People like to buy on credit. They often buy more and higher-priced items when credit is available. And they are often less price-conscious when purchasing on credit.

Many small retailers use bank card credit systems such as VISA and MasterCard. Such systems cost money, but they do offer several advantages over operating your own credit plan. They also offer advantages over accepting personal checks from persons who are not regular customers. Checks from regular customers also have been known to bounce. Whatever credit plan you use, be sure to include the cost of operating the credit plan in the prices of your products. No credit plan is free. Even if you operate your own plan on which you charge interest, you may or may not be making money when all the costs are figured.

Despite what some retail salespeople may think, cash is not all bad. You can train your salespeople to request payment in cash when possible. But you must be careful to always cheerfully extend credit to those customers who want it and are credit-worthy. If your credit is granted "free" for a period of time, use it as you would any other customer service to enhance your sales. Should you give a discount for cash? You and some of your regular customers may be able to save some costs this way. Most customers don't ask for a discount for cash, but it may be important to some. In fact, some stores and consumers are organized for cash discounts in much the same way credit card systems are organized.

Pricing for Small Retail Service Firms

Much of what has been said about pricing in this and the previous chapter does apply to small retailers whose product is mostly a service rather than goods. However, some differences do exist. From personal experience, most of us are aware of differences in pricing practices in retail service firms. Regarding the marketing issues in the pricing of services, one expert source says:

There are at least five dimensions of service output which could provide criteria for a more effective pricing strategy in services. Two are objective and fairly widely used: (1) the time required to perform a particular service and (2) the extent to which capital goods are utilized in performance. . . .

Pricing can take on a more dynamic character through consideration of three output criteria of a subjective nature, currently: (1) the quality of performance, (2) the specialization content of performance, and (3) the value of performance to the buyer or client.[4]

Retail service firms are quite diverse, but it does appear that all are capable of using a pricing strategy if they desire to do so. Many small retail firms do not. The alternative pricing strategies presented earlier in this chapter in step 4 of the eight-step process do apply. For example, an auto service firm can use a loss leader such as a lube and oil change for $4.88 to get customers to bring their cars in. Once the customer is there, the firm can attempt to sell other needed (and sometimes unneeded) services.

Pricing in small retail service firms is dominated by a cost orientation—even though many small operators really don't know their costs. Normally, price is derived by multiplying either actual or standard time required to perform the service by an hourly rate (which may or may not be the actual pay rate), and adding the list price for materials used. A multiplier such as 2 or 2.5 is sometimes applied to the labor cost to cover indirect costs such as supervision and down time. From a competitive point of view, the operator of a small retail service firm may feel compelled to use prevailing price schedules in his locality or standard rate books for his industry, especially when the services being performed are rather standardized. One difficulty in service firm pricing is that customers do not understand the allocations (which are often quite arbitrary) of indirect costs to each service job. Flat-rate pricing (even though it is based on allocations) helps to solve this problem. Retail service firms that are members of franchise organizations are usually quite restricted by the franchisor in their pricing practices.

Services that are customized to the desires of the customer, or that are unique according to the talent and reputation of the one performing the service, need not be priced on a cost-oriented approach. The best price will be considerably above the cost floor and will bear little relationship to cost. Prices for these services depend more on demand than cost. Likewise, services performed on an emergency basis are often priced according to "what the traffic will bear." Some services, such as real estate sales and employment office services, are priced on a contingency commission basis where payment is contingent upon performance. Examples of discrimination can also be found in pricing of services. For example, movies charge different prices to different classes of customers, and the price also varies by time of day and day of week. Airlines, resorts, hotels and motels, and many other service firms also practice price discrimination in an attempt to operate at or near capacity.

As this discussion has shown, there is much diversity among the pricing practices of small retail service firms. Remember, pricing practices are not the same thing as pricing strategies. You may easily understand and follow some of the pricing practices discussed above, even in the absence of a pricing strategy. However, you should first formulate a pricing strategy as a part of your overall marketing strategy. The selection of pricing practices to implement your strategy will then make more sense and hopefully more profit.

Appendix to Chapter 10:[5] "A Pricing Checklist for Small Retailers"

FIRST PRINTED
JUNE 1976

This Aid is a checklist for the owner-manager of a small retail business. These 52 questions probe the considerations—from markup to pricing strategy to adjustments—that lead to correct pricing decisions. You can use this checklist to establish prices in your new store, or you can use it to periodically review your established pricing policy.

The author of this Aid is Bruce J. Walker, Associate Professor of Marketing at Arizona State University, Tempe, Arizona.

A retailer's prices influence the quantities of various items that consumers will buy, which in turn affects total revenue and profit. Hence, correct pricing decisions are a key to successful retail management. With this in mind, the following checklist of 52 questions has been developed to assist small retailers in making systematic, informed decisions regarding pricing strategies and tactics.

This checklist should be especially useful to a new retailer who is making pricing decisions for the first time. However, established retailers, including successful ones, can also benefit from this Aid. They may use it as a reminder of all the individual pricing decisions they should review periodically. And, it may also be used in training new employees who will have pricing authority.

THE CENTRAL CONCEPT OF MARKUP

A major step toward making a profit in retailing is selling merchandise for more than it costs you. This difference between cost of merchandise and retail price is called *markup* (or occasionally *markon*). From an arithmetic standpoint, markup is calculated as follows:

$$\text{Dollar markup} = \text{Retail price} - \text{Cost of the merchandise}$$

$$\text{Percentage markup} = \frac{\text{Dollar markup}}{\text{Retail price}}$$

If an item costs $6.50 and you feel consumers will buy it at $10.00, the dollar markup is $3.50 (which is $10.00—$6.50). Going one step further, the percentage markup is 35 percent (which is $3.50 ÷ $10.00). Anyone involved in retail pricing should be as knowledgeable about these two formulas as about the name and preferences of his or her best customer!

Two other key points about markup should be mentioned. First, the *cost of merchandise* used in calculating markup consists of the base invoice price for the merchandise *plus* any transportation charges *minus* any quantity and cash discounts given by the seller. Second, *retail price,* rather than cost, is ordinarily used in calculating percentage markup. The reason for this is that when other operating figures such as wages, advertising expenses, and profits are expressed as a percentage, all are based on retail price rather than cost of the merchandise being sold.

TARGET CONSUMERS AND THE RETAILING MIX

In this section, your attention is directed to price as it relates to your potential customers. These questions examine your merchandise, location, promotion, and customer services that will be combined with price in attempting to satisfy shoppers and make a profit. After some questions, brief commentary is provided.

1. Is the relative price of this item very important to your target consumers?

Yes ☐ No ☐

The importance of price depends on the specific product *and* on the specific individual. Some shoppers are very price-conscious, others want convenience and knowledgeable sales personnel. Because of these variations, you need to learn about your customers' desires in relation to different products. Having sales personnel seek feedback from shoppers is a good starting point.

2. Are prices based on estimates of the number of units that consumers will demand at various price levels?

☐ ☐

Demand-oriented pricing such as this is superior to cost-oriented pricing. In the cost approach, a predetermined amount is added to the cost of the merchandise, whereas the demand approach considers what consumers are willing to pay.

3. Have you established a price range for the product?

☐ ☐

The cost of merchandise will be at one end of the price range and the level above which consumers will *not* buy the product at the other end.

4. Have you considered what price strategies would be compatible with your store's total retailing mix that includes merchandise, location, promotion, and services?

☐ ☐

5. Will trade-ins be accepted as part of the purchase price on items such as appliances and television sets?

☐ ☐

SUPPLIER AND COMPETITOR CONSIDERATIONS

This set of questions looks outside your firm to two factors that you cannot directly control—suppliers and competitors.

6. Do you have final pricing authority?

☐ ☐

With the repeal of fair trade laws, "yes" answers will be more common than in previous years. Still, a supplier can control retail prices by refusing to deal with non-conforming stores (a tactic which may be illegal) or by selling to you on consignment.

7. Do you know what direct competitors are doing price-wise?

☐ ☐

8. Do you regularly review competitors' ads to obtain information on their prices?

☐ ☐

9. Is your store large enough to employ either a full-time or part-time comparison shopper?

☐ ☐

These three questions emphasize the point that you must watch competitors' prices so that your prices will not be far out of line—too high *or* two low—without good reason. Of course, there may be a good reason for out-of-the-ordinary prices, such as seeking a special price image.

A PRICE LEVEL STRATEGY

Selecting a general level of prices in relation to competition is a key strategic decision, perhaps the most important.

10. Should your overall strategy be to sell at prevailing market price levels?

Yes ☐ No ☐

The other alternatives are an above-the-market strategy or a below-the-market strategy.

11. Should competitors' temporary price reductions ever be matched?

☐ ☐

12. Could private-brand merchandise be obtained in order to avoid direct price competition?

☐ ☐

CALCULATING PLANNED INITIAL MARKUP

In this section you will have to look *inside* your business, taking into account sales, expenses, and profits before setting prices. The point is that your initial markup must be large enough to cover anticipated expenses and reductions *and* still produce a satisfactory profit.

13. Have you estimated sales, operating expenses, and reductions for the next selling season?

Yes ☐ No ☐

14. Have you established a profit objective for the next selling season?

☐ ☐

15. Given estimated sales, expenses, and reductions, have you planned initial markup?

☐ ☐

This figure is calculated with the following formula:

$$\text{Initial markup percentage} = \frac{\text{operating expenses} + \text{reductions} + \text{profit}}{\text{Net sales} + \text{reductions}}$$

Reductions consist of markdowns, stock shortages, and employee and customer discounts. The following example uses dollar amounts, but the estimates can also be percentages. If a retailer anticipates $94,000 in sales for a particular department, $34,000 in expenses, and $6,000 in reductions, and if the retailer desires a $4,000 profit, initial markup percentage can be calculated:

$$\text{Initial markup percentage} = \frac{\$34,000 + \$6,000 + \$4,000}{\$94,000 + \$6,000} = 44\%$$

The resulting figure, 44 percent in this example, indicates what size initial markup is needed *on the average* in order to make the desired profits.

16. Would it be appropriate to have different initial markup figures for various lines of merchandise or services?

☐ ☐

You would seriously consider this when some lines have much different characteristics than others. For instance, a clothing retailer might logically have different initial markup figures for suits, shirts and pants, and accessories. (Various merchandise characteristics are covered in an upcoming section.) You may want those items with the highest turnover rates to carry the lowest initial markup

STORE POLICIES

Having calculated an initial markup figure, you could proceed to set prices on your merchandise. But an important decision such as this should not be rushed. Instead, you should consider additional factors which suggest what would be the best price.

17. Is your tentative price compatible with established store policies?

Policies are written guidelines indicating appropriate methods or actions in different situations. If established with care, they can save you time in decision making and provide for consistent treatment of shoppers. Specific policy areas that you should consider are as follows:

18. Will a one-price system, under which the same price is charged every purchaser of a particular item, be used on all items?

The alternative is to negotiate price with consumers.

19. Will odd-ending prices, such as $1.98 and $44.95, be more appealing to your customers than even-ending prices?

20. Will consumers buy more if multiple pricing, such as 2 for $8.50, is used?

21. Should any leader offerings (selected products with quite low, less profitable prices) be used?

22. Have the characteristics of an effective leader offering been considered?

Ordinarily, a leader offering needs the following characteristics to accomplish its purpose of generating much shopper traffic: used by most people, bought frequently, very familiar regular price, and not a large expenditure for consumers.

23. Will price lining, the practice of setting up distinct price points (such as $5.00, $7.50, and $10.00) and then marking all related merchandise at these points, be used?

24. Would price lining by means of zones (such as $5.00-$7.50 and $12.50-$15.00) be more appropriate than price points?

25. Will cent-off coupons be used in newspaper ads or mailed to selected consumers on any occasion?

26. Would periodic special sales, combining reduced prices and heavier advertising, be consistent with the store image you are seeking?

27. Do certain items have greater appeal than others when they are part of a special sale?

28. Has the impact of various sale items on profits been considered?

Sale prices may mean little or no profit on these items. Still, the special sale may contribute to *total* profits by bringing in shoppers who may also buy some regular-price (and profitable) merchandise and by attracting new customers. Also, you should avoid featuring items that require a large amount of labor, which in turn would reduce or erase profits. For instance, according to this criterion, shirts would be a better special sale item than men's suits that often require free alterations.

29. Will "rain checks" be issued to consumers who come in for special-sale merchandise that is temporarily out of stock?

You should give particular attention to this decision since rain checks are required in some situations. Your lawyer or the regional Federal Trade Commission office should be consulted for specific advice regarding whether rain checks are needed in the special sales you plan.

NATURE OF THE MERCHANDISE

In this section you will be considering how selected characteristics of particular merchandise affect planned initial markup.

	Yes	No
30. Did you get a "good deal" on the wholesale price of this merchandise?	☐	☐
31. Is this item at the peak of its popularity?	☐	☐
32. Are handing and selling costs relatively great due to the product being bulky, having a low turnover rate, and/or requiring much personal selling, installation, or alterations?	☐	☐
33. Are relatively large levels of reductions expected due to markdowns, spoilage, breakage, or theft?	☐	☐

With respect to the preceding four questions, "Yes" answers suggest the possibility of or need for larger-than-normal initial markups. For example, very fashionable clothing often will carry a higher markup than basic clothing such as underwear because the particular fashion may suddenly lose its appeal to consumers.

34. Will customer services such as delivery, alterations, gift wrapping, and installation be free of charge to customers? ☐ ☐

The alternative is to charge for some or all of these services.

ENVIRONMENTAL CONSIDERATIONS

The questions in this section focus your attention on three factors outside your business, namely economic conditions, laws, and consumerism.

	Yes	No
35. If your state has an unfair sales practices act that requires minimum markups on certain merchandise, do your prices comply with this statute?	☐	☐
36. Are economic conditions in your trading area abnormal?	☐	☐

Consumers tend to be more price-conscious when the economy is depressed, suggesting that lower-than-normal markups may be needed to be competitive. On the other hand, shoppers are less price-conscious when the economy is booming, which would permit larger markups *on a selective basis*.

37. Are the ways in which prices are displayed and promoted compatible with consumerism, one part of which has been a call for more straightforward price information? ☐ ☐

38. If yours is a grocery store, it is feasible to use unit pricing in which the item's cost per some standard measure is indicated? ☐ ☐

Having asked (and hopefully answered) more than three dozen questions, you are indeed ready to establish retail prices. When you have decided on an appropriate percentage markup, 35 percent on a garden hose for example, the next step is to determine what percentage of the still unknown retail price is represented by the cost figure. The basic markup formula is simply rearranged to do this:

$$\text{Cost} = \text{Retail price} - \text{Markup}$$
$$\text{Cost} = 100\% - 35\% = 65\%$$

Then the dollar cost, say $3.25 for the garden hose, is plugged into the following formula to arrive at the retail price:

$$\text{Retail price} = \frac{\text{Dollar cost}}{\text{Percentage cost}} = \frac{\$3.25}{65\% \text{ (or .65)}} = \$5.00$$

One other consideration is necessary:

39. Is the retail price consistent with your planned initial markups? ☐ ☐

ADJUSTMENTS

It would be ideal if all items sold at their original retail prices. But we know that things are not always ideal.Therefore, a section on price adjustments is necessary.

	Yes	No
40. Are additional markups called for, because wholesale prices have increased or because an item's low price causes consumers to question its quality?	☐	☐
41. Should employees be given purchase discounts?	☐	☐
42. Should any groups of customers, such as students or senior citizens, be given purchase discounts?	☐	☐
43. When markdowns appear necessary, have you first considered other alternatives such as retaining price but changing another element of the retailing mix or storing the merchandise until the next selling season?	☐	☐
44. Has an attempt been made to identify causes of markdowns so that steps can be taken to minimize the number of avoidable buying, selling, and pricing errors that cause markdowns?	☐	☐
45. Has the relationship between timing and size of markdowns been taken into account?	☐	☐

In general, markdown taken *early* in the selling season or shortly after sales slow down can be smaller than *late* markdowns. Whether an early or late markdown would be more appropriate in a particular situation depends on several things: your assessment of how many consumers might still be interested in the product, the size of the initial markup, and the amount remaining in stock.

46. Would a schedule of automatic markdowns after merchandise has been in stock for specified intervals be appropriate?	☐	☐
47. Is the size of the markdown "just enough" to stimulate purchases?	☐	☐

Of course, this question is difficult—perhaps impossible—to answer. Nevertheless, it stresses the point that you have to carefully observe the effects of different size markdowns so that you can eventually acquire some insights into what size markdowns are "just enough" for different kinds of merchandise.

48. Has a procedure been worked out for markdowns on price-lined merchandise?	☐	☐
49. Is the markdown price calculated from the off-retail percentage?	☐	☐

This questions gets you into the arithmetic of markdowns. Usually, you first tentatively decide on the percentage amount price must be marked down to excite consumers. For example, if you think a 25 percent markdown will be necessary to sell a lavender sofa, the dollar amount of the markdown is calculated as follows:

Dollar markdown = Off-retail percentage × Previous retail price

Dollar markdown = 25% (or .25) × $500. = $125.

Then the markdown price is obtained by subtracting the dollar markdown from the previous retail price. Hence, the sofa would be $375.00 after taking the markdown.

50. Has cost of the merchandise been considered before setting the markdown price?

Yes ☐ No ☐

This is not to say that a markdown price should never be lower than cost; on the contrary, a price that low may be your only hope of generating some revenue from the item. But cost should be considered to make sure that below-cost markdown prices are the *exception* in your store rather than being so common that your total profits are really hurt.

51. Have procedures for recording the dollar amounts, percentages, and probable causes of markdowns been set up?

☐ ☐

Analyzing markdowns is very important since it can provide information that will assist in calculating planned initial markup, in decreasing errors that cause markdowns, and in evaluating suppliers.

You may be weary from thinking your way through the preceding sections, but don't overlook an important final question:

52. Have you marked the calendar for a periodic review of your pricing decisions?

☐ ☐

Rather than "laying an egg" due to careless pricing decisions, this checklist should help you lay a solid foundation of effective prices as you try to build retail profits.

11

How to Plan Your Retail Promotion Strategy

Your promotion strategy has a number of elements. The activities of (1) advertising, (2) personal selling, (3) sales promotion, and (4) public relations and publicity are all combined to form an integrated promotion strategy. Besides these, you will also be concerned with such matters as formulating an overall promotion strategy, how to determine the effectiveness of your promotion efforts, the image created by your promotion, and how to work with outsiders such as advertising agencies and media representatives. This chapter and the next will discuss these concerns.

Promotion as a Part of Your Retail Marketing Mix

The promotion of your retail business offers you many opportunities to achieve excellence or to make mistakes. Promotion should create excitement. It may use an old idea but with a new twist. It should not merely be an ego trip for you, but good promotion will bring you much personal satisfaction. The worst promotion mistake you can make is to have no promotion strategy at all but simply be led in several different directions by the various media salesmen. Some common promotion mistakes among small retailers are:

1. Advertising over too large a geographic area.

2. Spreading promotion efforts too thin to reach a threshold level.
3. Irregular scheduling on an "on-again, off-again" basis.
4. Failure to integrate all parts of the promotion mix.
5. Using poor timing.
6. Poor allocation of the promotion budget.
7. Occasional use of promotion gimmicks that conflict with the desired image.
8. Amateur production of the promotion message.[1]

The list could go on, but let's go to the positive side.

Promotion is all the informative and persuasive communication you use to make your target market aware of the rest of your marketing mix. Is promotion really necessary? You may do some business simply because you are there. However, retailing is a very competitive field. Competitors are after your present and potential customers. **Yes,** you must promote. Some promotion is necessary simply to replace customers who are lost over time. And, if you want to grow, you need to add new customers and sell more to present customers. For example, if you could gain one new customer each day while retaining all present customers, the cumulative effect on your sales growth would greatly overshadow your expenditures for promotion. The life of your business depends on promotion.

What about word-of-mouth advertising? Isn't that enough? Customers do exchange information among themselves. Some of this information is favorable and some is not. What is said is largely beyond your control, but you should be aware that a web of word-of-mouth communication does exist among consumers. Some consumers are opinion leaders and others are followers. Make an effort to use word-of-mouth

by asking your satisfied customers to tell their friends about your business. However, don't rely totally on word-of-mouth. It often works too slowly, and its impact is usually overestimated by many small retailers.

What do you want promotion to do for your retail business? The answer gives you what may be called your promotion objectives. Your basic objective is to promote your retail business. You wish to inform, persuade, or remind customers. Examples of general objectives might be to give information, to stimulate demand, to differentiate your store, or to accentuate the value of the products you sell. However, you will also want to decide upon your specific promotion objectives. For example, you might want your promotion to bring in a certain amount of store traffic, build a particular store image, stimulate sales of certain products or product groups, or attract certain types of new customers. For your individual retail store, you can set more specific objectives in each of these areas.

Depending on what your objectives are, you will decide what to promote. For example, if you want to draw maximum customer traffic, don't waste time and money promoting less important goods. Concentrate on products and departments that do draw traffic. Then use good display and merchandising techniques to help sell other merchandise. Make up a list of your specific promotion objectives. Then check your advertising, personal selling, sales promotion, publicity, and public relations. Do your promotion efforts conform to your objectives?

For most small retailers, promotion is an important part of the retail marketing mix. Within the area of promotion, how do you as a small retailer decide how much emphasis to place on advertising, or personal selling, or sales promotion, or public relations and publicity to get the best overall promotion mix? In general, advertising and personal selling are the two most important components of the promotion mix. However, this is not always so. Also, some small retailers will rely more heavily on the so-called supplementary forms of advertising such as specialty advertising, point-of-purchase displays, and direct mail. The optimum promotion mix varies from retailer to retailer depending on such factors as type of merchandise sold, amount of service given, location, type of customers served, and funds available.

The best promotion mix for small retailers often involves a different combination than that used by his big business competitors. Small retailers are generally more likely to rely more heavily on more targeted types of promotion. This is because some retailers are target marketers rather than mass marketers. To avoid wasted promotional effort, selective promotional methods and media are used to zero in on the target market of the small retailer.

The Image Your Promotion Creates

Go to a strange city or town where you are not familiar with the local stores. Read the retail advertisements in the local newspaper, listen to the radio advertisements, watch local TV. All the time you are doing this, you are forming mental pictures about the stores advertised. The advertising has created a store image for each one in your mind. Some of the store images are clear and strong; others are quite fuzzy and weak. Now, go visit some of these stores in person. Is the store image created by advertising carried out in the rest of the promotional effort? Is the advertising image consistent with the product image, the place image, the price image, and the people image? And is the overall store image held by customers and potential customers the image the retail store is trying to project? To answer these questions for your own store, you might ask an objective person from some other area to take a look at your promotion and store image.

Your promotion activities influence the image your store has. In fact, for potential customers who have not yet entered your store, the image they receive through advertising and other promotion may be the only one they have of it. Small things can cause a different image to be projected. For example, generous white space in a newspaper ad can be used to project a quality image, whereas an ad in heavy black print usually projects a bargain or low-priced image. Using a radio station which plays rock music may project a different image than a station with a classical music format or one with a country format. The voice of the radio announcer can also affect the image.

Your store's on-premise sign is one of your best advertising methods. A stark sign of simple materials may suggest discount prices with no frills. A sign made of elegant and expensive materials may suggest high-quality or luxury goods along with extensive customer services and high prices.

Decide what you want your store image to be. Then use promotion to help you project that image.

The Eight-Step Approach to Planning Your Promotion Strategy

By now you are familiar with the eight-step process for strategy planning. You can use it to help plan your promotion strategy. The eight steps are given below. After formulating your overall promotion strategy, you can use the tools of advertising, personal selling, sales promotion, and publicity and public relations to implement your strategy. In addition to your overall promotion strategy, you may wish to develop substrategies for using each of these promotion tools.

Because your promotion strategy is an integral part of your overall retail marketing strategy, we will assume that you have already fairly well defined (a) your overall company and marketing objectives, (b) the differential advantage upon which your strategy is based, (c) your target market, (d) your retail environment, and (e) tentative strategies for at least some of the other areas such as product, place, price, and people strategies. The eight steps in forming your promotion strategy are as follows:

1. Record your current retail promotion strategy.
2. Identify your strategic retail promotion problems.
3. Divide your current strategic retail promotion problems into core-strategy and supporting-strategy areas.
4. Formulate alternative retail promotion strategies at both core and support levels.
5. Evaluate the alternatives in various combinations.
6. Choose your new retail promotion strategy.
7. Plan the details of implementation for your new retail promotion strategy.
8. Set performance standards and monitor feedback.

As noted in previous chapters, this is a framework that will work for you. However, it is merely a framework. You also must work to turn it into a successful promotion strategy.

Step 1: Record Your Current Retail Promotion Strategy. If a promotion strategy does exist and you have not yet recorded it, this is the time to do so. Remember, making promotion decisions and having a promotion strategy are not the same thing. Strategy involves the rationale behind the decisions. Items to be recorded include the answers to such basic questions as the following:

1. Who are the target audience(s) to whom your promotion is directed?
2. What specific responses are you seeking from the members of the target audience? In other words, what are your specific promotion objectives?
3. What promotion tasks have been assigned to each of the promotion tools (advertising, personal selling, sales promotion, and publicity and public relations)?
4. What is the overall importance of promotion in your retail marketing mix?
5. In what ways does promotion relate to the other parts of your retail marketing mix?

Once these and other related questions have been answered, be sure to record the answers. Also, record the weaknesses as well as the strengths of your current retail promotion strategy.

Step 2: Identify Your Strategic Retail Promotion Problems. In this step you attempt to identify problems (and opportunities) in your current promotion strategy. Some of these problems may have surfaced when you were recording in step 1. Some will be strategic and others tactical.

You find problems by actively looking for them and by attempting to analyze the symptoms of problems. If you fail to recognize some problems, it may be because you do not have adequate feedback (see step 8 below). Ask yourself whether or not your promotion objectives are being met. Are your promotion objectives what they should be? Are promotion tasks being accomplished in an efficient and effective manner? Have environmental changes (such as a new competitor, a new neighborhood newspaper, or the changed format of a radio station) taken place that affect your current promotion strategy? You are looking for strategic rather than tactical promotion problems. For example, selecting radio station X, Y, or Z is a tactical decision that you can easily make, once a promotion strategy incorporating an advertising strategy has defined the role of radio as one of the advertising media for reaching the target market.

Step 3: Divide Your Current Strategic Retail Promotion Problems into Core-Strategy Areas and Supporting-Strategy Areas. Some of the core-strategy areas where promotion problems may arise have been suggested by the questions raised in steps 1 and 2. Other examples of core-strategy problem areas would be (a) determining the promotion message to be communicated and (b) planning for changes in the basic promotion strategy over time.

Whether a problem is in the core or a supporting promotion strategy will depend on its importance to your business. Core problems are usually the result of some major change, such as a change in your target market, the environment, your differential advantage, or your company goals. Problems in the core usually call for

greater strategy revisions than do problems in a supporting strategy.

Supporting promotion strategies are those that support either the core promotion strategy or some other core (or supporting) strategy. For example, a core strategy calling for increased customer awareness of a relatively new product or service being offered by your store could be supported by a change in your advertising media and message strategies (both supporting in this case) to emphasize demonstration of the new product or service.

Having recorded the current promotion strategy, identified strategic promotion problems, and divided these into core and support areas, you now have a sound basis for planning for the future.

Step 4: Formulate Alternative Retail Promotion Strategies at Both Core and Support Levels. Your promotion objectives—the things you want your promotion to do for your retail business—act as the guide for formulating new alternative promotion strategies. The setting of your promotion objectives is, in itself, a core promotion strategy decision. Once objectives have been set, other strategy questions can be meaningfully considered. In this step you are merely formulating alternatives; you are *not* yet evaluating or selecting an alternative.

Your promotion objectives should be realistic and specific, stating exactly what is to be accomplished, when, and by whom, and how success is to be measured. The scope of realistic promotion objectives is not the same for small as for large retailers. For example, if Sears opens a new location, it may budget, on an investment basis, thousands of dollars to gain an immediate share of market for its new store. Many small retailers, on the other hand, must gradually build up their business because funds to invest in extra-heavy promotional effort are not available.

The alternative promotional strategies available to any small retailer are almost innumerable. Many of the alternatives will revolve around the tasks you assign to advertising, personal selling, sales promotion, and publicity and public relations. You will probably want to customize your promotion according to what you and your people do best. For example, if you and your sales people are extremely good at personal selling, you may wish to build your entire promotion strategy around this strength. Or if attractive displays are one of your strengths, you'll want to build your promotion strategy to take advantage of this strength.

Step 5: Evaluate the Alternatives in Various Combinations. Once a number of core- and support-level promotion strategy alternatives have been generated, you are in a position to evaluate them in various combinations. In this step you are evaluating; in the next step you will make a choice. Your evaluation involves assessing the reactions of competitors, the chances for successfully reaching your objectives, and the costs of different alternatives. You will ask yourself: To what extent will this or that promotion alternative help solve the promotion problems identified in step 2 above? Remember, you are evaluating alternative promotional strategies—not alternative promotional campaigns, themes, or individual promotions. During the implementation of your promotion strategy you will evaluate these latter items.

Step 6: Choose Your New Retail Promotion Strategy. The time has arrived for you to choose among the alternatives. Your choice will be a combination of core and supporting promotion strategies. Your plans should allow enough flexibility in both the structure and the budget for the tactical adjustments that will be desired later. If you came up with several good alternatives, you will select one that meets the promotional needs of your business and with which you personally feel compatible.

In some ways your promotion strategy will be novel and different. A major part of it probably will be similar to your current promotion strategy.

Step 7: Plan the Details of Implementation for Your New Retail Promotion Strategy. This is the how, when, and where, the by-whom and by-what-means, of the implementing of your new promotion strategy. For smooth implementation, such details must be planned. For example, in this step you will (a) assign various promotional tasks among the tools and within each tool—for example, to the major advertising media (newspapers, radio, television, and so on) and supplementary advertising media (specialty advertising, directories, on-premise signs), (b) determine the exact nature of the message to be communicated, (c) provide for coordinating the promotion schedule, and (d) plan the working relationships with outside people such as media salespeople, advertising agencies, and shopping center promotion managers.

Step 8: Set Performance Standards and Monitor Feedback. Here you set the criteria by which you will later evaluate the ways and the degree to which your new promotion strategy has been successful. You also plan for a constant flow or feedback of information so that you can make tactical adjustments as you implement your strategy. In practice, you will find it difficult to measure precisely the effectiveness of promotional activities. Nonetheless, you will want to get some idea of how well you are doing.

More is said in the next chapter about measuring promotion effectiveness. Our attention now turns to the four tools by which promotion strategies are implemented: (1) advertising, (2) personal selling, (3) sales and promotion, and (4) publicity and public relations.

Using Advertising in Your Retail Promotion Strategy

Retail advertising is mass communication by an identified sponsor (the retailer) of a promotional message. It is paid for and placed by the retailer to inform, persuade, and remind customers and potential customers through nonpersonal advertising media. Our brief discussion of advertising will first examine what advertising can do for your small retail business. Then we shall discuss advertising in terms of your message strategy and your media strategy.

Since it is impossible to give comprehensive coverage in a few pages, you may want to consult some additional sources of information on advertising that are helpful to small retailers:

1. *How to Advertise and Promote Your Small Business* by Gonnie McClung Siegel, a short paperback book published by John Wiley & Sons, Inc., 1978.
2. *Advertising Guidelines for Small Retail Firms*, Small Marketers Aid No. 160, an eight-page pamphlet published by the Small Business Administration.
3. *Selecting Advertising Media: A Guide for Small Business*, 2nd ed., Small Business Management Series No. 34, a 133-page booklet published by the Small Business Administration.
4. *Advertising Small Business*, a twenty-page booklet in the Small Business Reporter series published by the Bank of America.[2]

What Advertising Can Do for You. Advertising can help you reach some of your promotional objectives. Within the framework of the promotion strategy you have established, you can create a successful advertising program. Circumstances favorable to the advantageous use of advertising include the availability of sufficient funds, products where emotional motives are important, a favorable demand trend, consistent product quality, hidden product qualities, and a product that can be sold impersonally to a mass market. The retailer does not always find himself in such circumstances. What, then, can the small retailer expect from advertising? The following comments on what advertising *can* and *cannot* do give you a realistic idea of what to expect:

Advertising has two top objectives: to draw in new customers, and to help hold the old ones. Advertising can also identify a business with the goods or service it offers. It can build confidence in a business. It can create good will. It can increase sales and speed turnover. It can reduce your expenses by spreading them over a larger volume. However, there are a number of things advertising cannot do. Advertising can't make a business prosper if that business offers only a poor product or an inferior kind of service. Advertising can't lead to sales if the prospects that it brings in are ignored or poorly treated. Adver-

tising can't create traffic overnight, or increase sales with a single ad. (Unfortunately, many smaller businesses follow this kind of touch-and-go advertising policy.) Advertising that is untruthful or misleading will not build confidence in the business that sponsors it.[3]

Your Advertising Message Strategy. The planning and implementing of your message strategy is largely a creative process. Determining what to say and how to say it is more an art than a science. Especially for the "how to say it" portion, you may get some outside help, such as from a small advertising agency.

In thinking about your advertising message, you may wish to think in terms of the so-called AIDA checklist, which reduces message strategy to four major points:

1. Get *ATTENTION* through such devices as size, color, and headlines.
2. Arouse *INTEREST* by using a theme that is interesting to your intended audience.
3. Create a *DESIRE* on the part of your audience by showing how your store and the products you sell can meet their needs.
4. Get *ACTION,* such as moving people to visit your store or ask for an advertised item.

In somewhat more practical terms, the finer points of message strategy for newspapers and other print media are presented in checklist form in Table 11-1. Many retailers are careless in observing these basic requirements of good advertising. For example, a survey of the American Newspaper Publishers Association showed that "only 33 percent of the ads studied carried informative headlines, 50 percent failed to include all pertinent facts, only 52 percent gave the store's complete address, only 44 percent the phone number, and only 39 percent its hours of business."[4] How do

your advertisements stack up on these requirements of good advertising?

Your Advertising Media Strategy. Advertising media are the vehicles by which advertising messages are communicated to your audience. Examples are newspapers, radio, television, and your on-premise store signs. Some advertising media are called mass media because they reach large audiences. However, most small retailers are target rather than mass marketers. Their intended audience is the target market, not the entire mass. To use advertising media successfully, therefore, small retailers must act quite selectively when deciding which media to use and how to use them. A four-step approach is suggested.[5] Each step represents one of the strategic media questions faced by small retail advertisers.

1. Define the specific requirements of the media program.
2. Select the medium or combination of media that best fits those requirements.
3. Select a vehicle or vehicles (e.g., a specific TV station or a specific newspaper) within a chosen medium.
4. Schedule insertions within the vehicle and determine size or length of time of the message.

In other words, determining media requirements is the first step of what turns out to be a matching process between the target audience and the available means for effectively reaching them with the advertising message. Creative requirements such as the need to display the product in color may limit media selection. The characteristics of your target market, the type of store you operate, and the funds you have available will all be requirements to consider in media selection.

Table 11–1.

Checklist for Promotional Advertising (Newspaper)

*Merchandise	Does the ad offer merchandise having wide appeal, special features, price appeal, and timeliness?
Medium	Is a newspaper the best medium for the ad, or would another—direct mail, radio, television, or other—be more appropriate?
Location	Is the ad situated in the best spot (in both section and page location)?
Size	Is the ad large enough to do the job expected of it? Does it omit important details, or is it overcrowded with nonessential information?
*Headline	Does the headline express the major single idea about the merchandise advertised? The headline should usually be an informative statement and not simply a label. For example, "Sturdy shoes for active boys, specially priced at $6.95," is certainly better than "Boys' Shoes, $6.95."
Illustration	Does the illustration (if one is used) express the idea the headline conveys?
*Merchandise information	Does the copy give the basic facts about the goods, or does it leave out information that would be important to the reader? ("The more you tell, the more you sell.")
Layout	Does the arrangement of the parts of the ad and the use of white space make the ad easy to read? Does it stimulate the reader to look at all the contents of the ad?
Human interest	Does the ad—through illustration, headline, and copy—appeal to customers' wants and wishes?
*"You" attitude	Is the ad written and presented from the customer's point of view (with the customer's interests clearly in mind), or from the store's?
*Believability	To the objective, nonpartisan reader, does the ad ring true, or does it perhaps sound exaggerated or somewhat phony?
Type face	Does the ad use a distinctive typeface—different from those of competitors?
*Spur to action	Does the ad stimulate prompt action through devices such as use of a coupon, statement of limited quantities, announcement of a specific time period for the promotion or impending event?
*Sponsor identification	Does the ad use a specially prepared signature cut that is always associated with the store and that identifies it at a glance? Also, does it always include the following institutional details: Store location, hours open, telephone number, location of advertised goods, and whether phone and mail orders are accepted?

* The seven items starred are of chief importance to the smaller store.

Source: John W. Wingate and Seymour Helfant, *Small Store Planning for Growth,* 2d ed., Small Business Management Series No. 33 (Washington, D.C.: Small Business Administration, 1977), p. 69.

If you feel that media selection represents quite a challenge, you are not alone. One study of small retailers in small towns showed that (a) marketing was their most frequently reported business problem, (b) within the area of marketing, advertising was their most frequently reported marketing problem, and (c) within the area of advertising, media selection was their most frequently reported advertising problem.[6] The four-step approach outlined above should help, especially if you use it within the framework of your overall promotion strategy.

Your media strategy calls for some combination of your message *impact* in terms of media reach, frequency, and continuity. *Reach* is the total number of persons to whom your message is delivered. *Frequency* is the number of times your message is delivered during a given period (often a four-week period). *Continuity* is the total length of time over which the schedule runs. You should decide what is the ideal balance of these items within the limitations of your advertising budget. For each small retailer there will be situations and circumstances such as objectives, size of target market, existence of available media (and vehicles), available schedules, and media strategies of competitors that will determine the ideal media mix. One general guide is suggested by the principle of market dominance described in earlier chapters. This principle suggests that, as a small retailer, you will want to limit the number of advertising media you use (and the number of vehicles within each medium) to such a point that at least the threshold level of impact will be achieved. In other words, be a target advertiser as well as a target marketer.

The advantages and disadvantages of all the major advertising media are discussed at great length in nearly every advertising book. Therefore, such a discussion will not be presented here. However, a comparison chart for advertising media from the perspective of a small business is given in Figure 11-1. In addition, some of the so-called supplementary or minor advertising media will be discussed. This is done because some of these media often assume major importance for small retailers. This is so because they can be used very effectively, at a reasonable cost, to reach the target market. Sometimes these minor media are used alone, and quite often they are used in conjunction with the selective use of so-called mass media. They are also often combined with sales promotion and other parts of the total promotion effort.

Window displays vary in importance from retailer to retailer. Their primary purpose is to attract the attention of passersby. Some retailers use window displays over the entire front end of the store. Others with almost no pedestrian traffic may not use windows at all. However, for retailers in shopping centers, in downtown areas, near bus stops, or even near major intersections where automobile traffic stops, store windows can be effectively used to attract customers. In addition to helping create your image and selling specific merchandise, window displays can lend prestige to your store.

Window displays should be evaluated in much the same way as any other kind of advertising. Try to determine (a) the number of people passing your window during a given period, (b) the number of people who glance at your window, (c) the number who actually stop to look, and (d) the number who then come into your store. The brief checklist presented below may help you to increase these numbers.[7]

*Several boards must be purchased for these GRPs.

MEDIUM	MARKET COVERAGE	TYPE OF AUDIENCE	SAMPLE TIME/SPACE COSTS	PARTICULAR SUITABILITY	MAJOR ADVANTAGE	MAJOR DISADVANTAGE
DAILY NEWSPAPER	Single community or entire metro area; zoned editions sometimes available.	General. Tends more toward men, older age group, slightly higher income and education.	Per agate line, weekday: Circ: 5,000:$ .16 25,000:$ .40 250,000:$ 1.50	All general retailers.	Flexibility.	Nonselective audience.
WEEKLY NEWSPAPER	Single community usually; sometimes a metro area.	General; usually residents of a smaller community.	Per agate line: Circ: 1-5,000:$ .13 5-10,000:$ .26 10-20,000:$ .31	Retailers who service a strictly local market.	Local identification.	Limited coverage.
SHOPPER	Most households in a single community; chain shoppers can cover a metro area.	Consumer households.	Per agate line: Circ: 23,000:$ .19 57,000:$ .40 88,000:$ .40	Neighborhood retailers and service businesses.	Consumer orientation.	A giveaway and not always read.
TELEPHONE DIRECTORIES	Geographic area or occupational field served by the directory.	Active shoppers for goods or services.	Yellow Pages, per half column, per month: Pop: 14-18,000:$ 13.00 110-135,000:$ 24.53 700-950,000:$ 77.65	Services, retailers of brand name items; highly specialized retailers.	Users are in the market for goods or services.	Limited to active shoppers.
DIRECT MAIL	Controlled by the advertiser.	Controlled by the advertiser through use of demographic lists.	Mailing of 11"×17", 2-color, 4-page letter and business reply card in #10 envelope; label addressed; third class mail: $.25 each.	New and expanding businesses; those using coupon returns or catalogs.	Personalized approach to an audience of good prospects.	Number of variables that can thwart success of a mailing.
RADIO	Definable market area surrounding the station's location.	Selected audiences provided by stations with distinct programming formats.	Per 60-second one-time AM morning drive time spot: Pop: 20,000:$ 10.00 357,000:$ 17.00 2,754,500:$250.00	Business catering to identifiable groups: teens, commuters, housewives.	Market selectivity, reach and frequency.	Must be bought consistently to be of value
TELEVISION	Definable market area surrounding the station's location.	Varies with the time of day; tends toward younger age group, less print-oriented.	Per 30-second daytime spot; one time; highest priority status: Pop: 743,600:$ 40.00 1,656,800:$190.00 2,957,600:$475.00	Highly personal, owner-oriented businesses; sellers of products or services with wide appeal.	Dramatic impact, wide market coverage.	Cost of time and cost and complexity of ad production.
TRANSIT	Urban or metro community served by transit system; may be limited to a few transit routes.	Transit riders, especially wage earners and shoppers; pedestrians.	Per inside 11"×28" card: per month: 25 buses:$ 75.00 225 buses: $380.00	Businesses along transit routes, especially those appealing to wage earners.	Repetition and length of exposure.	Limited audience.
OUTDOOR	Entire metro area or single neighborhood.	General, especially auto drivers.	Per 12"×25" poster; 100 GRP per month: Pop: 2,400: $125.00 109,000: $108.08* 461,000: $157.60*	Amusements, tourist businesses, brand name retailers.	Dominant size, frequency of exposure.	Cost.
LOCAL MAGAZINE	Entire metro area or region; zoned editions sometimes available.	General; tends toward better educated, more affluent.	Per one-sixth page; black and white: Circ: 25,000: $185.00 40,000: $295.00	Restaurants, entertainments, specialty shops, mail order businesses.	Delivery of a loyal, special interest audience.	Limited audience.

Figure 11-1. Advertising Media Comparison Chart. (Reprinted with permission of Bank of America, N.T. & S.A., *Small Business Reporter,* "Advertising Small Business," Vol. 13, No. 8, Copyright © 1976, 1978.

1. *Merchandise selected*
   a. Is the merchandise timely?
   b. Is it representative of the stock assortment?
   c. Are the articles harmonious in type, color, texture, and use?
   d. Are the price lines of the merchandise suited to the interests of passersby?
   e. Is the quantity on display suitable (that is, neither overcrowded nor sparse)?

2. *Setting*
   a. Are glass, floor, props, and merchandise clean?
   b. Is the lighting adequate (so that reflection from the street is avoided)?
   c. Are spotlights used to highlight certain parts of the display?
   d. Is every piece of merchandise carefully draped, pinned, or arranged?
   e. Is the background suitable, enhancing the merchandise?
   f. Are the props well suited to the merchandise?
   g. Are window cards used, and are they neat and well placed?
   h. Is the entire composition balanced?
   i. Does the composition suggest rhythm and movement?

3. *Selling power*
   a. Does the window present a readily recognized central theme?
   b. Does the window dramatically use light, color, size, motion, composition, and/or item selection?
   c. Does the window arouse a desire to buy (as measured by shoppers entering the store)?

Interior or *point-of-purchase displays* will help you sell more products to customers who are already in your store. A point-of-purchase (P-O-P) display can be used to reinforce other advertising and to act as a silent salesperson that provides information to your customers. Such a display hits customers when they are in the store and ready to buy. It can also trigger "impulse" sales by suggesting better or additional merchandise to customers. Selling additional merchandise to your present customers is one of the least expensive ways to increase sales.

Common forms of P-O-P are floor displays, racks, counter displays, window displays, over-the-wire banners, shelf talkers, and other temporary items. Functional fixtures such as soft-drink dispensers and permanent displays such as those for Timex watches, various brands of panty hose, Hartz Mountain pet products, and various brands of beer and liquor also act as advertisements at the point-of-purchase. All these advertisements reach customers when and where they are ready to buy.

Much P-O-P advertising is provided either free or at a very reasonable cost by manufacturers and wholesalers. In fact many retailers receive more P-O-P materials than they can possibly use. In order, then, to decide what and how much to use, ask yourself: Will this display increase total store sales and profits or merely shift sales from one brand to another within a product group? Will the materials fit in with the store's overall appearance and image or will they create a cluttered effect? Does the display promote the store or merely the manufacturer's brand? Does it help sell related products? Does the material feature a store-wide theme? How will my customers react to the materials?

On-premise signs are the major means of identifying your retail store. Compared to other promotion methods, signs can be a very economical way of communicating with customers, especially if your store has a good location. Even though the initial cost (or lease payments) may seem high, a sign provides long-term benefits that should more than pay its way.

Signs perform three major communication functions for a retail store. First, signs provide information about your business and direct people to its location. Second, signs act as a format for street advertising. Third, your sign is a very important part (perhaps even the center of attention) of your store image.

Consider the following advantages of signs listed in a publication of the Small Business Administration:

1. Signs are oriented to your trade area. Signs do not waste your resources by requiring you to pay for wasted advertising coverage. The people who see your sign are the people who live in your trade area.

2. Signs are always on the job repeating your message to potential customers. Your on-premise sign communicates to potential customers twenty-four hours a day, seven days a week, week after week, month after month, year after year. Every time people pass your business establishment they see your sign. The mere repetition of the message will help them remember your business.

3. Nearly everyone reads signs. Signs are practical to use, for nearly everyone is used to looking at signs and using signs, even small children. Studies have shown that people do read and remember what is on signs. When special items are displayed, sales increase for these particular items within the store.

4. Signs are inexpensive. When compared to the cost of advertising in some other media, the on-premise sign is very inexpensive. . . . Unless your trade area encompasses an entire city or region, where you must rely upon broad based media coverage, there is no better advertising dollar value than your on-premise sign.

5. Signs are available to each and every shop-owner. There is no need to schedule the use of your sign. Your sign is available to you whenever you need it and to be used however you please.

6. Signs are easy to use. No special skills or resources are needed to operate a sign once it has been installed. If it is an illuminated sign, all you need to do is flip the switches and that may not be necessary with timing equipment. Once the initial expenditures are made, no special resources or professional services are needed. You need only operate and maintain your sign.[8]

Because you will be using the same sign for a long period, it might be wise to seek the assistance of your local sign company before making your selection. You may also wish to incorporate some of your own ideas into the store sign. Before doing so, you may wish to consult an interesting book call *The Sign User's Guide*,[9] which not only covers how to assess the sign needs of a business, evaluate the effectiveness of signs, and select appropriate sign types, sizes, and copy, but also provides some technical hints on sign design. For example, the most legible color combinations to use in lettering of outdoor signs are, in order of legibility, (1) black on yellow, (2) black on white, (3) yellow on black, (4) white on blue, (5) yellow on blue, (6) green on white, (7) blue on yellow.[10]

Specialty Advertising provides another opportunity to make your promotional efforts more effective. In this type of advertising, your message is imprinted on a useful device such as a yardstick, calendar, matchbook, pen, pencil, key chain, or even a custom-built product such as the campaign described below and illustrated in Figure 11-2. For the small retailer, specialty advertising has the advantage of being customized to fit your individual promotion needs.

Figure 11-2. An Example of Specialty Advertising

It is limited only by the creativity of the specialty-advertising representative serving you. Specialties have a long life. For example, a calendar will display your message for an entire year. Although unit cost per item may seem high at first, the cost per exposure of the often-repeated advertising message can prove to be quite cost effective. Also, the total cost of an advertising specialty campaign is sometimes fairly small compared to that of using other media.

Figure 11-2 illustrates the specialty advertising used quite successfully by a small retailer in a small college community. In order to increase student trade in the Pour House Lounge, the retailer and Hastings Advertising Agency pursued the following strategy at a cost of less than $600:

Strategy: *To appeal to the college trade, the lounge designated one evening each week as Central Technical College night and another evening was set aside for a local liberal arts school. The specialty-advertising counselor con-* *verted a commonplace fruit jar into a novel beer mug imprinted with the name of the lounge and message announcing the entertainment staples, "Foozin,' Boozin' and Pool." The customer's name was printed on the jar, and he had the choice of keeping the jar or leaving it on a display shelf. On subsequent visits, he could then order drinks served in his personal jar. Inasmuch as the mug was a 16-ounce (one liquid pound) jar, it became customary for guests to step up to the bar and order "one pound of beer." A second advertising specialty, a T-shirt portraying Pour House entertainment, was issued the following month to customers, who had an opportunity to purchase extra shirts.*

Result: *More than half the initial supply of jars was exhausted the opening night of the promotion.*[11]

The *Yellow Pages* (in some parts of the world they are other colors) can be one of the best places for small retailers to advertise. Their major advantage is that consumers who look in the Yellow Pages are usually ready to buy. They are simply in the process of determining *where* to buy. For example, if a consumer in a major city had decided to buy a particular brand of canoe, he can look in the Yellow Pages to find the name, telephone number, and address of all boat dealers who carry that brand of canoe.

The Yellow Pages are especially important to many small retail service firms. The telephone company has done much marketing research on how and to what extent consumers use the Yellow Pages. Ask your local representative for help. If you are going to use the Yellow Pages as a part of your advertising program, fit them into your total advertising and promotion strategy. Make your ad result in more than just an increase in the size of your monthly telephone bill!

Other Media can also be used by small retailers. For example, handbills may be distributed at the store, on cars, or at residences at a low cost. Be sure to select reliable people to circulate them and remember that some potential customers may consider handbills a nuisance and act accordingly. You might also consider advertising in religious, fraternal, high school, and college newspapers.

Using Cooperative Advertising to Stretch Your Advertising Dollars. Cooperative advertising is an arrangement between a manufacturer and a retailer whereby the retailer advertises the manufacturer's product in his retail advertising and the manufacturer pays a portion of the cost (often 50 percent of the advertising cost up to an amount equal to 5 percent of the retailer's purchases of merchandise). To qualify for co-op funds, the retailer must meet certain conditions set forth by the manufacturer. Because

some media (such as local newspapers) charge retailers lower rates than manufacturers, the manufacturer may also be stretching his advertising dollar through cooperative advertising. Otherwise, co-op may amount to a form of price concession that is more often taken advantage of by large than by small retailers.

Co-op advertising provides the small retailer with an incentive to carry and advertise a product. If the product sells well, both you and the manufacturer are benefited. However, co-op does have some disadvantages. You are required to keep records and submit tear sheets to insure reimbursement. Payment is sometimes slow, and vendor relations can become strained.

If you use co-op effectively, it can be profitable for you. Help is probably available through your wholesaler or trade association. For example, *Hardware Retailing* magazine provided its readers with a list of lawn and garden manufacturers who were offering co-op advertising programs for the coming season. The brief magazine article went on to offer the following advice and help:

By merely concentrating on the 8 or 10 lawn and garden lines you advertise most heavily and collecting co-op on those, a dealer can significantly enhance his promotional might.

An inquiry number accompanies each manufacturer's name for your convenience. Circle the appropriate number on the inquiry card located at the back of the issue for information on the specific plan available. The cards will be forwarded to manufacturers for their response.

A complete list of hundreds of manufacturers offering co-op money in all departments is available in the National Retail Hardware Association's 1979 Advertising Planning Calendar.[12]

12

How to Plan Your Retail Promotion Strategy

(continued)

This chapter continues our discussion of retail promotion strategy. It will cover how to use personal selling, sales promotion, public relations, and publicity in your retail promotion strategy, as well as how to de-termine your total promotion budget, how to measure the effectiveness of your promotion efforts, and how to find outside help to make your promotions more successful.

Using Personal Selling in Your Retail Promotion Strategy

You and your salespeople can use good salesmanship to personally promote your business. Our brief discussion here will not cover the operational aspects of retail sales-manship. Rather, we will look at some strategic decision areas of personal selling such as what should be the role and impor-tance of personal selling in your overall promotion strategy, what selling tasks need to be performed, who should do the selling and to whom, what selling processes are ap-propriate, and how is personal selling to be integrated into the overall promotion strat-egy? Once you have answered such ques-tions, you have a framework within which you can consider the day-to-day opera-tional questions (such as those related to recruiting, selecting, training, motivating, and compensating) retail salesforce man-agement.

Advantages and Disadvantages of Personal Selling. Many successful small retailers use personal selling as a major form of promotion. After all, it doesn't take a large promotion budget to do a good job of personal selling. Personal selling also provides you with immediate feedback from you customers. It is a direct one-on-one form of communication that effectively engages the customer's attention. Your promotion message can be adjusted to suit each customer's needs. You can use personal selling before, during, and after an actual transaction.

One disadvantage of personal selling is that the cost may be high. Self-service and self-selection of merchandise by customers are often less expensive, and other forms of promotion such as advertising may be able to perform certain tasks at a lower cost per contact. Also, salespeople are not usually able to actually attract people into your store; rather, they are effective only after the customer has entered. Finally, an unskilled salesperson may end up chasing away more customers than just about anything else in your operation.

Importance of Personal Selling. Personal selling tends to play a more important role in the retail promotion mix when one (or more) of the following conditions is met:

1. The retailer's own management philosophy has for a long time strongly emphasized personal selling. You can probably think of some stores where this is true.
2. The nature of the product favors personal selling because of such factors as complex product features, installation, customization, the need for demonstration, infrequent purchase, and natural sales resistance.
3. Because of trade-ins or price bargaining, the sales transaction process itself calls for personal selling.

4. The markup percentage and dollar amount are high enough to more than cover the expenses involved in personal selling.
5. The customer's needs are not well defined in his or her mind. In this case, personal selling can be used to create a desire and to build confidence in your store.
6. The number of potential customers is very small, or appropriate advertising media at a reasonable cost are unavailable.

Over the past several years, a substantial shift has taken place in many lines of retail merchandising. Its direction has been away from personal selling and in favor of pre-selling through advertising supported by retail display on a self-service basis. The nature and extent of this shift can be seen in mass retailing. Speaking of this shift, one noted retailing book reports:

Some observers believe that the era of informed, creative personal selling has passed and that impersonal selling now prevails. As one discount house operator has said: "We don't want salesmen in our organization. . . . Our clerks are trained to be courteous, to answer customers' questions and give them what they want, but not to waste time trying to sell them anything. . . . Selling has become an unnecessary vocation."[1]

To determine the importance of personal selling in your promotion mix, first decide what promotion tasks should be performed by personal selling. Order-taking and order-getting are the two major tasks assigned to retail salespeople. Order-takers perform service selling, usually for regular customers on a routine basis. However, good order-takers may be creative in their work. They are important for good customer relations, since they may be the only personal contacts the store has with many customers. In effect, they *are* the store. In addition to performing routine clerical and sales functions such as answering questions, stocking shelves, and ringing up sales, your order-takers should be trained to deal effectively with customers. If a customer has an exchange, a return, or a complaint, your order-takers should know how to handle it.

Order-getters, on the other hand, who are not nearly so numerous, use creative selling to sell both tangible and intangible products. For example, order-getters often sell higher-priced and more complex items such as insurance, automobiles, pianos, real estate, furniture, and appliances. These salespeople are usually more highly skilled and better paid than order-takers.They perform more of the persuasive part of the promotion job. Whether you employ order-takers, order-getters, or a combination of both will depend on your objectives and the tasks you assign to be performed by personal selling.

Theories of Selling. As we have seen, sales situations vary from retailer to retailer. Your personal selling strategy may be more effective if you base it on some sort of theoretical framework. The following four theories have been put forth as a basis of sales strategy formulation:

1. Stimulus-response theory.
2. Mental-states theory.
3. Need-satisfaction theory.
4. Problem-solving theory.[2]

The simple stimulus-response theory is based on the principle that every sensory stimulus provokes a response. This Pavlovian view of personal selling results in a standardized or "canned" sales presentation that is memorized by the salesperson. Such an approach can be used only in very simple selling situations in which the prod-

ucts being sold are inexpensive and economizing on salestime is important.

Mental-states theory (also known as selling-formula theory or the AIDA—attention, interest, desire, action—theory of selling) is based on the idea that the mind of the customer passes through several successive stages during the course of the sales presentation. This approach encourages the salesperson to plan the presentation. However, it may be difficult to determine the buyer's exact mental state at any given time. This method is used when the product is complicated or when the customer is called on by the salesperson several times before the sale is made.

Need-satisfaction theory is based on the consumer-oriented theory that products are purchased to satisfy needs. The salesperson identifies the prospect's need, makes the prospect aware of the need, and then shows how the product will satisfy the need. Small retailers who have adopted the marketing concept will feel very comfortable basing their personal selling strategies on this theory. However, this approach does require trained salespeople with the time to analyze customer needs. It is not appropriate for all kinds of selling situations.

Problem-solving theory is a customer-oriented approach that applies the scientific method to need-satisfaction theory. The salesperson acts as a professional consultant; he or she helps the customer identify needs, analyze alternative solutions, evaluate advantages and disadvantages, and choose a solution. This approach is more often used when buyer and seller have a long-term relationship and is appropriate in only a limited number of retail selling situations.

You should select a sales strategy based on a sales theory that fits your particular selling situation. If you don't, your salespersons will choose their own strategies or they will choose none at all, in which case selling will be a weak link in your overall promotion strategy.

Personal Selling and People Strategy. A very subtle distinction can be made between heavy emphasis on personal selling as a method of promotion and *people* strategy as an element of your retail marketing strategy. (People strategy is the topic of the next chapter.) A small retailer can use people strategy even if personal selling is not an important part of his promotion. Consider, for example, three major supermarkets in a small, rural midwestern city. One is part of a national chain, one is part of a regional chain, and one is an independent who is a member of a voluntary group. All are mass marketers; all use self-service, mass display, mass-media advertising, and mass merchandising; and all have about the same sales volume. None uses much personal selling to promote its store or products. The independent operator, however, uses a people strategy in his retail marketing. In the chain stores, the clerks are too busy completing their assigned work to talk to the customers. In the independent store, clerks talk with customers as part of the normal course of events. Although the two chains advertise their "friendliness," one trip to their stores reveals the wide gap between what the advertising department says and what the store employees actually do.

Two points can be drawn from this story. First, even if personal selling is not an important part of your promotion strategy, an effective people strategy can and should be a part of your small business retail marketing strategy. Second, personal selling, even if it is simply an excellent job of order-taking, offers the small retailer an opportunity to gain his or her store a differential advantage.

Improving Your Personal Selling. Improving your personal selling will require some effort. Fortunately, help is available from suppliers, trade associations, sales training courses, and many other sources. You might also want to teach your sales people (when the store is not busy) some commonsense rules. For example, you can post helpful hints to keep your employees aware of good sales practices. The following list on how to sell was originally prepared by the New York State Department of Commerce and was published by the SBA:

1. *Greeting:*
   Be friendly, courteous, prompt, business-like.
   Learn consumer's name and use it.
   Make customer feel important.
   Talk favorably about merchandise.
2. *Presentation:*
   Ask questions, listen, learn what he wants.
   Place customer's interest first.
   Suggest merchandise which best fits his need.
   Demonstrate as in actual use.
   Give at least three benefits for each item.
   Let customer handle the merchandise.
   Don't talk too much.
3. *Close:*
   Help customer to decide.
   Ask which item customer prefers.
   Remove unwanted merchandise from sight.
   Use utmost tact.
   Assume sale has been made.
   Write all details on the order.
4. *Pleasing:*
   Assure satisfaction.
   Show a related item.
   Show it is a pleasure to serve him.
   Keep all promises to customers.
   Be cheerful whether you make the sale or not.

When a customer returns, he has been well served.[3]

Numerous materials—books, cassette tapes, slide presentations, and so on—on personal salesmanship are available. Their use will be facilitated by having a framework for developing your personal selling strategy. Use the familiar eight-step approach or combine it with one given in Small Marketer Aids No. 159, entitled *Improving Personal Selling in Small Retail Stores*, available free from the SBA.

Using Sales Promotion in Your Retail Promotion Strategy

In addition to advertising, personal selling, public relations, and publicity, you will wish to use a host of other means to promote sales in your retail store. These other means, which taken together are called *sales promotion*, include sampling, premiums, trading stamps, coupons, contests, demonstrations, shows, special events, community and joint promotions, and other nonrecurring selling events. Many of these forms of sales promotion can be included in your promotion strategy to make it more exciting and effective.

Sales promotion usually calls for a quick response from the customer. Its purpose may be to get customers to buy before the heavy selling season, to attract new customers to the store, to persuade present customers to try new products, to maintain customer loyalty over time, or to supplement other promotion efforts in achieving the overall promotional objectives. Because retailers often speak about "promotional gimmicks," you may have the impression that sales promotion is a tactical rather than a strategic decision area of your retail promotion strategy. It is true that sales promotion can be viewed as a group of tools or gimmicks that can be tactically employed on rather short notice. However, a complete view of sales promotion would regard the individual tools (for example, a coupon, a contest, or a premium) of sales promotion as tactics that may or may not be appropriate for your sales promotion strategy. In other words, you should tactically use the appropriate tools within the strategic framework of your sales promotion strategy. Plan to use these tools as a regular part of your total promotion and integrate them into the total promotion effort. Spur-of-the-moment promotions can be counterproductive if they conflict with your desired image.

In using sales promotion, remember that it has both advantages and limitations. Some retailers think promotions divert attention from the store's products and their merits. The frequency and format of promotions may affect the store's image. Some promotions may borrow sales from the future rather than generate new sales. Competitive retaliation may neutralize some promotions. The too-frequent use of a promotion may make it expected rather than exceptional in the eyes of many customers. On the positive side, however, small retailers can give themselves an edge over their larger rivals by selecting promotions that cannot be easily duplicated by large retailers. For example, a local contest such as picking team winners in a local football "pool" would probably not be duplicated by a chain store competitor.

For optimal success, the right promotion should be presented at the right time. Promotions run in cycles with peaks and valleys of popularity. Many seem to be most effective just before they reach their peak. Some lessons for using sales promotion techniques follow:

1. The use of promotional techniques that are readily available to other retailers cannot replace sound retailing/merchandising strategies and planning.
2. Consumer preferences and response to promotional techniques may shift in short periods of time, so that what was in vogue last year is the villain this year.
3. The first retailers to use new promotional techniques may easily capture larger market sales and gain greater profits in the short run; however, once the technique becomes widespread, they may easily be in a worse competitive condition than other, more powerful, retailers who adopt the same technique.
4. Dependency upon a promotional technique overlooks the fact that strong new retailers and retailing concepts may emerge while the older retailers are engaged in a competitive promotional battle.
5. It is evident that a particular market segment is attracted to stores that offer particular promotional techniques such as stamps and games. As a result, it may be possible for certain retailers, particularly independent stores and chains, to use these techniques as long as large competitors do not adopt the practices. This is particularly true after larger competitors have tried and discontinued the techniques.[4]

Price Promotion and Deals. Price promotions that offer the consumer a special price for a limited time are very popular. They take such forms as one-day sales, red-tag sales, discount days, cents-off merchandise, price packs of manufacturers, and "free" deals such as buy three and get the fourth one free. The keys to success are selecting the best form in which to express the price deal, selecting the right amount of price reduction, selecting the right product(s) on which to offer the price deal, and using good timing. The chapter on pricing should help you make these decisions.

Nonprice Sales Promotions. Some of the more popular forms of nonprice retail sales promotions are briefly discussed below. If you decide to use some of these methods, be sure to integrate them into your overall retail promotion strategy. Also, ask yourself how you can use each promotional technique in a different and better way than other retailers.

Sampling. Providing free or low-cost samples is a method of getting your customers to try a product at almost no cost or risk to them. Sampling usually works best for low-unit-value products of small size that are frequently purchased. However, more expensive products can be sampled if customers are allowed to use them for a limited period.

The sampling of tasty food products is especially effective in stimulating impulse sales. Providing small samples of cloth, wallpaper, and other decorating materials is also quite common. Sampling can be used both to promote the sales of new and additional products to present customers and, when sampling is described in your advertising, to attract curious new customers. A small nut shop in Michigan used sampling on the sidewalk in front of the store as its major promotional tool. Have you ever tried to eat just one or two salted peanuts in the shell?

Premiums and Gifts. Getting something for nothing is the basic appeal of premiums and gifts. These promotional tools are often tied to a purchase and, unlike advertising specialties (which were discussed in the previous chapter), are usually not imprinted with an advertising message. Nonetheless, your specialty-advertising representative may be a good source of premiums and gifts. Manufacturers also supply them free of charge or at a low cost. For example, comic books, kites, and other small gifts are often given to young customers by children's shoe stores. These gifts may or may not carry an advertiser's name. Either way, they can be very effective. The franchise fast-food chains, too, are well aware of this fact.

Gifts may be outright to all takers, along with a purchase, or, as a self-liquidating premium offer, they may require the customer to make a payment at a "good value" price. Premiums can be for a single transaction or can be used in a continuity program that keeps customers coming back every week or so to get the next item until the set is complete. Examples of items used in continuity programs are encyclopedias, silverware, dishes, glasses, and anything else that comes in a series or a set.

A good gift or premium is something your customers want. It should encourage repeat sales. It should also be easy to administer. One easy approach is to tie a premium to so many dollars' worth of cash register tapes over the given period. A unique item that is not readily available from other stores often makes a good premium—especially if it bears some relationship to your line of business.

Trading Stamps. This sales promotion tool became so common a few years ago that many retailers, both large and small, felt that it lost its effectiveness. Unlike some other forms of sales promotion, trading stamps tend to be a long-term commitment

for the retailer. Stamps are still popular in some areas among some types of consumers. If you are considering the use of stamps, ask yourself such questions as the following: Do I currently have excess capacity so that if sales actually increase 10, 20, or 25 percent, my revenue will increase without increasing overhead costs? Are my target customers the kind of people who would want to save stamps (local vs. transient, middle-aged or older vs. younger, thrifty, and so on)? Could the cost of stamps (about 2 to 3 percent of sales) be better spent for some other type of sales promotion? What other complementary and competing retail stores in the market area are offering the same or competing stamps? What stamp plans are available? And how good are the redemption facilities for each trading stamp?

Coupons. You may promote your store and sales of your products by actively redeeming cents-off coupons issued by manufacturers. You may also issue and redeem your own coupons. For example, an important promotional tool of a garage is to use special coupons in a free shopping newspaper. A special on a specific service, which is usually tied in with seasonal needs, is used to bring customers to the garage. For example, a coupon for low-cost mounting of snow tires would be used in October and November.

An independent supermarket made imaginative use of manufacturer coupons to promote its sales by starting a coupon exchange box in its store. On the honor system, customers could deposit coupons they didn't want and take any coupons they wished to use to make a purchase in the store. Even though the retailer actually "gave away" many coupons to get the exchange started, the idea had a very good payoff in terms of increased sales. The grocer said that many coupon exchangers used coupons for nonfood items that represented additional sales and often carried generous markups.

One danger in using your own retailer-issued coupons is that you might overuse them. An advantage is that you can control the number of coupons issued, the value of each, and the timing. Your rate of redemption is affected by the coupon's value and its mode of distribution. For example, a small boat-rental marina passed out thousands of coupons at a local boat, sports, and travel show. Many of these coupons (which were good on weekdays for an additional two hours free on a canoe, sailboat, or paddle boat after the customer paid full price for the first hour) were discarded on the floor near where they were passed out. The redemption rate was quite low as a percentage of all coupons passed out. Even so, the owner's promotion objective of increasing business during the week was achieved. Another danger of using coupons is that they become so customary that almost no sales are made without them. Some dry cleaners have reached this point.

Couponing may be especially effective for the small retailer who has a small share of market and wants to increase it. A cents-off or other type of coupon can be used to reach many noncustomers, rather than simply acting as a price reduction for present customers.

Sometimes local groups such as the Junior Chamber of Commerce sponsor and sell coupon books to raise money. These books contain the coupons of many retailers. If you use such a coupon book, plan your coupon offer to fit both the intended audience and your specific promotion objectives.

Contests and Sweepstakes. Contests and sweepstakes are good in that the customer gets a chance to participate. If they fit in with your image, they are also a good way to build a mailing list. In a contest the entrant usually performs some skill activity, whereas in a sweepstakes chance determines the winners. Both are very popular despite some bad publicity a few years back. As a small retailer, you should view contests not in terms of the size of the prizes you give away but in terms of local interest. You simply cannot compete with large chain stores in terms of the amount of the prize, because many chains spread the cost of prizes and the prizes themselves over many stores. Sponsor a contest with simple rules and several chances for winning, based on some local event or item of interest, and don't forget to publicize the contest both before and after it is over. If contests as such do not fit the image of your store, you may be able to get good promotional value by providing products as prizes (free or at low cost) for the contests of other retailers. Finally, some retailers will use contests and sweepstakes only if every entrant wins something. The idea of having "no losers" is a good one, even if the minimum prize is quite small.

Demonstrations. Anyone who has attended a state fair is aware of the promotional value of demonstrations. Products such as sports equipment, farm equipment, food processors, and household appliances are too expensive to be sampled and are of such complexity that a demonstration of their actual use can be very effective. Manufacturers will sometimes provide trained demonstrators. Because demonstrations are expensive, you should promote the demonstration to get a large audience over which to spread the cost.

Shows. For retailers selling sporting goods, recreational vehicles, vacation merchandise, home furnishings, automobiles, and many other products there are shows and exhibitions that convene on a regular basis. These shows bring together in one place large numbers of people who have similar interests. Renting space and having an interesting and exciting message to tell those persons who stop at your booth can put you in contact with many new potential customers. A little imagination may even make you a substantial profit at the show itself. For example, a photographer developed a series of outstanding wildlife and outdoor photographs suitable for framing. These were displayed in an attractive setting at several sport shows, and sales of both photos and frames were very good. A family shoe store set up a special booth for hiking boots and other sport shoes at a sports show. The people who attended bought more freely in this "circus" atmosphere. Of course, they were helped by the reputation of the store, the quality brand names, and the easy use of bank credit cards.

Special Promotional Events. From the grand opening with free balloons, hot dogs, and soft drinks to the final legitimate going-out-of-business sale, there are many special events you can use to build a promotion around. Here are a few: (1) a joint sale of some kind with all stores in your shopping center or business neighborhood jointly participating, (2) an anniversary sale, (3) a sidewalk sale, (4) a fashion show, (5) a community event such as a parade, (6) the sponsoring of a team in a youth league, (7) a visit by a celebrity to your store, (8) the sponsoring of an event such as a marathon to help a popular charity, (9) an income tax refund promotion, and (10) the Christmas holiday gift-giving season. A complete list of such events would take pages. Find special events appropriate for your type of retail business. Use them. Evaluate them. And the next time you use them, in a year or so, try to improve on last year's performance. Look for good places to find ideas for new and unusual special promotional events, such as local organizations and the Chamber of Commerce.

Using Public Relations and Publicity in Your Retail Promotion Strategy

You can use good public relations and favorable publicity to strengthen your overall promotion strategy. Good *public relations* is part of the marketing concept. However, it is really nothing more than a positive organized effort on your part to be friendly and on good terms with the several groups (or publics) with which your retail business has contact. Some of these groups are customers, employees, suppliers, competitors, other business and professional persons in your community, and community organizations such as schools and religious groups.

Publicity differs from other forms of promotion in that it is free (or not paid for in dollars for space or time) and you do not have much control over the content that is communicated. Good publicity makes the public aware of the good things you do in relating to your various publics.

Although many small retailers tend to overestimate the promotional value of a single piece of favorable publicity or a single act of good public relations, you cannot afford to do a poor job in either area. Poor relations and bad publicity can negate thousands of dollars spent on advertising.

Building a good public relations (or community relations) program requires some effort by you and by all your employees. The following sixteen searching questions are raised in an SBA publication; how would you honestly answer them?[5]

1. Do you have a policy that good community relations is a matter of top management concern?
2. Do you constantly guard against your business activities conflicting with public policy?
3. Do you recognize each of the groups that make up an important segment of your firm's public?
4. Do you take regular steps to see that each group receives the appreciation it deserves?
5. Do you maintain sympathetic and wholesome employee relations even with temporary help?
6. Do you have an established system for informing employees what your firm stands for and how it functions?
7. Do you try to keep informed on what the public thinks of your firm?
8. Do you try to check what you hear and make improvements where needed?
9. Do you avoid high-pressure tactics in your community relations activities?
10. Do you make continuous and constant efforts to improve your community relations skills instead of merely putting on sporadic drives?
11. Do you make a conscious effort to understand how government affects your business and to improve your relations with government agencies?
12. Do you insist that all your company's actions be completely honest and sincere?

13. Do you remind your employees constantly that selling, serving, and good community relations are inseparable?
14. Do you make it a point to consider what is best for the public at large as well as for your own private interest when major business decisions are being made?
15. Are your premises well kept and pleasing to the eye?
16. Do you have a policy of encouraging your employees to be active in community organizations of their choosing?

If you can answer *Yes* to all the above questions, you don't need any suggestions for specific techniques to help you build better public relations. If not, try joining and actively participating in community organizations, giving talks to groups, contributing to and helping charitable organizations, and helping to promote community projects. As an example, a small-town supermarket operator found a way to do some good for his community and his retail store at the same time: he paid the cost for purchasing a local daily newspaper for every patient every day in the local hospital. The hospital volunteers distributed the newspapers with a small note attached to each, conveying a "get well" message and a statement that the newspaper was compliments of the owner of the supermarket. Although the supermarket owner (my father) had been doing this for years, it was not until I was hospitalized that I found out about it and realized how much this relatively inexpensive gesture meant to hospital patients.

Publicity about the good things your retail business does may be hard to get, except in some free shopping newspapers where all advertisers seem to take turns at getting feature news stories on the front page. One way to get the publicity you deserve is to assign the responsibility to yourself or some other manager in your store. Make it a regular part of someone's duties. Then give that person at least minimal training (perhaps from a book in your library or from a local newspaper reporter) in how to write a press release. A well-written press release and a good photo will make it easy for the local news media to give you some good publicity.

How to Determine Your Total Promotion Budget

How much should you spend to promote your business? Consider here not only what you spend for advertising media costs but also what you spend for all other forms of promotion. You have already made some marketing strategy decisions about the role and importance of promotion. The present budgeting process is a way to operationalize these decisions.

In considering decision criteria and approaches to decision making, here are some factors you will take into account:

1. The minimum amount that can be spent for promotion (or each form of promotion) for you to reach the threshold level of impact. Anything less than this minimum might be wasted.
2. The amount of promotion that would be too much.
3. Economies of scale you can realize at different levels of promotion.
4. The strengths and weaknesses of the rest of your marketing mix. For example, a newer store should spend more than an established store, and a store with a poor location needs to spend more than a store with an excellent one.
5. Your competitive climate, the size of your marketing area, and the economic environment. Many successful small retailers move with economic trends by increasing promotion when the economic outlook brightens and reducing it when a recession is approaching.
6. The promotion tools available to you. For example, a retailer may lower prices and the

promotion budget as a way to implement the decision to discontinue trading stamps. However, there may be a lag in reducing the size of the promotion budget.

Whether you are dealing with the size of your total promotion budget or the size of your advertising budget, the economic principle of marginal analysis applies in theory. However, marginal analysis is pretty much ignored in practice because the necessary data are not available. Most successful small retailers use somewhat arbitrary rule-of-thumb methods for budgeting promotion. Examine the methods discussed below to see how each relates to your situation. Perhaps some combination of those methods will work best for you.

Percentage of sales. This method is easy to understand and easy to use. It is, therefore, quite popular among small retailers. Here, your promotion budget is set at some fixed percentage of sales. The sales base may be past sales, expected future sales, or some combination. Expected future sales is probably the most logical base. The rationale for selecting a certain percentage figure is usually derived from your past experience. For example, if 4 percent worked in previous years, you budget 4 percent of sales for the coming year.

A variation of this method is the fixed sum per unit sold. The per-unit variation would be workable only if you sold expensive items such as automobiles or recreational vehicles.

Because sales are often the major intended result of promotion, it seems somewhat backward to assume a sales level and then determine how much promotion will be used to achieve it. However, as a starting point, the percentage-of-sales method does have merit. From this starting point you may wish to make adjustments for such factors as expansion, new competition, and changing business conditions.

Competitive parity. Under this approach, competition sets your promotion budget. This method may be realistic for large retailers who rely heavily on mass-media advertising, but it is not too applicable for small retailers, who often have unique promotion mixes. Competitive parity means that you monitor what competitors spend on promotion and act accordingly by budgeting the same dollar amount, the same percentage of sales, the industry average, or some other competitive amount. This method assumes (1) that market shares and promotion expenditures are directly and/or proportionately related, (2) that the small retailer knows what competitors are doing and are going to do, (3) that competitors know what they are doing, (4) that you should do what competitors are doing, and (5) that you can afford to match competitive promotion budgets. Any of these assumptions may be incorrect. This "copycat" method is not a comprehensive one.

Available funds. If you budget "all you can afford" for promotion, the result may be either too little or too much. This method involves allocating to promotion the residual (if there is one) after planned expenses for all other items and a planned profit have

been established. Although this method has been used successfully to promote a new business or a new retail location during the introductory period, in general it is dangerous and is not recommended.

Objective task. In this approach you (1) define all the specific tasks to be done by promotion, (2) assign a cost to each task, and (3) add up the costs. In effect, your total is a series of task budgets lumped together. This problem-oriented approach may appeal to many students and others because it appears scientific. Tasks can be given priorities according to their importance if funds are not available to accomplish all tasks.

In a practical sense, what this approach does is to break the budgeting problem down into several small budgeting problems. The question you must ask is: Are you in a good position to properly define and accurately determine the cost of each of these smaller problems? Even if you don't use the objective task method of budgeting, you can and should set promotion objectives. Also, the promotion tasks necessary to accomplish your specific promotion objectives should be spelled out in detail as part of your planned promotion strategy.

Each of the above approaches deals basically with a single variable, such as sales or competition. None is comprehensive, but each has something to offer. The percentage-of-sales method tends to be favored by small retailers.

After you have determined your overall promotion strategy, determine your promotion budget and its allocation by using a combination of approaches. Also, save in reserve some small portion of your budget for emergencies, opportunities, and experimentation.

How to Measure the Effectiveness of Your Promotion Efforts

A famous retailer is reported to have once said that he was convinced that half the money he was spending for advertising was being wasted. When asked why he didn't stop spending the money that was being wasted, the retailer replied that he didn't know which half it was that was being wasted. His was the common and difficult problem of measuring the effectiveness of promotion. In the opinion of the author, the overall effectiveness of promotion cannot be measured accurately. Nor can the overall effectiveness of advertising, personal selling, sales promotion, or public relations and publicity be measured accurately. Many activities and objectives are included in these related areas. In effect, if your total marketing program is working well, your promotion is probably doing a good job along with your product, place, price, and people strategies. If things are not going well, your promotion may or may not be part of the problem.

What can you measure? You can measure the effectiveness of some parts of your promotion. For example, you can measure the effectiveness of an individual advertisement, one newspaper against another, or the performance of each retail salesperson. Our discussion here will be limited to measuring the effectiveness of ads, especially direct-action ads as opposed to image-building ads, which take longer to work. Keep in mind that many factors besides advertising affect your sales.

Direct mail advertising gives you the best opportunity to measure effects. Other good opportunities for small retailers to measure the sales effects of advertising are provided by the following:

Coupons bought in. Usually these coupons represent sales of the product. When the coupons represent requests for additional information or contact with a salesman, were enough leads obtained to pay for the ad? If the coupon is dated, you can determine the number of returns for the first, second, and third weeks.

Requests by phone or letter referring to the ad. A "hidden offer" can cause people to call or write. Include—for example, in the middle of a paragraph—a statement that on request the product or additional information will be supplied. Results should be checked over a one-week through a six- or twelve-month period, because an ad of this type may have considerable carry-over effect.

Split runs by newspapers. Prepare two ads (different in some way you would like to test) and run them on the same day. Identify the ads—in the message or with a coded coupon—so you can tell them apart. Ask customers to bring in the ad or coupon. When you place the ad, ask the newspaper to give you a split run—that is, to print "ad A" in part of its press run and "ad B" in the rest of the run. Count the responses to each ad.

Sales made of particular item. If the ad is on a bargain or limited-time offer, you can consider that sales at the end of a week, two weeks, three weeks, and four weeks came from the ad. You may need to make a judgment as to how many sales came from display and personal selling.

Check store traffic. An important function of advertising is to build store traffic, which results in purchases of items that are not advertised. Pilot studies show, for example, that many customers who are brought to the store by an ad for a blouse also bought a handbag. Some bought the bag in addition to the blouse, others instead of the blouse.[6]

The following example illustrates one of the many ways that coupons brought in can be used for making advertising decisions:

A successful independent food retailer in a small Michigan town tested the effectiveness of ads in a free shopping guide and a paid-circulation weekly by counting coupon returns from identical ads in both publications. While 120 customers had clipped coupons from the newspaper (a remarkable rate of return, since it had but 1800 subscribers), only 80 had clipped them from the "shopper" (which was delivered to over 4000 homes). He therefore concluded that most of his customers were in the area where the newspaper's circulation was heaviest (i.e., in the town's natural trading area), and that the paper was his best bet for steady advertising. But he also concluded that since the free publication did draw some extra business, and since it had very low rates, it was a worthwhile medium for advertising periodic special promotions.[7]

Getting Outside Help for More Successful Retail Promotions

A promotion decision for many small retailers is whether to use a small advertising agency or to make advertising (and other promotion) a do-it-yourself project. The do-it-yourselfer takes the risk of making costly amateurish mistakes. However, outside help short of using your own ad agency is available. In deciding how much outside help you need and cannot afford to be without, ask yourself: If I'm so good at retail advertising, why don't I sell my store and go into the advertising business?

For the Do-It-Yourselfer. If you are going to do your own advertising management, you nevertheless will call on the skilled expertise of others such as media salespeople, graphic artists, printers, and your major suppliers such as manufacturers and wholesalers. An SBA publication lists the following sources of advertising help for small retailers:

1. The advertising departments of newspapers offer assistance in copy preparation, art work, and layout. They are often willing to advise the retailer on his general merchandising and sale promotional planning.

2. The firms that supply the retailer with his merchandise often provide advertising materials free of charge; grant advertising discounts; and participate cooperatively in the retailer's advertising by sharing a portion of the cost.

3. Direct-mail agencies compile specialized mailing lists which can be used by the retailer to contact selected customer groups. These agencies also assist in the preparation of the mailing literature.

4. The trade newspapers and magazines of his particular field of retailing often provide useful information to the store manager concerning the advertising practices of his fellow retailers. Trade associations, Chambers of Commerce, and Better Business Bureaus also frequently provide information on advertising and advertising ethics.[8]

Some examples of how small retailers can benefit by their wholesalers' advertising to consumers are provided by the hardware industry. In a recent year, hardware whole-salers spent $20 million to $25 million on such advertising. Here are some ways hardware wholesalers have helped their retailers have more effective promotion programs:

Ace Hardware Corp., Oak Brook, Illinois, [helps] with its emphasis on "The Helpful Hardware Man" image for retail stores. Ace also advertises basic products that most of its retail customers would carry.

Other wholesalers, such as the Pro Hardware organization, headquartered in Stamford, Connecticut, have keyed radio or television consumer advertising to sale circulars. This way, the advertising can feature specific products and prices and every retailer who uses the circular identifies himself with the commercials. Retailers can also tie in with local newspaper ads featuring the same products. 1978 was Pro's first venture into broadcast advertising of this type and the program is being expanded next year from a 20-week schedule in 20 markets to a 40-week schedule.

Our Own Hardware in Burnsville, Minnesota, uses a similar approach with its radio advertising program. During 1978, Our Own will run some 52,000 sixty-second radio spots throughout its 11-state trading area. These commercials, which tie in with monthly specials and sale circulars, leave time for the retailer to add his own identifying tag at the end of the commercial.

Hardware Wholesalers Inc., Ft. Wayne, Indiana, has run a market area radio advertising program for several years, using an institutional, problem-solving approach. HWI concentrates on cities with 50,000-watt broadcasters throughout its 26-state area. Retailers can tie into this advertising through their own newspaper ads or by adding personalized material to the radio spots.

Gamble Stores Div. of Gamble-Skogmo, Inc., Minneapolis, also uses radio commercials to help retailers. Called Gamble's Radio Network, the commercials are broadcast on 475 stations in Gambles' 24-state marketing area.

The commercials are primarily oriented to product-advertising and include local retailer tags. At appropriate times of the year, the radio spots are tied in to sale circulars.[9]

Using an Advertising Agency. If you are going to use an advertising agency, remember that you are still responsible for working with that agency to formulate your overall promotion strategy. Also, you will want to make certain that the agency's advertising plans are coordinated with your personal selling, sales promotion, and public relations and publicity efforts. The role of the ad agency could vary from full service to the writing and placing of advertisements. Full service might include creating a campaign theme, logo design, creating a slogan or jingle, writing copy, doing layouts, copy testing, audience measurement, other advertising research, sales promotion, and publicity. An ad agency is, in effect, composed of a diversity of advertising specialists who are available to you at an economical cost because other clients are sharing the cost of supporting them. Before beginning the agency selection process, you should know what you expect from the agency and the kinds of expertise the agency should have.

You may begin the actual agency selection process by simply finding out who is available in your area. The size of the ad agency is important. Of course, you want an agency that is large enough to offer some specialization and expertise. However, you should *not* select an agency that is too large. If your account is not an important part of the agency's business, the agency is not likely to service your account in a first-rate way. A smaller agency that is interested in growing by increasing your profitability may be the best choice.

At some point, your store and one or two small agencies will mutually select each other for more serious consideration. You should plan to spend a few hours at each agency to become familiar with the people who will actually work on your account. Being able to work well together is very important for the success of your advertising campaign. You may wish to ask each "finalist" agency to prepare a presentation that outlines the ideas the agency has for your advertising. If your account is quite small, however, ad agencies may be reluctant to invest in a presentation until they have a reasonable assurance that they have the account, or that presentation costs will be covered.

For your agency-client relationship to last over a period of time, it must be profitable for both parties. How should you pay your ad agency? You may pay a commission, a fee, or a combination of commission and fees. Whatever is mutually agreeable can work, so long as you are not paying for more than you are getting and the agency considers your account to be profitable.

13

How to Plan Your Retail People Strategy

What People Strategy Is

People strategy is the fifth "P" of the marketing mix for small retailers. If you have a people strategy as part of your retail marketing mix and if you use it well, it can interact with product, place, price, and promotion to make your overall retail marketing strategy more effective. Your people strategy will be unique to your firm, much as the people of your firm are unique. As such, it represents an opportunity for a significant differential advantage. Because your big business competitors are organized into bureaucratic hierarchies rather than being built around individual people, big retailers (even though they may try) cannot effectively use people strategy in their marketing mixes. People strategy is reserved for small businesses. You and some of your

small retail competitors may choose to use this powerful element of the small business marketing mix.

In this chapter we describe what people strategy is. Key people strategy areas discussed are (1) a strategy for matching your people with the customers of your target market, (2) people organization strategies, (3) people image strategy, (4) the use of good personnel policies as supporting strategy, and (5) strategies for using outside people. The eight-step approach to planning your retail people strategy is outlined.

As an element of your retail marketing mix, *people strategy* refers to all the people of your retail firm. *People* includes you (the owner/operator), other managers, all employees, whether they are salespeople or not, and some outsiders such as consultants and suppliers.

The need for you as a small retailer to have a people strategy is based on the proven fact that many consumers are responsive to good people strategy. The better your potential customers know you and the other people of your store, the more good customers you will have and the greater will be your sales to each customer. Your people are a major reason why customers patronize your store (or your competitor's stores). So why not recognize people strategy as a regular part of your retail marketing mix? The impersonal world of bigness has influenced many consumers to seek something more than a computer account number and an automatic "Have a nice day!" from the chain-store clerk. The customer who deals with the owner in a small retail store may receive much psychic satisfaction unavailable to him from the large retailer. In the small store, he deals directly with the top person, and that person probably treats him as an individual by talking with him after greeting him by name. A professor in the field of small business said it this way:

Interaction of this type is increasingly important for retailers because of the consumer's increasing search for self-actualization through consumption. Interpreted as the expression of individual priorities and preferences reflecting different life styles and going beyond those related to satisfying basic wants and needs, self-actualization implies a highly individualized approach to need-satisfaction which requires a high level of personal sales efforts. The selling efforts of the independent firm's top management should be more effective than those of the larger retailer's sales personnel, who are usually far removed from their own top managers and often unmotivated.[1]

The rest of this chapter will describe in detail what people strategy is, but first let us briefly see what people strategy is not. In the retail marketing mix, people strategy is *not* simply the personal-selling part of your promotion strategy. Although your people do the personal selling, people strategy is a broader concept. Second, people strategy is *not* how to manage people; rather it is using people as a part of your marketing mix. Third, people strategy does *not* refer to the people of your target market (i.e., your customers). Although there is no denying that customers are usually people, the term is being used here to mean the people of your firm. Fourth, people strategy is *not* concerned primarily with personnel matters, but personnel policies can be used to support people strategy as part of the marketing mix. Finally, people strategy is *not* people tactics.

As mentioned above, people strategy is appropriate for small business but not for big business, because small businesses do not organize and operate in the rigid formal structure of a bureaucratic hierarchy. The absence of such a bureaucracy makes it possible for the small retailer to build the team around the players (people) rather than force the players into predetermined slots. If you build your retail people into a team by always thinking in terms of the consumer-oriented marketing concept, *people* can become an effective part of your marketing mix.[2]

Some *examples* of people differences and how people can become a part of the small retailer's marketing mix may be helpful at this point.

Example 1. Ever since 1908, the Radicia family has operated a successful outdoor newsstand on the corner of 17th and Farnam in Omaha, Nebraska. Even with competition from nearby book departments and book stores, the newsstand supports two families. People strategy is part of the reason. Many customers probably go out of their way to buy at their stand. The following quote tells why:

There is competition. Within a block are at least three businesses—in comfortable indoor quarters—which stock almost every publication the Radicia brothers offer.

"We stay on our toes to keep ahead," said Joe. "We know a lot of our customers and we're ready with what they want. They don't have to wait. Nobody does."

"And they like us," his brother said. "We smile a lot—even when it's cold. You bet we get cold. There's no way to stay warm when it's below zero and the wind is blowing. But we smile anyway."

The businessman in the warm car paid for his newspapers and nodded when Joe said, "Have a good day."

"You, too," he replied. Then he felt foolish. A good day with a minus-40 wind chill factor?[3]

Example 2. The differential advantage that can be gained by using the people element in the marketing mix is illustrated by a small bank in Alexandria, Virginia. The bank doesn't have a computer, but it does have a parrot that shares the president's office. The Burke & Herbert bank likes to point out how small it is rather than boast about large assets. It emphasizes old-fashioned service rather than a lengthy string of services. Tellers make it a point to greet customers by name, and loans are negotiated somewhat as a family affair. The point of all this is not that the bank is backward, but that this bank has purposely fitted its operation (through its people) to exactly meet the wishes of a selected target market.[4]

Example 3. This example is illustrated in Figure 13-1. Here the owner of a supermarket takes a minute to chat with one of his customers. He could be spending this time in some other way, but could it be spent better? He also encourages all his employees to take a few seconds to visit with customers and to make a special effort to get to know their names. He says his chain-store competitors are often too concerned about man-hour productivity to take a brief moment to be friendly with customers. This small retailer really believes in it. Customers spend more time shopping and more money as a result.

Example 4. An example of people strategy can be found in organizations such as the Omaha Executives Association. This group of about one hundred business men and women meets every Thursday noon. The major purpose of the organization is to provide business leads for the members. Most of the businesses are small. Many are retail. By providing leads for each other and by getting to know each other better, the members of this group are increasing sales and profits for each other. The cost of doing so is minimal. An effective people strategy does not have to be an expensive part of your marketing program.

Role of People Strategy in Your Retail Marketing Mix

As an element in your retail marketing mix, what can people strategy do for you? It all depends on how much you emphasize it. Some small retailers are probably in a better position than others to give a major role to people strategy. However, many small retailers are probably not using people strategy at all (or they are not aware that

Figure 13-1. (Photo courtesy Harvey Berner)

people are a part of their overall marketing strategy). Many other small retailers are using people strategy sometimes. And a few small retailers are using people strategy as a regular part of their total retail market strategy. In summary, people strategy is probably underutilized by most small retailers.

People strategy plays an especially important role in the marketing efforts of small retailers whose target market customers are responsive to it. When the personal treatment received by the customer is affected very greatly by the personalities of employees, people strategy is important. Close customer interaction of this sort is found in such retail businesses as taverns, restaurants, and personal service firms. Other examples are the bank, newsstand, and supermarket cited earlier. Retailers who are involved in fashion merchandising for either men or women can also profit greatly from a good people strategy, because they are regarded as opinion leaders by their customers.

Your target market customers, your environment, and the roles assigned to the other four P's (product, place, price, and promotion) of your marketing mix will all combine to determine the role of people strategy in your total marketing strategy. For most small retailers, the chances are pretty good that people strategy can advantageously play a more important role than it has in the past. The major areas of your people strategy include, but are not limited to, the following:

1. A strategy for matching your people with your target market customers.

2. Your people organization strategy.
3. Your people image strategy.
4. Your personnel supporting strategy.
5. Your strategies for using outside people.

A Strategy for Matching Your People with Your Target Market Customers

When you first began formulating your marketing strategy, you selected the target market you would serve. Since then, you have gathered many facts about your target market. (See Chapter 3.) You are now ready to use your close knowledge of your target market customers to help you determine the people you should have in your store to serve these customers. In effect, you are going to match your people with the people of your target market. Customers like to do business with people they like and with whom they feel comfortable. The more your target market customers can identify with the people of your store, the more sales you will have. Try to match your people to your target market in much the same way you matched your product to your market. For example, if you operate a store that sells to children (for example, children's clothing, toys, ice cream, pizza, or a variety store), you don't want a grouchy old man who doesn't like kids as one of your salespeople. You want people who really like kids and who, regardless of their ages, can really identify with kids. If the kids don't like your people, they won't shop at your store and they'll also tell their parents not to shop there. However, if they do like your people, the reverse will tend to be true.

How far should you go in attempting to get the ideal people-market match? Your people and your customers do need some common frame of reference based on background and experiences. For example, if you operate a clothing store for petite women or one for big and tall men, the physical appearance of your salespeople should not be the direct opposite of that of your target customers. A sporting goods store would want people who were interested in sports. A music store would want people interested in music. A health food store would want people interested in good nutrition, food preparation, and good health. These matches are obvious. Matching along some other dimensions is not always so obvious. Some dimensions to consider are age, sex, temporary and permanent help, part time and full time, ethnic background, hobbies, training, personality, social class, interest in the job, and compatibility with the desired store image. In effect, you can use demographic and other dimensions to segment the people you want for your sales and other positions in much the same way you used dimensions to segment your target market.

Many successful retailers, when asked what is responsible for their success, respond, "Good people!" As a small retailer you have the opportunity to have good people who are also matched with your target market customers. Don't settle for anything less. Then work with your people to personalize and individualize the communications between them and your customers. For example, the most common greeting to a customer is "May I help you?" This is followed very closely in popularity by "Can I help you?" One successful small retailer trains his people not to use these opening remarks. Instead, his people are trained to say "GOOD MORNING" or "GOOD AFTERNOON" or "GOOD MORNING, Mrs. Williams." Such individualized recognition is important to the customers of a small retailer.

How can you help your people learn to know your customers by name? Here are some suggestions. First, make it a point to let them know they are supposed to do this. Second, do it yourself. This not only sets a good example but also lets your people hear customers' names. Third, teach them to notice names on charge cards, checks, and service tickets. For example, have them say, "Thank you, Mr. Johnson" when they return Mr. Johnson's charge card. Fourth, have them learn both the first and last name. Also, have them try to learn the names of children who are shopping with or without their parents.

Your People Organization Strategy

The organization and management of people is less difficult for a small than for a large retailer. However, it does call for your attention. You need a customer-oriented strategy for effectively organizing all your people into a marketing team. As your business grows larger, the need increases for a formal organization structure, which can be either production- or marketing-oriented. The way in which you organize the work activities of your employees will influence how well they respond to the needs of your customers.

One study of small businesses discovered that departmental organization is not often found in companies with annual sales below $100,000. Companies with annual sales between $1 million and $3 million usually have two or three formalized departments. Firms with annual sales of $3 million to $6 million have three to five departments. Firms with annual sales from $6 million to $20 million have from five to eight departments.[5] These broad guidelines would not necessarily apply to your particular line of retailing. Basic organizational principles such as clear lines of authority, written statements of comparable responsibility and authority, the requirement to report to only one boss, minimization of layers of management, appropriate span of control, flexibility, and simplicity do apply to all small retailers.

In using such principles, however, small retailers should keep in mind the unique capabilities of the people involved. Build the organization around the people. You should be reluctant to give up unnecessarily the natural people advantage of a small firm. Such things as close personal relationships, direct communications, and person-to-person motivation may prove to be more important than a neat-looking organization chart. Your strategy should always take into account that your people are an important part of your marketing mix. Your people are important to your target market customers.

Your People Image Strategy

Your people image is every bit as real as your product image or price image. It is a major part of your overall store image. For a small retailer it may be especially important, since a good people image is not easily duplicated by competitors. You must decide exactly what people image you are trying to project.

People image is the perception that someone has regarding the reality of the people of your retail firm. The perception and the reality may differ. Also, the perception may vary from one observer to another. You may think your people image is one thing; your employees may think it is something else. Your present customers may have another image of your people, and potential customers may have yet another.

Images can be more important than reality, because people usually act as they perceive. For example, a drug store may have an excellent pharmacist whose own personal image is ideal among customers who come into the store. However, some potential customers may get the impression that the drug store is careless in filling prescriptions when they witness careless driving by the person who delivers prescriptions in the store's vehicle.

Your people image is formed by a variety of things. The strongest influences are those things that are most easily perceived—friendliness, manner of dress, speech patterns and mannerisms, cleanliness, knowledge, poise, general appearance, personal interest, courtesy, and other noticeable outward signs.

People image is but one part of your total image. Images are also generated from your products, your place (such as location and layout of your store), your price (bargain price or high price), and your promotion (advertising image). Consistency among all these areas of image is desirable. To the extent that you yourself are heavily involved in all phases of your retail marketing mix, such consistency is likely to occur. It is also likely that the resulting total store image will be a projection of yourself.

Building the desired favorable image will take a long time and much hard work. Changing an established favorable image to another favorable image can also be very difficult and quite expensive. However, changing a favorable image to an unfavorable or unclear image is not too difficult: a little neglect is all it takes.

Every small retailer who employs people projects some kind of people image. In the absence of a strategy for forming it, your people image may be weak, inconsistent, and ineffective. It may even be negative. Your people image is projected and to some extent can be controlled by you. It is the personality of your retail store as demonstrated by you, your managers, your employees, and the outside people who help you. Take a positive approach in deciding what you want your people image to be and how best to project it.

Your Supporting People Strategies

You can support your core people strategy by good personnel practices and policies—such things as recruiting, selection, developing, and motivating activities directed toward all people of your firm. Unlike some of the other people strategy areas mentioned in this chapter, this area is a supporting- rather than a core-strategy area. It is viewed from a retail marketing perspective as well as a personnel perspective. In other words, good personnel management can be used to provide the right people to interact with your target market customers. Some of the personnel management items that often call for unique treatment in small business are management succession, family business problems, the owner/manager, recruiting and selection, developing people, and motivating and working with people.

Management Succession. Although it would seem that a successful small retailer would be quite concerned with planning for his own successor, such is not always the case. A retail store may have a continuity of top management over the long career of the owner/operator, but a sudden break may occur if the retailer retires, leaves to start a new business, dies, becomes seriously ill, or for some other reason leaves the business. Because the personality of the owner is often the people image as well as the driving force of the business, a sudden unplanned change has serious marketing implications. The same personality characteristics that may have been responsible for building a successful business may make it hard to hand over control and customer loyalty to a successor. Among the approaches to management succession that could be used are heir apparent, internal management strug-

gle, and bringing in an outsider. Any approach will affect the people portion of the retail marketing mix.

Family Business Problems. Many small retail firms are family businesses. This entails both pluses and minuses for people strategy. Greater concern, involvement, long hours, and a better overall people strategy is the biggest advantage. On the other hand, the emotional involvement of family members can sometimes cause problems. The following advice on how to make your family business more profitable may be helpful:

1. Cash in on increased flexibility to rapidly increase or decrease resources in order to gain an edge in the marketplace.
2. Keep emotions outside the business.
3. Make objectivity a fetish.
4. Depersonalize key business decisions.
5. Make employment attractive to nonfamily candidates in order to attract and keep outstanding people.
6. Apply businesslike financing techniques.
7. Personalize your approach with customers, suppliers, employees, and others, but don't do everything yourself.
8. Put man-woman roles in perspective.
9. Make hereafter plans for your business.[6]

The Owner/Manager. The small-store owner/manager is certainly part of the solution but sometimes may also be a part of the problem. And who is going to tell the boss that the boss is wrong? The periodic advice of a consultant may be one answer. The use of an outside board of directors or board of advisors may also prove effective. An open mind and a desire for constant improvement are very important. Because the leadership of the owner/manager is so vital to the successful planning and implementation of a good people strategy, you should not neglect your own personal and managerial development. If the functions you perform in the business are important, it is also important that your performance of these functions be objectively evaluated.

Recruiting and Selection. Your recruiting and selection activities are important parts of building the ideal people strategy for your marketing mix. You don't have to hire just anyone who comes along. First of all, know your requirements. Then devise a plan for getting those people who meet the requirements.

Some small retailers have been very successful in hiring good people. For example, one hardware retailer found that active retired people with mechanical skills were ideal because they had good product knowledge and related very well to the store's customers. Another small retailer had great success in using school teachers on a part-time basis.

Attracting top management people to a small retail business is somewhat more difficult. An opportunity to participate in the profits through partial ownership or a bonus plan is sometimes offered.

Factors other than money are important in hiring good people at all levels. Some of the things that attract good people to small businesses are a greater chance for involvement, opportunities for growth, more freedom of action, an informal and friendly atmosphere, and a chance to learn many aspects of the business.

Developing People. You pay for a training program whether you have one or not. Many small retailers have not invested enough in people development. Large numbers of untrained, part-time sales people are used in retailing. They often chase away knowledgeable, full-time customers. Outside sources of training are schools, short courses, supplier training programs, and trade association programs. However, most training in small retail stores is on-the-job training. This means that you must do the training yourself on a person-to-person basis. The following suggestions from the Small Business Administration may be helpful:

HOW TO INSTRUCT

When he's ready to learn, you should be ready to teach.
Are you?

Prepare the Learner

Put the learner at ease.
Arouse the learner's interest.
Make him aware of the job to be learned.
Find out what the learner knows about the job.
Show the importance to his success.

Present the Task

Present one idea at a time, clearly, patiently and in order.
Tell—show—illustrate—ask him questions.
Stress key points of the task.
Show the learner how he will use it.

Practice the Job

Have the learner try his hand.
Have him tell you why he does each thing.
Have him discuss the new ideas.
Insist on correct use of timing, trade, terms, etc.
Correct errors—expand explanations.

Provide the Right Attitude

Check on his understanding—How? Why? Who? What? Where? When?

Perfect His Skills

Check his performance.
Commend good work.
Detect weaknesses—help him overcome them.
Suggest his next step ahead.

"IF THE WORKER HASN'T LEARNED, THE INSTRUCTOR HASN'T TAUGHT"

The principal of the local high school could help you. Ask for the Distributive Education coordinator.[7]

Motivating and Working with People. If you want to know whether your employees are highly motivated to do a good job, ask your customers. They know. No one had to tell them, either. The fact that customers do know means that motivating and working with your people is part of your marketing mix.

Motivation of personnel in a small firm can be personal. This is a distinct advantage a small retailer has over large competitors. Use your knowledge of human behavior to develop your own approach or philosophy for motivating your people.

Strategies for Using Outside People

Small retailers often need expertise and specialized skills not available within the firm. Examples of such outside people are attorneys, accountants, consultants, marketing researchers, advertising agencies, suppliers, service contractors, installers, delivery services, and finance firms. These outside people become a part of your people mix. This is readily apparent when one of them comes into direct contact with one of your customers. For example, who gets the blame if the firm you contract to deliver customer parcels makes a mistake? You do, of course. The customer is your customer and expects you to take care of things. You also get the credit when your outside people perform well.

Some strategy questions to consider in using outside people are: To what extent do you use outsiders rather than insiders? For what purposes do you use them? What are the costs and competitive advantages and disadvantages? To what extent do outsiders interact with insiders and with target market customers?

Earlier sections have described some of the more important areas of people strategy. There are others. For example, some retailers whose industry appears to be growing more automated face what might be called people-machine strategy. What is the optimum combination of people and machines to best serve the customers in their target markets? The least-cost or most efficient combination may not be the optimum. What do the customers really want?

An Eight-Step Approach to Planning Your Retail People Strategy

Of all the people-strategy areas discussed above, the one which is usually a core-strategy area is matching your people with the needs of your target market customers. The others tend to be supporting rather than core areas.

The exact nature and role of people strategy in your firm will depend on many factors, such as target market served, your differential advantage, your environment, and the rest of your marketing mix. With these things in mind, you can use the familiar eight-step process to formulate a people strategy designed specifically for your business:

1. Record your current retail people strategy.
2. Identify your strategic retail people problems.
3. Divide your current strategic retail people problems into core-strategy areas and supporting-strategy areas.
4. Formulate alternative retail people strategies at both core and support levels.
5. Evaluate the alternatives in various combinations.
6. Choose your new retail people strategy.
7. Plan the details of implementation for your new retail people strategy.
8. Set performance standards and monitor feedback.

Step 1: Record Your Current Retail People Strategy. This is probably the first time you have recorded your people strategy. Perhaps you haven't even previously recognized people as one of the strategy areas of your retail marketing mix. As a guide, you may wish to review the previous materials in this chapter. Ask yourself specific questions about how the people variable has been operating for you. For example, to what extent and in what ways have you been able to match your people with the needs of your target market customers? How has the organization of your people and their work been built around customer satisfaction at a profit? What image do your people project, and how desirable is that image? How are personnel practices used to support your overall people strategy? How do outside people fit into your retail marketing strategy?

Record as much information as you can about both good and poor practices in your current people strategy. Record both the things you are doing and the things you are not doing but might consider doing. Record not only *what* you are doing in people strat-egy but also *why* with respect to your total marketing effort.

Step 2: Identify Your Strategic Retail People Problems. In this step you try to identify problems and opportunities in your current people strategy. A major problem may be that no people strategy previously existed. If so, you have identified the need for a framework with which to create one. Some problems probably emerged as you performed step 1—many of them tactical problems, but some possibly strategic.

People problems may be suggested by raising such questions as: Are customer complaints too frequent? Is customer turnover too high? Is employee turnover too high? How does your people strategy differ from that of competitors? What changes have occurred in the target market, the environment, or the rest of the marketing mix that require changes in people strategy?

Step 3: Divide Your Current Strategic Retail People Problems into Core-Strategy Areas and Supporting-Strategy Areas. We noted above that your strategy for matching your people with your target market customers is usually a core strategy area; all others tend to be supporting strategies. Whether a problem is core or supporting depends on how important it is to you. Core people problems usually result from a major change such as loss of your differential advantage, a shift in your customer preferences and attitudes, an environmental change, or a change in your goals. Some examples would be the loss of a key executive whose personality heavily influenced the people mix and image, the entry of younger persons into the market, changes in laws regarding part-time employees, or a decision to expand your business by adding a new site. Such changes can result in core-strategy problems. Core people strategy problems will probably occur less often than supporting people problems, but they will call for more radical strategy revisions.

Don't ignore supporting people-strategy problems. Good supporting strategies enhance your chances for success. For example, supporting personnel strategies in recruiting, selection, developing, and motivating the right people to serve your customers are key factors to success.

You have now recorded your current people strategy, identified strategic people problems, and decided which problems are core and which are supporting. You are ready to begin planning your future people strategy.

Step 4: Formulate Alternative Retail People Strategies at Both Core and Support Levels. This process begins with a reappraisal of your differential advantage. Then you consider core strategies and supporting strategies in that order. Three ways in which your core people strategies may vary are (a) redefining who your target market customers are and how your people mix will match that target market, (b) calling for a different level of emphasis on people strategy in your marketing mix, and (c) calling for different levels of support for your core people strategy.

Formulating alternative people strategies is supposed to be a creative process. In this step you should not be inhibited by tradition or convention. A new people strategy may or may not involve new people. It takes place at both core and support levels, even though problems may have been identified at only one level. People strategies work in combination with each other and with product, place, price, and promotion to make up your overall marketing

strategy. Your people strategy also relates to the nonmarketing areas of your business.

Be wary of attempting to copy people strategies of other retailers. Successful strategy ideas travel quickly and the temptation to imitate may be very great. However, because individual people are unique, a strategy may not work as well with one group as with another. A good people strategy for one retailer to reach a certain market may not be very good for another retailer or another target market.

Step 5: Evaluate the Alternatives in Various Combinations. In this step you are merely evaluating the alternatives; you are not yet selecting one. Evaluate each alternative and combination of alternatives in terms of your goals and resources. Ask how effective each alternative would be in helping to solve the current people problems identified in step 2. Also consider the effects different alternatives would have on reducing people problems and other marketing problems in the future. Take into account both advantages and disadvantages. Weigh costs against expected returns. Try to get a consensus or at least some agreement among your management team as to what important criteria you will use to make your evaluations. Try to keep a positive tone to the evaluation process, and make sure that evaluations are restricted to evaluating alternative people strategies rather than alternative individual people.

Step 6: Choose Your New Retail People Strategy. The new people strategy you select should be one that you plan to live with for quite some time (although during that time you will make tactical adjustments). Your new people strategy may not differ much from your former one. However, you will probably make some changes in supporting-strategy areas. Probably you will find that several good people strategies are available to you; you should select the one that best capitalizes on the unique people advantages of your firm and that fits your business philosophy.

You must make a choice in this step, and your choice should be realistic in terms of your resources. A realistic plan is one that you can implement. Some compromise between the ideal people strategy and what can realistically be accomplished may be necessary.

Step 7: Plan the Details of Implementation for Your New Retail People Strategy. Here you plan not only *what* is going to be done to implement your new people strategy, but also the details of *how, when, where,* and by *whom.* Details that are not specifically spelled out will probably not get carried out, or else they may be performed in such a way as to be less effective than desired. For example, if a training program to correct some people problems is part of the new strategy, some details of the program must be specified. Otherwise nothing at all happens, or a token training effort is made for a short period, or training focuses on the wrong problems, or the like. If you or one of your managers does not plan the details of

people-strategy implementation, the outcome will be determined by chance, neglect, or the ideas of a lower-level employee.

Step 8: Set Performance Standards and Monitor Feedback. This is a planning step rather than an actual control step. Involved here is the setting up of quantitative and qualitative criteria by which you will later evaluate the success of your people strategy. In the control phase of our PIC marketing management process, these criteria will be used for the actual evaluation. A second question to be addressed in this final planning step is to make provision for continuous feedback on how well your people strategy is working. This feedback permits you to fine-tune by making appropriate tactical adjustments from time to time.

People do the work, and people make a retail marketing strategy work. By making people (along with product, place, price, and promotion) a part of your marketing mix, you can make your marketing program more successful.

In this and previous chapters, all five P's of the marketing mix for small retailers have been described. You are now ready to combine all these elements into a total retail marketing strategy.

14

How to
Fit it all Together:
Your Total Retail
Marketing Strategy

Planning Your Total Marketing Program: An Introduction

Chapter 2 summarized this book in outline form. Having read it and subsequent chapters, you should have a fairly complete idea of how to plan your overall retail marketing strategy. The framework acts as a step-by-step guide, which you fill in according to the goals, differential advantage, target market, and other aspects of your own specific retail business. Once you have the planning part of the management process (PIC) well in hand, you will also give attention to implementing and controlling your plan.

The PIC retail marketing management process was shown graphically in Figure 2-1. Also given in Chapter 2 was a ten-step outline, around which your retail marketing strategy should be planned, implemented, and controlled:

1. How to set your company goals and objectives.
2. How to set your marketing goals and objectives.
3. How to identify your differential advantage.
4. How to define your target market(s).
5. How to plan your dealing with your business environment.
6 How to plan your overall marketing strategy (steps 1–8 of the strategy formulation process) by first planning each of the following parts of your retail marketing mix:
   a. Product mix.
   b. Place mix.
   c. Price mix.
   d. Promotion mix.
   e. People mix.

7. How to integrate your overall marketing strategy plan into an overall retail marketing program.
8. How to implement your retail marketing program by
   a. Organizing.
   b. Directing.
   c. Tactical adjustments.
9. How to control your retail marketing program.
10. Your result is a successful retail firm that produces customer satisfaction at a profit.

Company goals, marketing goals, and differential advantage (items 1, 2, and 3) were discussed in Chapter 2 and elsewhere. Target markets (item 4) were the topic of Chapter 3. In Chapter 4 you learned how to deal with your environment (item 5). Most of the rest of the book (Chapters 5 through 13) helped you plan your overall retail marketing strategy by first planning a marketing mix and strategy for product, place, price, promotion, and people (item 6). In the present chapter you are going to put all these parts together into a meaningful whole. Your result will be an integrated overall retail marketing program that you can profitably implement and control. Profitable implementation and control (items 8, 9, and 10) is the subject of our final chapter, Chapter 15.

How to Put It All Together

Your overall retail marketing strategy is composed of two things: (1) the customers of the target market(s) you serve, (2) the marketing mix (composed of the controllable elements or five P's—product, place, price, promotion, and people) you have designed in order to satisfy those customers at a profit. You combine the five elements of the marketing mix in such a way as to create a whole that is greater than the sum of its parts. You do this by using the eight-step strategy formulation process introduced in Chapter 2. We will not repeat that process here, but if you review Chapter 2 you should now find it much more meaningful because you have used the process in forming strategies for each of the five P's.

A total retail marketing program results from integrating the marketing strategy plans for all the target markets you serve. If you serve only a single market, you will not have separate strategies to integrate. However, many small retailers can segment their customers into two or three distinct target markets. For example, a restaurant may serve the luncheon crowd at noon, the dinner group in the evening, and the theatergoers in late evening. The three separate marketing strategy plans for each group of customers will be combined to form an overall retail marketing program.

Ideally, the total program you develop should be in written form and communicated to those concerned. You may use a period of one year, or you may choose some other time frame. You may wish to follow the ten steps of the retail marketing strategy outline given earlier in this chapter. Writing it out will help you be certain that all the parts fit together.

Under the marketing concept, the "ideal" retail marketing mix would have just the right amount (neither too much nor too little) of each of the five P's. As a formula, this could be shown as a 100 percent marketing mix, and any mix of less than 100 percent would be less effective. In other words, a retail marketing mix with a score of 85 percent would be 85 percent as effective as the ideal marketing mix. However, an ideal mix would be almost impossible to achieve. In fact, an 85 percent mix would be extremely good.

For example, suppose that you had an ideal mix—exactly the right product, right place, right price, right promotion, and right people. These five elements would have to blend together in the right way. Expressed as an equation, a 100 percent retail marketing mix equals a 100 percent product times a 100 percent place times a 100 percent price times a 100 percent promotion times a 100 percent people mix—or

$$(100\%)(100\%)(100\%)(100\%)(100\%) = 100\%$$

If any of the five P's were at less than 100 percent, the total mix could not reach 100 percent. For example, a 90 percent product times a 90 percent place times a 90 percent price times a 90 percent promotion times a 90 percent people mix equals a 59 percent total marketing mix:

$$(90\%)(90\%)(90\%)(90\%)(90\%) = 59\%$$

This result is due to the reverse of the synergetic effect. However, we must also consider *suboptimization.* This means that you will sometimes have to shift resources, making a part of your mix less than 100 percent effective in order to make the total mix better. For example, what may have been your best or "ideal" price strategy may have to be adjusted to provide resources for promotion or to offset the cost of a better site location. Or you may have to spend less than the "ideal" amount of promotion so that inventories can be built up. What you want is the best total retail marketing mix,

made of elements that are as effective as possible when viewed individually, subject to the constraint that total effectiveness takes precedence over individual effectiveness. It's similar to eating a balanced diet made up of good food from all the basic food groups.

In the process of integrating and planning for the effectiveness of your total marketing program, you may wish to consider such issues as the following:

1. How productive in terms of dollar return on investment is your marketing program?
2. Would more or less emphasis on marketing be more profitable in the short run? in the long run?
3. What is the necessary threshold level for any of the five P's to contribute to the overall marketing effort?
4. How much lag time is involved when the composition of your marketing mix is changed?
5. What are the carry-over effects of your previous marketing efforts?
6. Which parts of your total marketing program are least vulnerable to attack by competitors?
7. Which parts of your retail marketing effort tend to be most reinforcing of other parts?

In doing your marketing planning, remember that time lags occur between the time you make your plans, the time you implement these plans, and the time your target market customers respond to your program. For example, a new retail salesperson should become more productive with more experience, a new location may take time to build up sales, or an increased expenditure for advertising may take some time to produce results.

Make a Comparative Marketing Strategy Chart

To become a more successful retailer, you may find it helpful to write down not only your own marketing strategy but also those of your competitors. This will give you a chance to view both the parts and the integrated totalities of these strategies at a glance. It will let you view any apparent shifts in competitive strategy for a total systems perspective. You will want to make such a comparison chart for each target market you serve. For example, the restaurant mentioned earlier would make three comparison charts: one for the luncheon target market, one for the dinner target market, and one for the late evening theater target market. You can set up the first draft of the comparison chart on a blackboard or a large sheet of paper in a conference room. You may include whatever items you wish to compare. As a guide you can use the format and items shown in Figure 14-1.

You use the marketing strategy comparison chart by listing for yourself and for all your important competitors whatever solid information you have about the ten numbered items listed down the first column. You list what the strategies are and the strengths and weaknesses of every item for yourself and for each competitor. Let's briefly go through each of the ten items.

1. *Description of tarket market:* Here you describe the target market as *you* have defined it. Your description is a summary statement of the extent and dimensions of the customer group now under consideration. Because you will make a separate marketing strategy comparison chart for each important target market you serve, include only one target market here.

2. *Any differences in defining target market:* Here you record any differences that exist between the way you define your target market in item 1 above and the way your competitors define their target market. Thus, for this item your box will be empty on the chart. Boxes for competitors will describe areas of overlap along any dimension, such as age, geographic, or income, where that competitor is defining his target market either more narrowly or more broadly than you are.

3. *Product strategy:* Stated here are your product strategy and the product strategies of your competitors. The major strengths and weaknesses are noted. See the chapter on product strategy to remind yourself of what the major product strategy issues are. Don't forget to make a detailed comparison of customer services.

4. *Place strategy:* Items compared here are sources of supply, site location, layout, and other place strategy decision areas covered in the chapters on place strategy. Because location is so much a part of retail success, you may wish to compare information in this item with target market definitions in items 1 and 2.

5. *Price strategy:* Remember that you are comparing price strategy and not simply prices. Compare all the price strategy areas as well as price-level strategies.

6. *Promotion strategy:* Compare here the role that promotion plays, the image it attempts to communicate, and the way in which advertising, sales promotion, personal selling, and public relations and publicity are combined into a promotion mix. How are promotion strategies similar and different for each competitor?

7. *People strategy:* Do all competitors have a people strategy as part of their marketing strategy? What role does people strategy play? What are the strengths and weaknesses for you and competitors in matching your people with target market customers,

1. Description of target market: _____

   _____

   _____

   _____

   _____

COMPETITORS ITEMS COMPARED	YOU	COMPETITOR ABC	COMPETITOR XYZ
2. Any differences in defining target market			
3. Product Strategy			
4. Place Strategy			
5. Price Strategy			
6. Promotion Strategy			
7. People Strategy			
8. Differential Advantage			
9. Summary of overall marketing strategy			
10. Implications and comments for further consideration			

Figure 14-1. A Comparative Marketing Strategy Chart

people organization strategy, people image strategy, supporting people strategies, and strategies for using outside people?

8. *Differential advantage:* Describe here the differential advantage around which you and each of your competitors has built (or could build) a successful overall marketing strategy. Chances are that the ability to be very competitive on prices is *not* the differential advantage; it is usually something more fundamental.

9. *Summary of overall marketing strategy:* This is a summary statement for each firm, telling in simple, straightforward language how the firm has used its resources to attempt to make a profit by serving the needs of the target market described in items 1 and 2.

10. *Implications and comments for further consideration:* Here you record ideas you may wish to consider in the future. These ideas will come to you as you complete the nine items above and when from time to time you look at your marketing strategy comparison chart. A good time to look at the chart is whenever you are contemplating a change in strategy or whenever it appears that a competitor's strategy is changing.

In making and working with your marketing strategy comparison chart, don't accept the popular stereotype of competitors. Get the facts rather than using guesses. Do this by visiting their stores and by gathering other information such as competitors' advertisements. Success requires objectivity.

Don't confuse a tactical adjustment with a change in strategy. Changes in marketing strategy will occur much less often than will tactical adjustments.

Keep a proper perspective. On that large sheet of paper or whatever you use to make up your comparative marketing strategy chart, you have recorded a still picture. It does not say much about the past or about future progress.

Remember, you don't have to rank number one in all categories (or even in any categories) to make a profit and successfully serve part of the target market. You can make profits by being number two or number three in total or in several of the items listed in the marketing strategy comparison chart. Whatever you do, don't give too much time and attention to your competitors. Spend your time and effort on your own business. And, if you are not yet number one, keep trying harder. If you are number one for this target market, keep improving your marketing program. The time it is easiest to do this is when you're on top.

Marketing Research Can Help

Consumer research that small retailers can do was discussed at the end of Chapter 3. Chapter 12 described some simple marketing research for testing promotion effectiveness. Several other types of marketing research also can provide useful information for planning, implementing, and controlling your marketing strategy. Marketing research is a tool to provide you with marketing information so you can make better decisions. Marketing research can provide information not only about the market but also about the environment and about any element of your marketing mix.

Our approach here is a managerial and nontechnical one. Many techniques of marketing research are complex and best left to an expert. However, some simple and unsophisticated marketing research can and probably should be done by the small retailer himself.[1] You may also secure assistance from a local college professor at a reasonable cost. Some marketing research can also be done by working with your local field office of the Small Business Administration.

Taking a survey by distributing a questionnaire is one of the most popular methods of gathering marketing information. Using available published statistics such as census data is another method. A third method is observation such as in a traffic count or by keeping good sales records. All these methods can be used by small retailers if they are careful to get the right information and apply it properly to the right problem. Another method, which you can use alone or in combination with some of the above methods, is the controlled experiment. Although experiments can become quite complex in their designs, this is not often necessary in a small retail business. You can perform a simple marketing experiment for such purposes as the following:

1. Comparing sales of one product against those of another.
2. Calculating the sales effect of a promotion.
3. Comparing regular against special display.
4. Measuring the effects of a price change.
5. Measuring what happens if the product is changed.
6. Determining the results of a change in people strategy.
7. Measuring the results of any other action you take in any part of your retail marketing program.

With a little imagination, and taking care not to read too much into your results, which will admittedly not be precise, you can use the experimental method to conduct a variety of simple marketing experiments. In effect, the experimental method is little more than trial and error backed up with good record keeping. Your own experience is a series of somewhat uncontrolled experiments.

For purposes of illustration our experiment will attempt to measure the effectiveness (in terms of sales) of building a special display of an item that we will call *Special*. Our experimental design is known as a pre-post design; its simplest form is shown in Table 14-1.

You have used this experimental design many times, perhaps without realizing it. The design can even be used after the fact. In terms of the sales effects of the display of our product Special, the design would be as shown in Table 14-2.

The experimental design used here is a crude one. It does not provide for control of other factors that might affect the sales of Special: the weather, a change in total store

Table 14-1.

Pre-Post Design

	Experimental Group		
	Symbol	$	%
1. Pre-measurement	A	—	—
2. Experimental variables introduced	Yes	—	—
3. Post-measurement	B	—	—
Effect of experimental variable = $B - A$			

Table 14–2.
Sales Effects of Building a
Display of Special

		Experimental Group (Special)	
	Symbol	$	%
1. Pre-measurement (e.g., last week's sales or average week's sales of Special)	A	$400	100%
2. Experimental variable introduced (e.g., building a display of Special)	Yes		
3. Post-measurement (e.g., test-week sales of Special)	B	$600	150%

B − A = $600 − $400 = $200, or 150% − 100% = 50%

The effect of introducing the experimental variable (building the display) is increased sales of Special of $200 or 50%.

traffic and sales, competitive promotions, promotion by the manufacturer of Special, and the price at which Special was sold. By using a control group, we can net out the impact of these and other outside factors. The control group could be sales of a very similar product in the same store; or, if you have more stores than one and they are quite similar, you could use another store as the control group. The control-group store could belong to you or to a friend. The display of Special is built in one store (the experimental store) but not in the other store (the control store). In all important aspects other than the display the two stores should be nearly identical. Then any changes taking place in the experimental store (the one with the display of Special) will be the result of two things: (1) introducing the experimental variable and (2) all the uncontrollable variables (which is the same thing as saying everything else). On the other hand, changes in the control store are the result of only item 2—all the uncontrollable variables. Thus, the *post* minus *pre* results of the control store are subtracted from the

post minus *pre* results of the experimental store, so that the remainder is the result of the experimental variable only.

The format for this design, known as a pre-post with control group design, is shown in Table 14-3. Even though a control has been added, the design is still fairly simple and easy to use. It is far from perfect, especially from the viewpoint of a research expert; however, from the practical viewpoint of a small retailer, the design can be very useful in providing reasonably good information for making better marketing decisions.

You can adapt the experimental designs discussed above to fit a wide range of marketing problems. Where appropriate, you should use the experimental method; at other times you will use observation and surveys. Always, before you collect any data on your own, go to secondary sources for information that is readily available. Information is much less expensive and relatively easy to obtain from suppliers, trade associations, newspapers, and government agencies.

Table 14-3.
Pre-Post Design with Control Group

	Experimental Group: SPECIAL IN STORE 1			Control Group: SPECIAL IN STORE 2		
	Symbol	$	%	Symbol	$	%
1. Pre-measurement (e.g., last week's sales or average week's sales for Special)	A	$400	100%	C	$420	100%
2. Experimental variable introduced (e.g., display of Special)	Yes in store 1			No in store 2		
3. Post-measurement (e.g., test-week sales for Special)	B	$600	150%	D	$435	104%

Effect of the experimental variable = $[(B - A) - (D - C)]$
in $ = [($600 - $400) - ($435 - $420)]$ in % = $[(150\% - 100\%) - (104\% - 100\%)]$
= $200 - $15   = 50% - 4%
= $185   = 46%*

* Discrepancies may result if A and C are not identical.

**EXAMPLE OF SEMANTIC DIFFERENTIAL QUESTIONNAIRE
AS PRESENTED TO PERSONS INTERVIEWED***

Extremely/Quite/Slightly   Slightly/Quite/Extremely

Pleasant Place to Shop	____:____:____ : ____:____:____	Unpleasant Place to Shop
High Priced	____:____:____ : ____:____:____	Low Priced
Informative Advertising	____:____:____ : ____:____:____	Uninformative Advertising
Unfair	____:____:____ : ____:____:____	Fair
Good Service	____:____:____ : ____:____:____	Poor Service
Narrow Selection	____:____:____ : ____ ____	Wide Selection
Store Like Others	____:____:____ : ____:____:____	A Unique Store
High Quality Merchandise	____:____:____ : ____:____:____	Low Quality Merchandise
Misleading Advertising	____:____:____ : ____:____:____	Believable Advertising
Reliable	____:____:____ : ____:____:____	Unreliable
Poor Value for Money	____:____:____ : ____:____:____	Good Value for Money
Helpful Sales People	____:____:____ : ____:____:____	Uninterested Sales People
Unattractive Decor	____:____:____ : ____:____:____	Attractive Decor
Current Fashions	____:____:____ : ____:____:____	Conservative Fashions
Few Brands	____:____:____ : ____:____:____	Many Brands
Unpleasant Sales People	____:____:____ : ____:____:____	Pleasant Sales People
Liked by Your Friends	____:____:____ : ____:____:____	Disliked by Your Friends

Note staggering by columns of the favorable and unfavorable alternatives.

Figure 14-2. (Source: adapted from Carter Grocott, "Newspaper Advertising and the Small Retail Store's Image," *Journal of Small Business Mangement* 12 (April 1974), p. 11)

Your Total Image

In previous chapters you have read about product image, place image, price image, promotion image, and people image. These five types of images should all be consistent with each other to form the overall image that you want to project to your target market customers. Your total image should also be consistent with the overall marketing strategy you have decided to use. You may wish to do some marketing research to see if your image and those of your competitors match the information you have recorded in your comparative marketing strategy chart. Such a check will tell you how well you (and your competitors) are communicating with your customers and potential customers. A questionnaire that you can adapt to measure your total image among present and potential customers, as well as your own management self-image, is given in Figure 14-2 (page 187). By profiling the summary results from each group of persons interviewed (customers, potential customers, and managers), you can see how your total image is seen by each group. You can also use such a questionnaire to check the images of your competitors, if you decide it is worth the cost.

Your total image is based on everything you are and everything you do. Some of the more important elements that go together to make up your image are listed below.

1. *Target market elements of image.*
   a. Type of clientele served.
   b. How customers dress.
   c. What customers say in the store.
   d. How customers act in the store.
   e. Whether or not customers smoke.
   f. How much time each customer spends in the store.
   g. Whether different types of customers visit the store at different times of the day.
   h. How many (or how few) customers are in the store at any given time.
   i. Whether customers are alone, with a family, or with other groups when shopping.
   j. How much customers interact with products, employees, and other customers.

2. *Product elements of image.*
   a. Quality of merchandise.
   b. Merchandise assortment.
   c. Merchandise availability.
   d. Fashionability of merchandise.
   e. The number and level of customer services offered and who pays for them.
   f. Packaging.
   g. Brands carried.

3. *Place elements of image.*
   a. Store location.
   b. How long store has been in business and at that location.
   c. Neighboring stores and buildings.
   d. Parking facilities.
   e. On-premise signs.
   f. Store front.
   g. Physical appearance of building.
   h. Fixtures.
   i. Width of aisles.
   j. Location and height of merchandise displays.
   k. General cleanliness.
   l. Atmospherics such as color, lighting, decoration, music, smells, motion and temperature.

4. *Price elements of image.*
   a. Price levels.
   b. Range of prices.
   c. How prices are physically marked.
   d. How prominently price is featured in advertising.
   e. Price/quality relationship.
   f. Discounts available.

5. *Promotion elements of image.*
   a. Advertising media used.
   b. Amount of promotion.
   c. Institutional versus item price promotions.
   d. Size and layout of advertisements.
   e. The advertising message communicated.
   f. Believability of advertisements.
   g. Types of sale promotion used.

h. Frequency of sales promotion events.

i. Characteristics of sales personnel, such as knowledge, cleanliness, speech patterns, friendliness, personality, and so on.

j. Extent of involvement in community relations.

6. *People elements of image*
   a. Personality of owner/manager.
   b. Personality of other managers and employees.
   c. How employees get along together.
   d. Physical appearance of people.
   e. How your people relate to customers.
   f. How well your people get to know customers.
   g. How your people treat customers.

Other elements such as the environmental areas may also affect your image. All these elements blend together to form an image in the minds of customers and potential customers. Accordingly, they may view your store as dull or exciting, clean or dirty, modern or old-fashioned, high-priced or bargain-priced, friendly or unfriendly, and so on. What do your target market customers expect? With what total image can they comfortably identify? Obtaining regular customers, satisfy their needs, and building repeat business is the best way to insure long-term profits. The right image can help you do this.

A few examples may help to emphasize the importance of image for a successful retail operation.

Example 1. A very successful restaurant had the reputation of being a place where only "old people" went. The new owner wanted to expand his business by appealing to a larger and younger target market. It was virtually impossible to do so. In spite of the fact that the restaurant offered a good value in dining out and very good food, the "older-people image" of the restaurant was so strong that younger people refused to go there.

Example 2. The importance of the atmospheric portion of your total image is illustrated by the bakery and the fish store cited below:

A new bakery was opened up in a shopping center and attracted considerable attention initially because of its fine fixtures, window treatment, and exotic pastry. Everything about the atmosphere suggested fine pastries fit for a king. Yet customers failed to materialize in sufficient numbers and the bakery went out of business. The owners made the mistake of overdesigning the shop for the clientele. The store's atmosphere suggested high prices and special-occasion pastries, whereas most shoppers wanted low prices and more everyday pastry. The owners had mismatched the atmosphere to the clientele.

A fish store in an ethnic neighborhood did a thriving business. The store was very unkempt and unattractive. Someone talked the owner into remodeling the store to give it a clean, attractive look. The owner did this, and business fell off. Somehow the modernization connoted higher prices to many customers, and also they felt less comfortable in the place than before. Once again, atmosphere was mismatched to the clientele.[2]

Example 3. What's in a name? Turn to the Yellow Pages of your local telephone directory and look at the business names the various retailers have given to their stores. Then ask yourself what image each name creates in the minds of potential customers who have not yet shopped at that store. Here are a few examples I have found:

(1) Electric lighting fixtures: Miller Electric or The Lighting Center.

(2) Draperies: JB Draperies or Window Expressions.

(3) Fences: Broski Bros., Inc., or Economy Fence Co.

(4) Florist: David's Florist or Flower Land Florist.

(5) Lawn care: Hooper's Lawn and Landscaping or Barefoot Grass Lawn Service.

You can see that different names do project different images. For the most part, businesses named after the owner do not project a clear image unless the owner is well known. For additional examples of image, see the chapters on product, place, price, promotion, and people.[3]

Customer Response to Your Marketing Program

If your retail marketing program works for you, it is a good program. The better it works, the better it is. It doesn't really matter that your program is different from those of your competitors.

Trial and error and the making of adjustments for the changes taking place in the market are part of the continuous retail marketing management process of planning, implementing, and controlling. Thus far in this book we have concentrated on planning your retail marketing strategy. In the final chapter we discuss implementing and controlling. Before we turn to that chapter, let's suppose for a moment that things are not 100 percent as they should be. How can you spot this? What are some danger signals that you can train yourself to look for so that potential problems can be corrected in the early stages? The SBA suggests that you train yourself to look for the danger signals shown in Figure 14-3.

A consumer-oriented marketing program based upon the five P's will make you a successful retailer and will also make you a nice *PROFIT*. When you respond to customers in a positive way, they in turn respond to your marketing program.

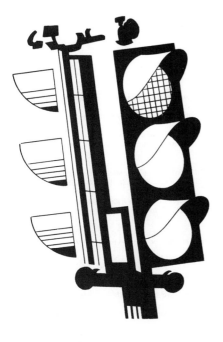

DANGER SIGNALS IN A SMALL STORE

By Bruce Goodpasture

SUMMARY

Danger signals warn the owner-manager that something has started to go wrong. They can be especially helpful to men and women in newly established businesses (firms that are less than 2 years old).

This *Aid* was written mainly for such individuals. Its purpose is to help them recognize their management problems in the early stages so they can look for assistance while there is time to help the business.

The idea for this *Aid* was suggested by members of SCORE (Service Corps of Retired Executives) chapters in Virginia. These volunteer small business counselors pointed out that often inexperienced owner-managers don't realize that they have a problem until it becomes acute. The author, Bruce Goodpasture, is a member of SBA's Office of Management Assistance. In compiling these danger signals, he drew on the experience and knowledge of many individuals in addition to his own.

Figure 14-3. (Source: U.S. Small Business Administration. Small Marketers Aids No. 141)

Figure 14-3
(continued)

**WHAT ARE THE DANGER SIGNALS IN MANAGING A SMALL STORE?
CAN YOU HEAR THEM AS YOU HEAR THUNDER?
CAN YOU TOUCH THEM AS YOU TOUCH A SHARP KNIFE?
CAN YOU SEE THEM AS YOU SEE A CAR RUNNING A RED LIGHT?
YES.**

You can hear customers complaining about the lack of service. You can hear employees giving customers misinformation about products. You can touch dusty counters and displays. You can touch shopworn and obsolete merchandise. You can see customers walk out without buying. You can see the loss when your cash register continuously checks up short.

Fortunately, you don't need super senses to hear, touch, and see some of the danger signals. They pop up like red flags on expired parking meters.

Here are some danger signals concerning CUSTOMERS.

A small store is flirting with danger if:

Many CUSTOMERS walk out without buying.
Many old CUSTOMERS no longer visit the store.
TRAFFIC (pedestrians and vehicles) in front of the store has fallen off.
Customers are NOT URGED to buy additional or more expensive items.
Customers are RETURNING more merchandise than they should.
Sales are DOWN this month over the same month last year.
Sales for THIS YEAR to date are DOWN over the same period last year.

Red lights are flashed on by DISPLAYS and MERCHANDISE.

A small store invites customers to stay away if:

The display window IS NOT TRIMMED with new and exciting merchandise.
Display racks, shelves, and counters are DUSTY.
Some of the stock looks SHOPWORN.
The store has a RUNDOWN look.
CROWDED aisles make it hard for people to reach merchandise.
Merchandise is often DAMAGED because of crowded displays and mishandling in the storage area.

Danger signals also pop up in BUYING AND SELLING.

A small store may not show a profit if:

Its prices are NOT IN LINE with those of competitors.
More than a few ODD sizes and colors accumulate in a short time.
DOLLARS that can be spent for NEW stock are limited because the backroom is full of slow-moving items.
Stocks are NOT FLAGGED to remind the owner-manager to reorder at the proper time.
MARKDOWNS on style items are not taken QUICKLY when customers begin to discard a style for a new one.
More than a few SEASONAL items are carried over.
CASH DISCOUNTS are not taken on purchases.

Here are some of the warning flags that are hoisted by EMPLOYEES.

A small store is in danger of driving away customers if:

Employees are slow in GREETING customers.
Employees appear indifferent and make customers WAIT unnecessarily.
Personal appearance of employees is not NEAT.
Salespeople LACK KNOWLEDGE of the store's merchandise.
Customers complain of employee LACK OF INTEREST in their problems.
MISTAKES which employees make are INCREASING.
QUALIFIED employees LEAVE for jobs with the store's competitors.

Early warning alarms can also be sounded by MONEY.

A small store is in financial trouble if:

The owner-manager BARELY MAKES ENDS meet from month to month.
The owner-manager has trouble MEETING PAYMENTS on bank loans.
The owner-manager makes ends meet but is PENALIZED for paying bills late.
The store's bank balance DECLINES for several months in a row.
The owner-manager PAYS HIMSELF more than is justified by the store's sales.
The bank is RELUCTANT to lend the owner-manager money

Loud and clear warnings come from RECORDS.

A small store is not using its records as management tools if:

The owner-manager pays his PERSONAL EXPENSES out of the same checking account as his BUSINESS EXPENSES.
The recordkeeping system does not help the owner-manager to PAY BILLS, including taxes, ON TIME.
Credit customers are BEHIND with their payments.
Stock turnover is SLOWER than the average for the type of merchandise.
Gross profit IS LESS THAN the average for the type of merchandise.
The net worth of the business HAS DECREASED.

TRAIN YOURSELF

TRAIN YOURSELF to look for danger signals. Catch trouble before it catches you.

First printed
February 1970

Reprinted
May 1979

RELATE the signals you've just read about to YOUR operation. HONE them down to where they'll hit you loud and clear while the problem is still small. Accountants and other outside advisors can help you SPELL OUT a more complete set of danger signals.

And volunteers, such as SCORE members are available at the nearest SBA office.

U.S. GOVERNMENT PRINTING OFFICE : 1979 O—290-808

15

How to Manage Your Retail Marketing Program

This book has stressed that management and marketing are different for small retailers than for large retailers. We have examined the target markets, the environment, and the five elements of the small retailer's marketing mix in detail. Our emphasis has been on strategy planning, although many references have also been made to implementing and controlling. The present chapter emphasizes the implementing and controlling parts of the PIC management process.

Small retailers implement and control

their marketing programs by organizing and directing people. Although such organizing does not result in a bureaucracy, the use of certain management principles—properly adapted to the small-firm situation—can help you become more successful. Likewise, the control function tends to be different for small than for large retailers. We shall discuss this difference. Finally, we take a look into the crystal ball to see what the future might bring for small retailers.

Implementing Your Retail Marketing Program

You implement your retail marketing program by implementing each of the parts to the full extent of your plan and by making the necessary tactical adjustments. You do this by *organizing* and *directing* the various work tasks to be performed by you and your people. In short, implementing is (1) using your planned strategy to (2) make decisions and then (3) putting those decisions into effect through actions.

Some Generalizations about Management in Small Retail Firms. A major strength of many small retailers has been in the implementation rather than in the planning and control phases of management. Although strategy planning is very important, success may often be determined by how well the small retailer implements a rather standard or common marketing strategy. Well-implemented plans work and pay off. The inherent potential a small retailer possesses for superior implementation is an advantage that few small retailers can afford to ignore.

You can avoid mediocre performance by working with people who really want to do a good job. In fact, many small retailers have built their success on the basis of getting the job done better than larger competitors. Quite often the owner/manager is physically involved in much of what gets done. On the other hand, large retailers have layer upon layer of management, each checking on the layer below, to make sure the work gets done. Management layers are very few (often there is only one layer) in a small retail firm. Either the owner/manager and his people do the work or it doesn't get done.

Work tasks are usually less divided in small retail firms than in large ones. Therefore the problems of organizing both people and work tasks are different for small retailers. Large retailers use a bureaucracy. Small retailers do not. However, this does not mean that some formal organization is unnecessary for small retailers. Organiza-

tion is needed. The basic principles of organization are much the same as in large firms, but they must be properly adapted to suit the small-firm situation. By analogy, the principles of navigation apply to both ocean liners and canoes, but not in quite the same way.

Knowledge of the industry, the market, and efficient marketing practices comes with experience and makes up an important part of the managerial skills of the small retailer. Such knowledge permits but does not guarantee good implementation. Some of the suggestions in the following subsections can help you to do a better job. Since the discussion here is brief, you will also wish to do some further study.

Implementing by Organizing. One author summarizes the most relevant organizational guidelines for small business managers as follows:

1. Maintain a flexible organizational structure.
2. Ensure that the manager is involved in those activities which will provide insights into changes taking place in the environment and provide feedback on the major developments in the firm.
3. Only when the manager cannot cope using a superficial approach should delegation be extracted from him or her and then only in those activities in which he or she does not have a comparative advantage, and in which he or she does not need to be involved in order to facilitate strategic decision making.[1]

The need for organization in any group is emphasized by another observer:

Many residents of communal living experiments, attracted by the potential for individual freedom that such arrangements promise, will tell you that the most frequent reasons for the failure of such organizations are disputes over responsibilities for doing the dishes and carrying out the garbage for the group. This inability to delineate jobs in such a way that they get done without unnecessary duplications of effort and with a reasonable level of morale is often experienced by more formal organizations. It suggests several of the most important reasons for organizing: (1) to differentiate between jobs and allow for specialization of effort, (2) to provide for coordination between tasks and people, (3) to define responsibilities and authority held by members of an organization, and (4) to reflect and support over-all strategies.[2]

Many small retailers do not have a clear understanding about who is to "take out the garbage" or perform other tasks of varying degrees of desirability. Pleasant duties may be performed too well and unpleasant ones may be neglected. Wasted time and arguments among employees may result. What principles of management organization can you use to insure that your marketing program is properly implemented? Lists of such principles may vary slightly from author to author. The following list represents the thoughts of many writers on small business management:

1. A good organization is designed to accomplish specific purposes.
2. There should be unity of command, with only one person responsible for any given activity.
3. Authority must be clearly spelled out.
4. Decision-making should be accomplished at the lowest level possible.
5. Communication is, desirably, a two-way street, working both from the top man down and from the bottom man up.
6. Employee performance in the organization is monitored and controlled.
7. The limits of control of any individual within the organization must be made clear.[3]

Let us use these seven principles of organization as a framework for discussion. As you review them, you may say to yourself, "Hmmm, that makes a lot of sense." Then ask yourself how you can use each principle to better implement your marketing program. Have you been ignoring some of these principles?

1. *Accomplishing specific purposes. Form follows function* is the shorthand way of saying that the structure of your organization should be determined by the function or purpose for which the organization was formed. Thus, if accomplishing your marketing objectives has a high priority, your formal organization structure should help rather than hinder the accomplishment of these objectives.

Your formal organization structure may be the result of grouping people and tasks in a variety of ways—for example, by function, by product area, by service process or service project, by customer type, and by areas of your people's expertise.

Function is often used as the basis for organizing the lowest level of the organization. Persons who perform similar functions are grouped together. For example, a supermarket may have stock clerks who place merchandise on the shelves, cashiers who check customers out, and carry-outs who put groceries into customers' cars. Some people perform different functions at different times.

Organizing by *product* is dividing your people according to the product lines or groups your store carries. In the supermarket, personnel may be assigned to groceries, meats, produce, frozen, nonfoods, and so on. In a clothing store catering to both sexes, some personnel would be assigned to men's and boy's wear while others would be assigned to women's, teen's, and children's.

Organizing by *service process* or *service project* would occur in small retail service firms. For example, a garage may have some employees who concentrate on engine repairs and others who do body and fender work. Service project organization would be applied to services performed off the firm's premises, such as installation, remodeling, and home care and maintenance. Here a crew or team organization composed of a few specialists is assigned to each project.

Organizing by *customer type* occurs when a small retail firm also has a wholesale division selling to contractors or institutional buyers.

Organizing by *area of expertise* is similar to some of the above, since your people may have expertise by product line, function, and so on. However, the starting point here is the expertise of certain employees and/or the lack of expertise of others.

The method you use to organize could lead to a differential advantage over your competitors. Analyze your current organization (and those of your competitors). Does your organization run smoothly and does it meet the needs of your customers? Is your organization flexible enough that one person can help out another or replace another in case of illness or emergency? Do customers have to wait around needlessly because your method of organization has created bottlenecks?

2. *Unity of command.* This principle means that one person is charged with getting a job done and that each employee reports to only one boss, to whom in certain matters he is directly responsible. Small retailers often violate this organization principle, especially in firms that are family owned and operated. One family member tells an employee to do one thing and another family member says to do something else. The employee is frustrated and doesn't know what to do.

3. *Clearly defined authority.* This principle calls for clearly assigned work responsibilities and the authority needed to accomplish tasks. Some judgment is involved here. Responsibilities should be specific enough to avoid vagueness and jurisdictional conflicts, but they must also be stated in such a way that some things not specifically mentioned do get done. Written definitions of authority can be useful and may also help you to delegate. The inability to delegate is a major managerial shortcoming of many small retailers. As your business grows from very small to not-quite-so small, you must gradually shift from being a doer to being a manager of your people. In view of the value of your own personal talents and time, consider the following guidelines for delegating. As a general rule, delegation should be practiced when someone within the organization can do a job:

a. Better than the small business manager.
b. Instead of the small business manager.
c. At less expense than the small business manager.
d. With better timing than the small business manager.
e. In a way that makes a greater contribution to training and development than if performed by the small business manager.[4]

4. *Lowest-level decisions.* Small retail firms do not have many levels of management, so it should not be hard to follow the principle of lowest-level decisions. Your marketing strategies should be communicated to all managers by clear policies, practices, and procedures so that appropriate decisions can be made at the lowest possible level.

Then you are able to practice management by exception: only the exceptions to the routine decisions need take your time. You use your time for more important things, and lower-level persons with a first-hand knowledge of each situation are prepared to handle most routine matters.

5. *Two-way communication.* Communication should flow freely both up and down (and across) your organization. Communication tends to be less formal in small businesses. Sometimes it may even be too informal to be effective. Channels of communication should be established, kept open, and used by you and all your people. Short-circuiting or going around a manager is a communication problem sometimes found in small firms.

6. *Monitor and control.* This is sometimes called the principle of accountability. It involves checking up to see that what was supposed to get done does get done in the way it should be done. More is said about control later in this chapter.

7. *Span of control.* There is a limit to the number of people that you or any of your managers can effectively manage. The number is not necessarily the same for all managers or all situations. For example, if you are managing people who are performing very similar tasks in close physical proximity to each other, you may be able to manage twenty people or more. However, there is less similarity (as there is at the top level of your organization), the span of control must narrow. For the owner/manager of a retail business, the optimum span of control may be from three to ten direct subordinates, depending on the nature of the operation. Assistant managers, department managers, and other managers are needed for a more effective organization. Specialized staff assistants can also help you manage a larger number of subordinates.

Other management organization guides could be listed besides the seven described above. For small retailers, the key is to keep the organization simple, flexible, and easy to understand for all employees. An organization chart may help to communicate how the organization is supposed to work. Keep in mind, however, that the organization chart is not the organization itself. In fact, it is often said that organizations tend to change before the ink on the chart is dry. Build your organization around your people. And put names of your people on your organization chart. If a person holds more than one position, list that name again for each additional position. Discuss your organization with all your people at one of your store meetings.

Organizations are usually some combination of the following pure types: functional, line, line-and-staff, and informal. In *functional* organization each manager is responsible for a specific function, and subordinates report to several managers—one for each function. In this extreme form, functional organization violates the principle of unity of command. In practice, although organizations may be divided along functional lines, a line-and-staff organization is usually superimposed. In a very small firm, such as in a new business, functional organization may work. Even here, however, the implicit line authority of the top manager is present. *Line* organization is a command authority relationship among superiors and subordinates. Although it also may exist in very small firms, the need for some staff assistance is often present. *Line-and-staff* organization combines the command authority of line organization with the advisory role of staff. This form tends to be very popular, especially as the small firm grows.

No matter what the formal organization is, an *informal* organization will also exist. All social organizations tend to develop informal organizations, consisting of the structure and relationships resulting from group interaction. Friendships and rivalries develop, informal group leaders emerge, the grapevine communication system carries messages, and so on. The small retailer who is to be an effective manager must recognize the existence of the informal group and learn to use it in accomplishing firm objectives. For example, the attitudes of one or two key salespeople who are regarded by their peers as group leaders may be critical in the success of a proposed sales promotion effort.

Committees, whether temporary or permanent, are an organizational supplement that brings group thinking to a problem area. Those who have served on committees are well aware of the saying: "A committee never did anything." It was suggested earlier that marketing strategy formulation could best be done by a committee or marketing management team under the leadership of the owner/manager. The provision for communicating with relative freedom from barriers is perhaps the greatest benefit from the use of committees. Even though most committees are strictly advisory, they do provide a forum for idea exchange.

Beyond the areas of organizing that we have discussed are others that cannot be covered, or even mentioned, in this book. Some of these are theoretical; others are very operational. Many small business management books and periodicals go into more detail.[5]

Implementing by Directing. Directing the work of other people is somewhat like telling a joke: some people do it extremely well and others fail miserably. To succeed in your small retail business, you need to do it extremely well. Management books are full of discussions of such concepts as leadership, communication, and motivation. These concepts are certainly too complex to cover here. Even the management books are not in complete agreement on how managers should use these ideas to direct people at work. However, one thing is clear: just as with telling jokes, you get good at directing people by practicing and constantly trying to improve.

Leadership in a small retail firm involves relatively few people. Often these leaders are a given—that is, they are the owner/manager and a few other people. Changes in these key leadership positions do not occur often. Because the leadership is a given, the best strategy may be to (1) objectively define the leadership style with its strengths and weaknesses and then (2) attempt to build the organization around the leadership style. For example, if you are a dictator, seek employees who work well under such circumstances. The dictatorial boss is not too popular among most people, but if that is how you operate, admit it and build your organization accordingly. If you are a dictator, hopefully you will be a benevolent dictator. On the other hand, if your leadership style is one of charismatic enthusiasm and a team spirit, act accordingly. Whatever your style, you can improve your leadership ability.

Good communications from you to your people and from your people to you is an important part of directing. Small firms probably have too little rather than too much communication. The next time a task is not performed or is performed poorly or incorrectly, ask yourself whether or not the employee received the proper communication to let him know exactly what was expected of him. In addition to specific communications, you will also want to keep all your people informed on what generally is going on in the business. This helps them feel that they are part of the firm.

Motivation is also a part of directing. Providing your own good example and keeping your people informed can work with other things to motivate your people. Money alone will not motivate them; it takes more. Psychologists and other experts have studied and reported on motivation. You can read this extensive literature from the perspective of a small retailer. Your conclusion will probably be that motivation is a very complex subject.

Highly motivated people are certainly an asset to a small retailer. You can motivate your people more easily if you first get to know each and every one of them as individuals. Each one may require something a little different. But each person will be more highly motivated and a more productive person if he or she is known and treated as an individual.

A small firm is an ideal setting for good (or bad) person-to-person relationships. Because of the lack of specialization and the variety of jobs for everyone to do, the job enrichment and job satisfaction that many large firms would love to have are a natural in the small firm. If you try hard, you can employ and direct people who really *want* to work rather than those who are simply *willing* to work.

Implementing by Tactical Adjustments. You can also implement your marketing program by making tactical adjustments from time to time. A tactical adjustment can be made to (1) your overall marketing program, (2) the marketing mix for a single target market, (3) one of the five P's, and (4)

an element of one of the five P's such as the advertising part of promotion. Tactical adjustments may be made quite independently; they need not take place at the same time changes are made in strategy. Rather, they are the fine tuning of strategy so that it will work more smoothly.

Although tactical adjustments should be broadly planned for, they are not specifically put into the marketing program ahead of time. By way of analogy, a television receiver has fine tuning controls that may be used to make minor corrections that enhance considerably the quality of reception. However, when major adjustments are needed, the TV repair shop must be called. Likewise, tactical adjustments are not strategic adjustments.

Given below are several examples of tactical adjustments to the retail marketing program. Although these adjustments are classified separately under the five P's, in actual practice they interact.

1. *Product examples:* Within the present product strategy a small retailer emphasizes a substitute product while the more desired product is in short supply. A small retailer stops carrying a particular brand. An economy size of a fast-selling product is added. A customer service that formerly was "free" is now available at a slight charge. A new procedure for cashing checks is tried.

2. *Place examples:* A new supplier is secured by the small retailer. The shelf position of some products is changed. The parking lot is redesigned for easier parking. Special displays are changed to coincide with upcoming seasonal promotions.

3. *Price examples:* Within the present pricing strategy, the small retailer marks down the price of seasonal or perishable merchandise. Selling prices are adjusted up or down to reflect changes in the cost of merchandise. A retail cents-off coupon is used to temporarily

combat a competitor's lower price. The small retailer offers a temporary price reduction in the form of a rebate. Prices for a special sale are marked with "red tags" rather than regular tags.

4. *Promotion examples:* Without changing the present promotion strategy, the small retailer tests responses from two shopping newspapers. Part of the ad budget is used to experiment with a new radio station. The store slogan is given more emphasis in advertisements. A sales contest is discontinued after its effectiveness has diminished.

5. *People examples:* The owner/manager takes a two-day course in management-by-objectives. Outside people such as the marketing consultant and the advertising agency people are invited to the store picnic. A major supplier is invited to make a presentation at the next store meeting. An employee who did not project the right people image for the store is helped to change. A renewed emphasis is given to the ongoing program to call all customers by their names.

A complete list of tactical adjustments that you might use would be quite lengthy. The target market of customers you are serving is probably the best guide to which tactics are best suited to your business. Don't feel compelled to copy the tactics of large retailers or other competitors. It is your own retail marketing program you are trying to fine-tune, not theirs. If tactical adjustments won't help you do a better job of implementing your current strategy, perhaps it's time to get a better strategy.

Controlling Your Retail Marketing Program

In earlier chapters the final step in the eight-step process of strategy formulation was always to set performance standards and monitor feedback. In step 8 in those chapters we were formulating the plans for controlling our retail marketing program. In the present chapter we are speaking not of planning but of the actual retail marketing control process itself. This is the third part of our PIC (planning, implementing, and controlling) management process. The question you want to answer here is: In what ways (qualitative) and to what extent (quantitative) has your retail marketing program been successful in accomplishing its objectives? Another way of stating the question may be: In terms of the five controllable variables (product, place, price, promotion, and people) of your retail marketing program and the target market customers to whom your marketing effort is directed, how can you reduce any gap that may exist between planned and actual performance?

The Nature of Retail Marketing Control. The control function in retail marketing is the systematic comparison of the actual results of marketing effort with predetermined standards and plans in order that corrective action can be taken (if necessary) to insure that objectives are met. Control is a process rather than a one-time thing. For example, a steering system is used to control the direction of an automobile. It works all the time, not simply when you wish to change direction. Likewise, your marketing control system should be an active, continuous management process rather than an event that takes place once a year at budget time. Parts of your marketing program are continuously being implemented; therefore you need continuous control of such performance. You need control to tell you how things are going and how future plans may be affected.

Levels of Marketing Control. Your total retail marketing system is composed of subsystems at several levels. Therefore, control is also appropriate at various levels. The five levels of marketing control for a small retail firm could be as follows:

1. The total marketing program of the small retail firm, composed of all target markets, marketing objectives, and overall company objectives.
2. The marketing plan for each target market you serve.
3. The effectiveness of product, place, price, promotion, and people as elements of your marketing mix.
4. The effectiveness of the components that go together to make up each of your five P's—for example, the effectiveness of advertising as a component of your promotion mix.
5. The operational level of control—for example, the effectiveness of a particular advertisement, a particular salesperson, or a particular pricing tactic. Also included in operational control are such things as cash control, credit control, merchandise or inventory control, and control of shoplifting and employee pilferage.

A small retailer probably spends more time on control level 5, the operational level of control, than on the other four levels combined. However, this does not mean that the other levels should be neglected. It simply means that operational control is time-consuming. For example, controlling operating expenses (level 5) is extremely important in attempting to end up with a profit. However, the best expense control in the world is not much good if a lack of control in any of the other levels results in a retail marketing program that produces insufficient sales.

Many control techniques and systems have been developed for use by retailers of all types and sizes. Some of these are currently too expensive for many small retailers. Point-of-sale (POS) systems that use electronic equipment for processing sales and inventory data are more and more within the reach of many small retailers—especially if they plug into an existing system of a major supplier. Other kinds of operational control can also be improved by using outside help.[6]

The Control Process for Small Retailers. In planning for marketing control, you determine (1) the level or levels of control involved and (2) what standards are to be used against which actual performance will be measured. The marketing control process for small retailers can be broken down into the following three steps *after* planning for control has taken place:

1. Gathering information by measuring actual performance.
2. Management appraisal of performance in terms of deviations from predetermined standards.
3. Making decisions and taking corrective actions.

Step 1. The information that results from measuring and recording actual marketing performance should be about key marketing items at the appropriate level. When such performance measures involve the performance of people (and they usually do), the people being measured should have some participation in setting the standards of performance. Yes, by *people* we do mean managers, employees, and so on. Their amount of participation depends upon your own management philosophy. Also, the performance measure should be clearly understood in advance and the rules should not be changed in the middle of the game. It is also important that your performance appraisal is based only on those factors that are within the control of the person or unit being evaluated.

Step 2. By comparing performance information generated in the first step with predetermined standards, you can isolate the deviations. In fact, your reporting system may be set up according to the exceptions principle to highlight deviations beyond a certain tolerable limit. Deviations may be either positive or negative. A positive deviation is overperformance. Although it probably occurs less frequently than negative deviations, overperformance may not always be desirable. Further inquiry and action are sometimes warranted when overperformance occurs. Perhaps your objective should be raised. Or perhaps overperformance in one activity is at the expense of inadequate performance in another activity. Analysis of both positive and negative deviations may point out new marketing opportunities. After you have appraised the causes of deviations, you are ready for the next step.

Step 3. In making decisions and taking corrective actions where appropriate, you use what you have learned in the first two steps. Corrective actions may be aimed at any of the five levels of the marketing system mentioned earlier. If corrective action is needed at the overall marketing strategy level, you may consider planning an entirely new strategy. On the other hand, if corrective action is needed at the operational level, you may tighten up controls on expenses that were out of line. Corrective action often involves people whose performance was lacking in some way. Remember that discipline in a small retail firm begins with self-discipline of the owner/manager. Good example and positive reinforcement for other people will decrease the need for discipline. However, in a few cases disciplinary action is called for. When administering discipline, you should:

1. Know the rules.
2. Act promptly on violations.
3. Gather pertinent facts.
4. Allow employees an opportunity to explain their positions.
5. Set up tentative courses of action and evaluate them.
6. Decide what action to take.
7. Apply the disciplinary action, observing labor contract procedures.
8. Set up and maintain a record of actions taken.[7]

The importance of the control process (at all levels) is emphasized most when a small retail firm is growing. When the firm is very small, the owner can personally control almost everything directly by himself. Under such circumstances, control problems are not too great. As the firm grows, and perhaps expands to a second or third location, the need for indirect control increases. The small retailer must now rely more on reports and control systems. Many small retailers either have failed in an expansion move or have decided not to expand because they are either unable or unwilling to make the switch from direct personal control to forms of indirect control.

The Retail Marketing Audit. For the small retailer who wishes to do a complete review of retail marketing and other areas of the business, a complete retail audit may be advisable. One easy way to do this is to get a copy of Wingate and Schaller's *Management Audit For Small Retailers.*[8] This booklet has 170 questions and comments divided into eighteen areas of retail management. Many of these areas involve the marketing part of retailing. The questions in this audit are designed not as a test but as a guide for self-appraisal. They point to areas where you need to investigate further. The accompanying comments are not answers to the questions but give the "reasons why" for the questions and supply directions for further study. You can use the management audit to determine both your strong points and your shortcomings.

The Future Outlook for Small Retailers

Generally, the future for small retailers is BRIGHT. As long as there are consumer markets in a free market society, there will be many opportunities for small retailers. Your own future as a retailer is up to you. The opportunities are there and will continue to be there.

Predicting the future is very difficult. Even so, some things seem to be quite predictable. Every retailer knows that inflation, materials shortages, and high energy costs are going to be part of the future. Some other things that are going to affect retailing in the future are the growing desire of many consumers for more personalization and self-expression, a turning of consumer attitudes away from bigness, and a desire to be different. Population growth and age and geographic distribution, increased education, and higher real incomes will all affect retailing in the future. Technology will exert an influence through such devices as buying over closed-circuit television and electronic transfer of funds. These changes will affect different kinds of retailers in different ways. Some types of retailing will be the "hot new ways to get rich quick." Other types will be "warm" but not "hot," and others, will be "cool" or even "cold." Regardless of your type of retailing, you will have an opportunity to be successful in terms of both making money and serving target market customers. The key, as stated throughout this book, is to position your retail business in such a way that you are using a retail marketing strategy specifically designed for your target market customers.

The authors of a very good book on independent retailing title their last chapter, "There'll Always Be an Independent Retailer." Among the points they make in the summary of that chapter are the following:

1. Statistics show that the independent retailer is here to stay.
2. This is so because department and chain stores have a number of inherent weaknesses that the independent can exploit.
3. The basic weaknesses of chain and department stores are (a) lack of good human relationships, (b) inflexibility and inertia, and (c) they require 100 percent locations and large customer areas. These weaknesses can become the strongest part of the independent stores' operations.
4. Special department store weaknesses are (a) new ideas are accepted with great reluctance and (b) merchandise tends to be dull and unexciting. These department store weaknesses can be developed into small store strengths.
5. Special chain store weaknesses are (a) they can handle only standardized, mass-produced, large-volume merchandise and (b)

they lack consumer services. These weaknesses, too, can be made into small store strengths.[9]

What these gentlemen say is true. It is the application of the marketing concept and target marketing to retailing. If you use these ideas and work to implement them, your future as a successful small retailer will be **BRIGHT.**

Appendix 1: Management and Marketing Aids

Free Management Assistance Publications from the Small Business Administration

Three types of free management-assistance publications are available from the SBA: *Management Aids, Small Marketers Aids,* and *Small Business Bibliographies.* The *Management Aids* are primarily for use by small manufacturers, but some of them may be helpful to some small retailers. *Small Marketers Aids* contain many items of interest to small retailers. *Small Business Bibliographies* furnish reference sources, some of which are for individual types of retail businesses.

Free single copies of items for each of the three lists may be obtained by contacting the SBA at the following address or telephone number: Small Business Administration, P.O. Box 15434, Fort Worth, Texas 76119, or call toll-free 800-433-7212 (Texas only call 800-792-9801).

From time to time additional publications become available and older ones are updated and revised. A complete listing of the latest publications can be obtained in order-blank form by requesting from the SBA a copy of the most recent form, SBA 15-A.

Management Aids

170. The ABC's of Borrowing
171. How to Write a Job Description
178. Effective Industrial Advertising for Small Plants
179. Breaking the Barriers to Small Business Planning

Small Marketers' Aids

Small Business Bibliographies

"For Sale" Booklets from the Small Business Administration

The "for sale" booklets of the SBA are lengthier than the free publications. They are classified under the *Small Business Management Series,* the *Starting and Managing Series,* and *Nonseries Publications.* For the current listing, see form SBA 115-B, which is also written as an order form. Although these publications are published by the SBA, the SBA does not sell them. They are sold by the Superintendent of Documents and can be ordered by following these official instructions:

How to order from the Superintendent of Documents: Complete the order blank on page 4. Send it with your check or money order to the Superintendent of Documents, Government Printing Office, Washington, D.C. 20402. Make check or money order payable to the Superintendent of Documents. Do not send postage stamps or cash. These booklets are NOT SOLD by the Small Business Administration. Foreign remittances should be made by international money order payable to the Superintendent of Documents, by draft on an American or Canadian bank, or by UNESCO coupons. Both domestic and foreign customers may charge their orders to their Master Charge, Visa, or Superintendent of Documents deposit account. Please include your card number and date of expiration. Prices subject to change without notice.

Small Business Management Series

No.		Stock No.	Pgs.	Price
1. _____	An Employee Suggestion System for Small Companies	045-000-00020-06	18	$1.10
3. _____	Human Relations in Small Business	045-000-00036-2	38	1.60
4. _____	Improving Material Handling in Small Business	045-000-00041-9	42	1.25
15. _____	Handbook of Small Business Finance	045-000-00139-3	63	1.50
20. _____	Ratio Analysis for Small Business	045-000-00150-4	65	1.80
22. _____	Practical Business Use of Government Statistics	045-000-00131-8	28	1.40
25. _____	Guides for Profit Planning	045-000-00137-7	59	1.90
26. _____	Personnel Management Guides for Small Business	045-000-00126-1	79	1.10
27. _____	Profitable Community Relations for Small Business	045-000-00033-8	36	1.50
28. _____	Small Business and Government Research and Development	045-000-00130-0	41	1.25
29. _____	Management Audit For Small Manufacturers	045-000-00151-2	44	1.60
30. _____	Insurance and Risk Management for Small Business	045-000-00037-1	72	2.10
31. _____	Management Audit for Small Retailers	045-000-00149-1	50	1.80
32. _____	Financial Recordkeeping for Small Stores	045-000-00142-3	135	2.50
33. _____	Small Store Planning for Growth	045-000-00152-1	99	2.40
34. _____	Selecting Advertising Media—A Guide for Small Business	045-000-00154-7	133	2.75
35. _____	Franchise Index/Profile	045-000-00125-3	56	2.00
36. _____	Training Salesmen to Serve Industrial Markets	045-000-00133-4	85	2.20
37. _____	Financial Control by Time-Absorption Analysis	045-000-00134-2	138	2.75
38. _____	Management Audit for Small Service Firms	045-000-00143-1	67	1.80
39. _____	Decision Points in Developing New Products	045-000-00146-6	64	1.50

Starting And Managing Series

No.		Stock No.	Pgs.	Price
1. _____	Starting and Managing a Small Business of Your Own	045-000-00123-7	97	$2.40
19. _____	Starting and Managing a Pet Shop	045-000-00065-6	40	.75
20. _____	Starting and Managing A Small Retail Music Store	045-000-00107-5	81	1.30
22. _____	Starting and Managing an Employment Agency	045-000-00109-1	118	1.30
24. _____	Starting and Managing a Small Shoe-store	045-000-00127-0	104	1.35

Nonseries Publications

	Stock No.	Pgs.	Price
Export Marketing for Smaller Firms	045-000-00158-0	84	$2.20
U.S. Government Purchasing and Sales Directory	045-000-00153-9	169	4.00
Managing for Profits	045-000-00005-2	170	2.75
Buying and Selling a Small Business	045-000-00003-6	122	2.30
Strengthening Small Business Management	045-000-00114-8	158	2.75
Small Business Goes to College	045-000-00159-8	82	3.25

Appendix 2: Instructor's Appendix

Discussion Questions

Chapter 1

1. The chapter lists twelve personal characteristics of successful small retailers. Take any one of these twelve characteristics and give an example of how a successful small retailer that you know demonstrates it.

2. How would you define a small retailer?

3. In Figure 1-2 it can be seen that for department stores and grocery stores, large retailers tend to dominate, whereas for the other kinds of retailers shown, small retailers tend to dominate. How do you explain this?

4. Find evidence in the chapter to support the idea that small retailers are an important force in the U.S. economy.

5. In Figure 1-3 explain why furniture stores and liquor stores tend to be single-unit establishments, whereas department stores, variety stores, and grocery stores tend to be multiunit establishments.

6. What marketing advantages do small retailers have? Give some examples of firms that you are familiar with that demonstrate these advantages.

7. What marketing disadvantages do small retailers have? Give some examples.

8. What is meant by the consumer-oriented marketing concept?

9. How would you define success for a small retailer?

10. How would you define failure for a small retailer?

Chapter 2

1. How would you describe the parts of the visual model of retail marketing management shown in Figure 2-1?

2. How would you distinguish between company goals and objectives and marketing goals and objectives?

3. How do company goals and objectives differ for small and large retailers?

4. Give some examples of specific marketing goals and objectives for a small retail firm with which you are familiar.

5. What is a differential advantage?

6. Using small retail firms with which you are familiar, try to determine the principle differential advantage of each.

7. What is meant by target market?

8. How do successful small retailers deal with their environment?

9. What are the five P's of the small retail marketing mix and how do they interact to form a complete marketing mix? You may wish to use Figure 2-1 to aid your explanation.

10. Distinguish between strategy and tactics.

11. Distinguish between core strategy and supporting strategies.

12. Briefly describe each of the eight steps for planning your retail marketing strategy.

13. What is meant by planning, implementation, and control?

14. How can a small retailer implement a retail marketing program?

15. How can a small retailer control a retail marketing program?

Chapter 3

1. What is a retail market?

2. Use an example of a retail store with which you are familiar to show how that store defines its target market in relationship to its differential advantage.

3. What segments of the total market tend to be target markets that can most advantageously be served by small retailers? Give some examples.

4. Describe the market segmentation process for small retailers.

5. What is meant by a segmenting characteristic? See Table 3-1.

6. Explain the principle of market dominance for small business.

7. Explain the principle of market simplification for small business.

8. Using a retail store with which you are familiar, explain how the five-step process outlined in the chapter can be used to make the target market definition operational for that store.

9. Give some examples of how markets are changing for small retailers.

10. Take any one of the nine situations described in Table 3-2 and explain how the result comes about.

11. What can small retailers do to learn more about their customers?

Chapter 4

1. What can the small retailer do about the economic environment?

2. Briefly distinguish between the economic environment and the competitive environment.

3. Select a type of retail store such as a restaurant, a flower shop, or a retailer of personal services and show how ease of entry and exit affects the competitive environment for such a retailer.

4. Give your own assessment of the political and legal environment for small retailers at the present time and for the near future.

5. How should small retailers deal with the environmental variables?

6. Who is your competition as a small retailer?

7. How do taxes affect small retailers?

8. How do franchisees who do and do not have legal problems differ from each other?

9. What are some of the potential legal problems of small business?

10. Discuss the social responsibilities of a small retailer.

11. What is consumerism and how does it affect small retailers?

12. What can small retailers do about consumerism?

13. Give some examples of how the scientific and technological environment affects small retailers.

14. What are some of the more important services provided by trade associations?

Chapter 5

1. What is the total-product concept?

2. Describe the goods/services mix of a retail firm with which you are familiar.

3. Give examples of convenience goods, shopping goods, and speciality goods.

4. How might services by classified for purposes of planning a marketing strategy for a retailer?

5. Give examples to illustrate width, depth, and consistency.

6. How can stock turnover and the stock-to-sales ratio be used for purposes of controlling merchandise?

7. Use an example to illustrate how stock turnover should be calculated.

8. What is the 80/20 principle?

9. How can a small retailer make scrambled merchandising work?

10. Why is the customer services mix so important for small retailers?

11. What are the important strategy questions to be answered concerning the customer services mix?

12. Examine the list given in Table 5-2 to see how many services are offered by several retail stores with which you are familiar.

13. Explain why a service performed by a service contractor rather than a retail store is still part of the product mix of the retail store.

14. Should customer services be free or charged for?

15. How does product strategy affect the store image of a small retailer?

16. Using a store with which you are familiar, analyze how the brands carried affect the store image.

17. What decision criteria might a small retailer use to select new products?

Chapter 6

1. What is meant by the market-product matching strategy for a small retailer?

2. What does the small retailer record in step 1 of the eight-step process for planning retail product strategy?

3. Give some examples of strategic product problems.

4. Use the list on pp. 65–67 as a guideline for examining the product strategy of retail firm with which you are familiar.

5. How does a small retailer divide current strategic product problems into core-strategy and supporting-strategy areas?

6. How can all alternative product strategies be evaluated?

7. What are some details that must be planned for in a new product strategy?

Chapter 7

1. What major areas are included in retail place strategy?

2. Explain how small retailers may be part of a vertical marketing system.

3. What is the role of a small retailer as a follower in the channel of distribution?

4. What are some services a resident buying office performs for its retailers?

5. How can a small retailer build good relationships with suppliers?

6. In what way do channels of distribution change over time?

7. Discuss the importance of franchising.

8. See if you can name a type of retailing in which franchising is not involved.

9. Give some examples of franchisees involving wholesalers and retailers.

10. Give some examples of franchisees involving manufacturers and retailers.

11. Give some examples of franchisees involving service sponsors and retailers.

12. What are the advantages and disadvantages of franchising from the franchisors' point of view?

13. What are the advantages and disadvantages of franchising from the franchisees' point of view?

14. How would you describe the future outlook for franchising in a particular line of retail trade?

Chapter 8

1. How important to a small retailer is a good location?

2. What is the difference between having a retail location and having a strategy for retail location?

3. Explain what is meant by the inverse and disproportionate relationship between site-location quality and the amount of promotion expense necessary. See Table 8-1.

4. Why do many small retailers do an inadequate job of considering the market area in which to locate their business?

5. Using a map of the city in which you are located, plot the different site types available to a small retailer.

6. See if your local urban planning agency or your local newspaper has sales figures for the various shopping centers in your area.

7. How are small retailers treated differently from major chains and department stores by many shopping center developers and landlords?

8. Using a shopping center in your city, show how

some sites within that shopping center are better than others.

9. Examine the layouts of some retail stores with which you are familiar. Do they follow or violate layout principles?

10. How can sales per square foot be increased?

11. Discuss the advisability of locating items or departments that are natural traffic generators in the less accessible areas of a retail store.

12. Is there such a thing as impulse buying?

13. How do store location and store layout affect store image?

14. Give some examples that show how physical distribution affects retail marketing strategy.

Chapter 9

1. What is meant by the assertion that the setting of prices is not the same thing as having a pricing strategy?

2. How would you define price?

3. List some pricing objectives that would be realistic for a small retailer.

4. How important a role does pricing play in the marketing strategy of a small retailer?

5. How important are prices to customers?

6. Is a retailer's price image always a true reflection of the store's actual prices?

7. Explain the basic difference between calculating markup on cost and markup on selling price.

8. Why is it that the percentage markup on selling price cannot be equal to or greater than 100 percent?

9. Why is the percentage markup on cost always greater than its equivalent percentage markup on selling price?

10. How can retailers effectively use markdowns?

Chapter 10

1. Does a retailer who uses cost-plus pricing require a pricing strategy?

2. Comment on the statement that price-level strategies of small retailers are almost always to price above the market.

3. Give an example to illustrate product-line pricing strategy.

4. How does product-line pricing differ from price lining?

5. Give an example of a stability pricing strategy.

6. Give an example of a psychological pricing strategy.

7. Do you know any retailers who use discriminatory pricing strategies? If so, explain how these strategies work to the advantage of the retailer

8. What should be the role of the small retailer if price cutting and price wars occur?

9. Give some pricing guidelines for the small retailer to follow during a time of inflation.

10. In what way is credit a part of pricing strategy?

11. In what ways does pricing for retail service firms differ from pricing for retailers who sell mostly goods?

Chapter 11

1. What are some common promotion mistakes made by small retailers?

2. How effective is word-of-mouth advertising for small retailers?

3. What are some of the ways promotion helps to create your image?

4. Briefly go through the content of what would be included in step 1 of the eight-step process for planning your retail promotion strategy.

5. What are the implications for the small retailer of the observations quoted in the chapter listing the things that advertising can and cannot do?

6. Evaluate the advertising message strategy of a small retailer with whom you are familiar.

7. Using Table 11-1, the checklist for promotional advertising in newspapers, evaluate the newspaper advertising of a small retailer with whom you are familiar.

8. Use the advertising media comparison chart to determine which advertising media are best suited for a small retail firm with which you are familiar.

9. Using the checklist for window display, evaluate several windows of small retailers in your community.

10. What are the advantages of using on-premise signs for a small retail store?

11. How can cooperative advertising help to stretch the small retailer's advertising budget?

Chapter 12

1. Under what conditions does personal selling tend to play a more important role in the retail marketing mix?

2. Briefly discuss the four basic selling theories that serve as a basis for sales strategy formulation.

3. How does personal selling relate to people strategy for small retailers?

4. Think about a good retail salesperson you have encountered. Then decide who is the best salesperson you have ever encountered and attempt to determine what made that person so good.

5. Give examples of sales promotion that illustrates the quick-response objective of sales promotion.

6. Explain why trading stamps are not as popular a form of retail sales promotion as they were several years ago.

7. Describe a realistic publicity and public relations program for a small retail firm.

8. Briefly describe the approach you would suggest for determining the promotion budget for a small retail firm.

9. Can promotional effectiveness be measured? If so, how? If not, why not?

10. How would you advise a small retailer to go about selecting and using an advertising agency?

Chapter 13

1. In your own words, briefly describe what is meant by people strategy.

2. Give some examples of people strategy in small retail firms with which you are familiar.

3. Describe what is meant by a strategy that matches your people with your target market customers.

4. What is meant by a people organization strategy?

5. What is meant by a people image strategy?

6. Describe some of the supporting people strategies.

7. In what ways can the owner/manager create people problems for the small retail firm?

8. How can small retailers motivate their people?

9. How can small retailers use outside people?

10. Describe in detail the first step in the eight-step process for planning your people strategy in a small retail firm.

Chapter 14

1. In your own words describe the total process of planning your entire retail marketing strategy.

2. Explain the synergetic effect as it relates to the ideal retail marketing mix.

3. Is it possible that marketing plays a more important role for some small retailers than for others?

4. Make a comparative marketing strategy chart for two or three retailers with whom you are familiar.

5. In what ways can marketing research help a small retailer plan his retail marketing strategy?

6. Illustrate the use of the pre-post research design.

7. Illustrate the pre-post design with control group.

8. How is the total image of a retail firm developed?

Chapter 15

1. The chapter gives several generalizations about management in small firms. Discuss any one of these in terms of a small retail firm with which you are familiar.

2. Why is organizing necessary in order to implement?

3. Give examples of each of the seven principles of management listed in the chapter.

4. Why should the owner/manager delegate to others in the retail organization?

5. Give an example of an informal organization.

6. Give an example of a small retail firm using a committee.

7. What is meant by implementing by directing?

8. Give some examples of implementing by making tactical adjustments.

9. How is a retail marketing program controlled?

10. Name several levels of control for retail stores.

11. Briefly describe the control process for small retailers.

12. What is a retail marketing audit?

13. Will chain stores and large department stores eventually drive all small retailers out of business?

14. How do you assess the future outlook for small retailers in a particular line of retail trade?

True-False Questions

Answers to True-False Questions are found on pages 221–223.

Chapter 1

1. According to the text, the most important element for the success of your small retail business is marketing.

2. The chapter states that a small business is one that is independently owned and operated and not dominant in its field of operations.

3. Most retailers in the United States would be classified as large retailers.

4. According to Figure 1-3, about half of all retail trade is done by single-unit establishments.

5. One estimate of the Small Business Administration states that 99 percent of the total 2.3 million retail-trade businesses in the United States are small and that these small businesses account for 73 percent of total retail sales receipts.

6. Large and small retailers do not face the same sets of advantages and disadvantages.

7. Product characteristics such as perishability, customization, and the need for significant amounts of personal services tend to favor large retailers.

8. Small retailers are sometimes discriminated against by shopping centers, suppliers who offer quantity discounts, and advertising media who offer discounts.

9. A small retailer who is using the marketing concept should think of his retail business as one that sells manufacturers' products to customers.

10. Scholars of small business generally agree that the Dun and Bradstreet statistics on small business failure are extremely accurate.

Chapter 2

1. The framework given in Chapter 2 will tell you what your marketing strategy should be.

2. The first step in the retail marketing strategy outline is: how to set your company goals and objectives.

3. The goals of a small retail firm do not reflect a small retailer's own personal goals.

4. "Satisfying the needs of customers in order to make a profit" is a specific goals statement for a small retailer.

5. If you do not have some kind of differential advantage or cannot identify one after considerable thought, you should not become a small retailer.

6. Any ways in which a small retailer differs from his competitors constitute a differential advantage.

7. The process that many successful small retailers use to define their target markets is called market segmentation.

8. The political and legal environment has become a less important variable for small retailers in recent years.

9. Your overall retail marketing strategy is composed of (a) a target market and (b) a retail marketing mix designed to satisfy the target market at a profit.

10. A product includes goods but does not include services.

11. The price element of the retail marketing mix refers simply to how much the customer pays for the product.

12. *People* is the one element of a retail marketing mix that is unique to small retailers.

13. The core strategy is based on your differential advantage and is the central focus for competitive and/or innovative success.

14. The time dimension for a marketing program is usually one month.

15. A marketing program is implemented by organizing, directing, and tactical adjustments.

Chapter 3

1. If you are a small retailer located in a metropolitan area of one million people, the size of your target market is one million people.

2. A retail market is composed of people who have needs, with purchasing power in the form of money or credit, and the willingness to buy.

3. As a target marketer, you specialize by serving some specific needs for a well-defined homogeneous group of customers.

4. Market segmentation divides the heterogeneous total market into smaller groups of customers that each internally possess rather homogeneous characteristics of significance to the retailer.

5. Some examples of segmenting characteristics or dimensions are sex, age, marital status, income, occupation, and geographic area.

6. The principle of market simplification for small business says that it is simpler for a small retailer to define his markets along the same lines as a large retailer.

7. The principle of market dominance is exemplified by a small retailer's attempting to obtain 5 percent of the total market by obtaining approximately 5 percent of each of twenty different market segments.

8. The principle of market dominance is exemplified by a small retailer's attempting to obtain 5 percent of the total market by obtaining approximately 50 percent of two of the twenty market segments.

9. If your sales remain the same and the combined total sales of all competitors in the market remain the same, then you have maintained your share of a constant market.

10. If your sales remain the same and the combined total sales of all competitors in the market decrease, then you have lost some of your share of the market.

11. Whenever you have an increase in sales, you also have an increase in your share of the market.

12. If your sales increase and the combined total sales of all competitors in the market remain the same, you have gained a larger share of the market.

Chapter 4

1. Even though large retailers face a similar set of environmental variables as small retailers, it is very likely that large and small retailers are affected differently by the environment.

2. The small retailer deals with the uncontrollable environment by attempting to understand it as well as possible so that he can adapt his marketing strategy accordingly.

3. Although recession, depression, and inflation are economic conditions, they are not part of the economic environment of small business.

4. The competitive environment is another name for the economic environment.

5. The competitive environment is concerned primarily with the level of prices.

6. One of the most important common legal problems of franchisees is the sharing of advertising cost.

7. Many of the largest corporations pay only about 25 percent of their income in federal taxes because of loopholes, whereas many medium-sized firms pay more than 50 percent.

8. The federal government through the Small Business Administration has several assistance programs such as ACE, SCORE, and BOMB.

9. Consumerism is an official term of the U.S. government given to describe the activities of the President's Consumer Advisory Council.

10. The four rights of the consumer are the right to safety, the right to be informed, the right to choose, and the right to a fair price.

Chapter 5

1. In general, small retailers tend to offer products with a higher proportion of goods and a lower proportion of services then do large retailers.

2. A specialty good is purchased only after making comparisons for such factors as suitability, price, quality, and style.

3. A shopping good is one for which a consumer has such a strong preference that he or she is willing to make a special purchase effort.

4. In general, convenience goods are usually purchased at convenience stores, shopping goods at shopping stores, and specialty goods at specialty shops.

5. Consistency refers to how closely related the product lines are in terms of consumer purchasing habits and in use.

6. The rate of stockturn or stock turnover is the number of times during a given period (usually a year) that the average amount of inventory is sold.

7. It is customary among retailers to calculate stockturn in terms of cost or units but not in terms of selling prices.

8. The so-called 80/20 principle means that a smaller retailer should try to sell 80 percent of his products to 20 percent of his customers in order to maximize profits.

9. "Scrambled merchandising" is a product strategy that involves the offering of many unrelated product lines.

10. Large retailers offer more customer services than small retailers.

11. Customer services usually are not offered by self-service stores.

12. As a small retailer, you may be able to design some specific customer services for some rather small target markets.

13. The general rule to follow in customer services is that only those customers who use the service should pay for the service.

14. Trading up is an attempt to market products of higher status and quality at a higher price.

Chapter 6

1. Within the entire area of product strategy, a small retailer's market-product matching strategy is almost always a core product strategy.

2. The eight-step process for planning retail product strategy begins with the first step, which is to identify your strategic product problems.

3. If a small retailer finds no serious strategic problems, he should conclude that his product strategy is sound.

4. Most product strategy problems are in the supporting-strategy areas.

5. Successful new product strategies are usually kept secret rather than being reported at meetings and in the trade press.

6. Most of the time, a retailer's new product strategy will not be a radical change from the previous retail strategy.

7. The eight-step process for planning retail product strategy can be compressed to five steps for the knowledgeable retailer who knows what his product strategy is.

8. The differential advantage of Ed's Quick Market was the liberal credit policy used to attract customers.

9. Part of the new product strategy for Ed's Quick Market involved a decision to create a new method for dealing with new-product additions and old-product deletions.

10. The changes in retail product strategy by Ed's Quick Market resulted in a sales increase of 50 percent and a profit increase of 66⅔ percent.

Chapter 7

1. Wholesaler-sponsored voluntary chains and retail cooperatives are forms of contractual marketing systems.

2. Vertical marketing systems do not offer many advantages for small retailers.

3. Retailers, regardless of their size, are usually in the power position to lead the channel of distribution.

4. Retailers of apparel, home furnishings, and similar merchandise will often use the services of a resident buying office.

5. An example of a change in the channel of distribution at the retail level is the recent growth of specialty stores dealing exclusively in athletic shoes and apparel.

6. Surprisingly, franchise sales of goods and services declined from 1977 to 1979 by about 18 percent.

7. Fast-food restaurants accounted for the largest share of retail franchise sales in 1977.

8. In a voluntary group, ownership of the warehouse is by the cooperative retailers.

9. All of the following are sources of revenue to franchisors: initial franchise fees, royalties, rental of premises, sale or leasing of equipment, sale of supplies, sale of raw materials, sale of franchised products, sale of services, other fees, and operating their own retail outlets.

10. One of the newest areas of franchising is real estate.

11. All the good retail franchise opportunities are pretty much gone.

Chapter 8

1. In forming a retail location strategy, the first thing to do is get a good location.

2. Some successful retailers say that an inverse relationship does exist between the quality of a site location and some items in the marketing mix such as advertising and promotion expenses.

3. If a site is a substantial part of a differential advantage for a small retailer, such a differential advantage can usually be easily duplicated by a competitor.

4. The site-location strategy for a small retailer should be formulated before an analysis is made of a specific site or sites.

5. Secondary business-district stores and highway business-district stores are called planned locations.

6. Community shopping centers are usually larger than regional shopping centers.

7. The small retailer gains many more advantages than disadvantages by locating in a large shopping center.

8. One of the advantages to a small retailer of locating in a large shopping center is that his image can be easily built and maintained.

9. "Business interceptions" refers to a site's being on major routes to potential destinations for shopping for the same product types.

10. Many retailers prefer a store site that is on the right side of the street, on the sunny side of the street, and on the going home side of the street.

11. Space elasticity is the ratio of relative change in unit sales to relative change in shelf space.

12. The impact of shelf space on unit sales differs among products.

13. Regular-sized (or best-selling size) items tend to have more space elasticity.

14. Products that are natural traffic generators should always be located near the rear of the store.

15. Impulse items usually tend to be medium-to-higher-priced necessities, purchased on a self-service basis, and mass-advertised.

Chapter 9

1. Most retailers use some type of cost-plus formula pricing for similar groups of products.

2. Resale price maintenance, also known as fair-trade pricing, is legal for small retailers but not for chain stores.

3. The number of units sold times price per unit, less cost, equals profits.

4. Customers who are male, older, single, and of higher income tend to have very good price knowledge.

5. The ideal image for a small retailer is one of low price and high quality.

6. Markup percentages and stock turnover usually are directly related; that is, the higher the markup percentage the higher the rate of stockturn.

7. Dollar cost is equal to dollar selling price minus dollar markup.

8. Although markup may be expressed as a percentage of either cost or selling price or both, it is customary and conventional in retailing to express markup as a percentage of selling price unless specifically stated otherwise.

9. Percentage markup on selling price is equal to dollar markup divided by dollar selling price.

10. If a retailer buys a product for $1 and sells it for $2, the percentage markup on the selling price is 100 percent.

11. If a retailer buys a product for $5 and sells it for $7, the percentage markup on the selling price is more than 33⅓ percent.

12. If a retailer's percentage markup on selling price is 33⅓ percent, his equivalent percentage markup on cost is 50 percent.

13. If a retailer's percentage markup on selling price is 33⅓ percent, his equivalent percentage markup on cost is 25 percent.

14. Some retailers have markups as high as 300 percent on selling price.

15. In general, markdowns should be delayed as long as possible, and then the amount of markdown should be as little as possible.

Chapter 10

1. The unit-cost approach is the pricing strategy most often used by small retailers.

2. The reason most small retailers follow the cost-plus method of formula pricing is simplicity.

3. Supporting pricing strategy questions are those which deal directly with the retailer's differential advantage.

4. Product-line pricing strategies are sometimes referred to as price lining.

5. Under prestige pricing, the customer assumes that a high price means high quality.

6. Leader pricing and odd-even pricing are two forms of psychological pricing that have been determined to be unethical by the American Marketing Association.

7. Discriminatory pricing in all forms is illegal; however, many small retailers practice it without getting caught.

8. A variable price policy works best in self-service stores and in large retail stores such as department stores.

9. Whenever two competitive retailers have an identical price on an identical item, it can be concluded that they are acting in collusion rather than competition.

10. Because the retailer's selling prices are higher in times of inflation, profits are usually up, and capital for replacing inventories is readily available.

11. The general rule during inflation is to take all price increases as soon as possible and to take the increases on all existing inventory as well as on incoming merchandise.

12. Most small retailers can do better by using their own retail credit system than by using VISA or Master Card.

13. Retail services are rarely priced on a discriminatory basis.

Chapter 11

1. A common promotion mistake among small retailers is to advertise over too large a geographic area.

2. Word-of-mouth advertising is usually a sufficient form of promotion for most small retailers.

3. The best or ideal promotion mix for small retailers is usually very similar to that of large retailers involved in the same kind of retail trade.

4. A retail ad that uses heavy black print usually projects a bargain or low-price image.

5. Determining the promotion message to be communicated is an example of a core promotion strategy area.

6. The two top objectives of advertising are to draw in new customers and to help hold the old ones.

7. The AIDA checklist reduces message strategy to the four major points of a good advertisement: attention, interest, decision, and arrival.

8. A retailer's media strategy calls for some combination of message impact in terms of media reach, frequency, and continuity.

9. Continuity is the total number of persons to whom a retailer's message is delivered.

10. The principle of market dominance suggests that a small retailer would want to limit the number of advertising media used in order to achieve at least the threshold level of impact.

11. On a cost-per-thousand exposure basis, on-premise signs are more expensive than most other advertising media.

12. In cooperative advertising, two or more retailers share the cost of placing a single advertisement.

Chapter 12

1. A disadvantage of personal selling is that it does not usually bring customers into the store.

2. Such factors as complex product features, installation, customization, the need for demonstration, and natural sales resistance tend to diminish the importance of personal selling for a retail store.

3. Small retailers who are target marketers should follow the lead of mass marketers by decreasing the amount of emphasis they give to personal selling in their marketing mixes.

4. Order-getters, of whom there are not nearly as many as there are order-takers, use creative selling to sell both tangible and intangible products.

5. The need-satisfaction theory of selling is based on the idea that the mind of the customer passes through several successive stages during the course of the sales presentation.

6. Successful small retailers should attempt to use the problem-solving theory of selling whenever possible.

7. There is usually considerable lag in customer response to sales promotion effort.

8. The first retailers to use new promotional techniques may find it very difficult to capture larger market shares and gain greater profits in the short run.

9. Premiums and gifts are often tied to a purchase and, unlike specialty advertising, they are usually not imprinted with an advertising message.

10. Couponing may be especially effective for the small retailer who has a small share of the market and wants to increase it.

11. Contests and sweepstakes should not be used by small retailers because, unlike their larger competitors, they cannot afford the expensive prizes necessary to get customers interested.

12. The best method of budgeting advertising expenditures for the small retailer is to spend as much as he can possibly afford to spend.

13. Although the available-funds method of budgeting promotion expenditures has been successfully used to promote a new business or a new retail location during the introductory period, the method is sometimes dangerous and is therefore not recommended.

14. In general, a small retailer should not use an advertising agency unless he has at least four stores and is spending $400,000 a year on advertising.

Chapter 13

1. People strategy, as a part of a total retail marketing strategy, is equally available to both large and small retailers.

2. By *people,* the book means all the people of a retail firm including the owner/manager, other managers, all employees, and some outside people.

3. People strategy for a small retailer is essentially the same thing as the personal selling part of the promotion strategy.

4. An example of people strategy is a large university's identification of its students by their social security numbers.

5. Customers of taverns, restaurants, and personal service firms are especially responsive to a good people strategy as a part of the retailer's marketing mix.

6. A small retailer's strategy for matching his people with the target market customers is usually a core strategy.

7. Even for a retail firm, the formal organization can be either production oriented or marketing oriented.

8. The slogan "Untouched by human hands" is an example of the people strategy of a very successful small restaurant cited in the chapter.

9. The people image of a small retail firm often reflects the personality of the owner/manager.

10. Supporting people strategies can be found in personnel areas such as recruiting, selection, developing, and motivating.

11. Management succession is usually not a problem for small retail firms.

12. To find out whether employees are highly motivated to do a good job, the retailer should ask the customers.

13. Formulating alternative people strategies is not supposed to be a creative process; it should be done according to a preconceived plan.

Chapter 14

1. The three parts of the management process in a small retail firm are planning, implementing, and controlling.

2. A restaurant that services one target market during the breakfast hour, another during the luncheon hour, a third during the dinner hour, and a fourth during the very late evening hours can integrate all four marketing plans into a total marketing program.

3. An ideal marketing mix requires the ideal blend of exactly the right product, right place, right price, right promotion, and right people.

4. A comparative marketing strategy chart shows a small retailer's marketing strategy as it actually happened compared to the retailer's ideal plan.

5. A small retailer should make out a comparative marketing strategy chart for each month.

6. A comparative marketing strategy chart gives the small retailer a chance to view at a glance both the parts and the total marketing strategies for his competitors and for himself.

7. The use of marketing research is usually beyond the financial resources of small retailers.

8. Because marketing research experiments can become very complex, they should not be used by small retailers.

9. Before a small retailer collects data on his own, he should go to all available secondary sources of information.

10. How customers dress, what they say, and how they act in a retail store all help to form the store image.

11. Store customers and potential store customers may not have the same image of a retail store.

12. With so many other ways to help form a store image, it makes little difference what the name of the retail store is.

Chapter 15

1. The three parts of the management process for small business retailers are planning, implementing, and coordinating.

2. Retail marketing strategies are implemented by tactical adjustments and by organizing and directing the various tasks to be performed by the retailer and the people of the retail organization.

3. A major strength of many small retail firms has been in the implementation rather than in the planning and control phases of management.

4. Because of their smallness, most small retailers find it almost impossible to maintain a flexible organization.

5. The principle of unity of command means that all of the top managers of a small retail firm think alike.

6. The principle of span of control is another way of expressing the principle of unity of command.

7. Generally, in a small retail firm, a manager should not have more than three subordinates reporting to him or her.

8. The owner/operator of a small retail firm should attempt to discourage and disband any informal organization because it interferes with the formal organization.

9. The control function in retail marketing is the systematic comparison of the actual results of marketing efforts with predetermined standards and plans.

10. The operational level of retail marketing control deals with such things as the effectiveness of a particular advertisement, a particular salesperson, or a particular pricing tactic.

11. The retail marketing audit is usually performed by a certified public accountant.

12. The number of small retailers is decreasing rapidly.

Answers to True-False Questions

True = +   False = o

Chapter 1
1. o
2. +
3. o
4. +
5. +
6. +
7. o
8. +
9. o
10. o

Chapter 2
1. o
2. +
3. o
4. o
5. +
6. o
7. +
8. o
9. +
10. o
11. o
12. +
13. +
14. o
15. +

Chapter 3
1. o
2. +
3. +
4. +
5. +
6. o
7. o
8. +
9. +
10. o
11. o
12. +

Chapter 4
1. +
2. +
3. o
4. o
5. o
6. +
7. +
8. o
9. o
10. o

Chapter 5
1. o
2. o
3. o
4. o
5. +
6. +
7. o
8. o
9. +
10. o
11. o
12. +

13. o
14. +

Chapter 6
1. +
2. o
3. o
4. +
5. o
6. +
7. o
8. o
9. +
10. o

Chapter 7
1. +
2. o
3. o
4. +
5. +
6. o
7. o
8. o
9. +
10. +
11. o

Chapter 8
1. o
2. +
3. o
4. +
5. +
6. o
7. o
8. o
9. +
10. +
11. +
12. +
13. +
14. o
15. o

Chapter 9
1. +
2. o
3. +
4. +
5. o
6. o
7. +
8. +
9. +
10. o
11. o
12. +
13. o
14. o
15. o

Chapter 10
1. o
2. +
3. o
4. o
5. +
6. o
7. o
8. o
9. o
10. o
11. +
12. o
13. o

Chapter 11
1. +
2. o
3. o
4. +
5. +
6. +
7. o
8. +
9. o
10. +
11. o
12. o

Chapter 12

1. +
2. o
3. o
4. +
5. o
6. o
7. o
8. o
9. +
10. +
11. o
12. o
13. +
14. o

Chapter 13

1. o
2. +
3. o
4. o
5. +
6. +
7. +
8. o
9. +
10. +
11. o
12. +
13. o

Chapter 14

1. +
2. +
3. +
4. o
5. o
6. +
7. o
8. o
9. +
10. +
11. +
12. o

Chapter 15

1. o
2. +
3. +
4. o
5. o
6. o
7. o
8. o
9. +
10. +
11. o
12. o

Notes

Chapter 1

1. U.S. Small Business Administration, Office of Planning, Research, and Data Management, *Small Enterprise in the Economy,* 4:1 (March 1978), inside cover.
2. Dillard B. Tinsley and Danny R. Arnold, "Small Retailers in Small Towns: Is Marketing the Key?" *Journal of Small Business Management,* 16 (January 1978), pp. 7–12.
3. W. H. Kuehn, *The Pitfalls in Managing a Small Business* (New York: Dun and Bradstreet, 1973).
4. Michael Z. Massel, "It's Easier to Slay a Dragon than Kill a Myth," *Journal of Small Business Management,* 16 (July 1978), p. 44.
5. *Ibid.,* p. 45.
6. *Ibid.,* p. 48.

Chapter 2

1. Reprinted by permission of the *Harvard Business Review.* Adapted from "Formulating Strategy in Smaller Companies" by Frank F. Gilmore (May–June 1971). Copyright © 1971 by the President and Fellows of Harvard College; all rights reserved.

Chapter 3

1. Anthony J. Alessandra, Ugur Yauas, and Wayne D. Jennings, "Retailing Strategies for the Small Health Food Retailer," *American Journal of Small Business,* 1 (October 1976), pp. 12–22.
2. A. J. Strickland III and R. D. Parrish, "Locating an Organization's Target Market Using the New Computer-Based Census Data," *Journal of Small Business Management,* 12 (July 1974), p. 28.
3. Roger Ricklefs, "A 'Neatness Expert' Tidies Up after All the Rest of Us Slobs," *The Wall Street Journal,* March 3, 1975, pp. 1, 11.
4. Richard P. Carr, Jr., "Developing a New Residential Market for Carpeting: Some Mistakes and Successes," *Journal Of Marketing,* 41 (July 1977), pp. 101–102.
5. *Grey Matter,* 49:1 (1978), published by Grey Advertising, Inc.
6. Arthur W. Cornwell, *Sales Potential and Market Shares,* Small Marketers Aids No. 112 (Washington, D.C.: Small Business Administration, 1965).
7. For example, see C. Glenn Walters, *Consumer Behavior* (Homewood, Ill.: Richard D. Irwin, Inc., 1978), or see Chapter 6, "Consumer Behavior Affects Small

Business" in William H. Brannen, *Successful Marketing for Your Small Business* (Englewood Cliffs, N.J.: Prentice-Hall, Inc., 1978).

8. Appendix to Chapter 3 is reprinted by permission of the publisher, *Journal of Small Business Management,* 14 (October 1976), pp. 55–58.

Chapter 4

1. Paul Bausch and Joseph F. Hair, Jr., "Product Safety Legislation and the Small Retailer," *American Journal of Small Business,* 3:1 (July 1978), p. 47.

2. James L. Porter and William Renforth, "Franchise Agreements: Spotting the Important Legal Issues," *Journal of Small Business Management,* 16 (October 1978), p. 29.

3. *Marketing News,* November 7, 1975, p. 1.

4. William L. Call and Allan H. Savage, "Can Small Business Afford to Defend Itself?" *Journal of Small Business Management,* 13 (April 1975), p. 1–4.

5. For a comprehensive discussion, see Chapter 11, "The Technological Environment of Retailing," in Joseph Barry Mason and Morris Lehman Mayer, *Modern Retailing* (Dallas: Business Publications, Inc., 1978), pp. 283–315.

6. Revel W. Elton, "How Trade Associations Help Small Business," *Management Aids,* No. 32 (Washington, D.C.: Small Business Administration, 1971), p. 1.

Chapter 5

1. Gordon E. Miracle, "Product Characteristics and Marketing Strategy," *Journal of Marketing,* 29 (January 1965), p. 20.

2. John M. Rathmell, *Marketing in the Service Sector* (Cambridge, Mass.: Winthrop Publishers, Inc., 1974), pp. 10–17.

3. John E. Swan and Henry O. Pruden, "Marketing Insights from a Classification of Services," *American Journal of Small Business,* 2 (July 1977), p. 41.

4. Louis P. Bucklin, "Retail Strategy and the Classification of Goods," *Journal of Marketing,* 27 (January 1963), p. 53–54.

5. For a discussion of buying and merchandise management see John W. Wingate and Joseph S. Friedlander, *The Management of Retail Buying* (Englewood Cliffs, N.J.: Prentice-Hall, Inc., 1978), and Ralph D. Shipp, Jr., *Retail Merchandising* (Boston: Houghton Mifflin Company, 1976).

Chapter 7

1. William R. Davidson, "Changes in Distributive Institutions," *Journal of Marketing,* 34 (January 1970), p. 7.

2. Harold Schaffer and Herbert Greenwald, *Independent Retailing* (Englewood Cliffs, N.J.: Prentice-Hall, Inc., 1976), p. 40.

3. For more information see Richard M. Hill, *Profit by Your Wholesaler's Services,* Small Marketers Aids No. 140, U.S. Small Business Administration (Washington, D.C.: U.S. Government Printing Office, 1973), 6 pp., and Ernest A. Miller, *How to Select a Resident Buying Office,* Small Marketers Aids No. 116, U.S. Small Business Administration (Washington, D.C.: U.S. Government Printing Office, 1972), 4 pp.

4. Waylon D. Griffin, "A Profit Strategy for the Small Grocer," *Journal of Small Business Management,* 12 (January 1974), p. 49.

5. For example, see Donald W. Hackett, *Franchising: The State of the Art* (Chicago: American Marketing Association, 1977), 67 pp.; C. R. Stigelman, *Franchise Index/Profile,* Small Business Management Series No. 35, U.S. Small Business Administration (Washington, D.C.: U.S. Government Printing Office, 1973), 56 pp., or *Franchising in the Economy 1977–1979,* U.S. Department of Commerce (Washington, D.C.: U.S. Government Printing Office, 1979), 96 pp.

6. *Franchising in the Economy 1977–1979,* p. 1.

7. *Ibid.*

8. *Ibid.,* p. 3.

9. Ronald Tathum, Ronald Bush, and Robert Douglas, "An Analysis of Decision Criteria in Franchisor/Franchisee Selection Process," *Journal of Retailing,* 48 (Spring 1972), p. 13.

10. Frank N. Edens, Donald R. Self, and Douglas T. Grider, Jr. "Franchisors Describe the Ideal Franchisee," *Journal of Small Business Management,* 14 (July 1976), p. 47.

11. Stigelman, cited in note 5.

12. *Franchising in the Economy 1977–1979,* p. 4.

Chapter 8

1. William H. Brannen, *Successful Marketing for Your Small Business* (Englewood Cliffs, N.J.: Prentice-Hall, Inc., 1978), p. 214.

2. John E. Mertes, "A Retail Structural Theory for Site Analysis," *Retailing: Concepts, Institutions, and Management,* ed. Rom J. Markin, Jr. (New York: The Macmillan Company, 1971), pp. 181–182.

3. Dwayne Laws, *How to Evaluate Hardware Store Locations* (Indianapolis: Russell R. Mueller Retail Hardware Research Foundation, 1971).

4. Kimberly King, "Profile: Waterbed City," *Industry Magazine,* December 1977, p. 19.

5. "Furniture and Waterbed Together," *Industry Magazine,* May 1976, p. 82.

6. Carl Calvert, "New Sleep: Nurturing a Professional Image," *Industry Magazine,* September 1978, pp. 81–83.

7. Patricia Premselaar, "Waterbed's Cincinnati Kid," *Industry Magazine,* September 1976, p. 27.

8. Richard Lawrence Nelson, "Principles of Retail Location," *Management Perspectives in Retailing,* ed. Ronald R. Gist (2d ed.; New York: John Wiley & Sons, Inc., 1971), pp. 204–208.

9. Frank Moyer, "Separate Camping, Ski Stores Strengthen 'Specialist' Look," *Sporting Goods Business,* February 1979, pp. 1, 46, 48.

10. R. Ted Will and Ronald W. Hasty, *Retailing: A Mid-Management Approach,* pp. 360–362. Copyright © 1973 by R. Ted Will and Ronald W. Hasty. Reprinted by permission of Harper & Row, Publishers, Inc.

11. For more detail, see Ronald C. Curhan, "Shelf Space Allocation and Profit Maximization in Mass Retailing," *Journal of Marketing,* 37 (July 1973), pp. 54–60.

12. Thomas B. Doyle, "Expansion Up," *Selling Sporting Goods,* September 1977, p. 48.

13. Thomas B. Doyle, "Expansion Down," *Selling Sporting Goods,* September 1977, pp. 48–50.

14. Hawkins Stern, "The Significance of Impulse Buying Today," *Journal of Marketing,* 26 (April 1962), pp. 59–60.

15. Stern, pp. 61–62.

16. Mike Major, "At Magnolia Hi-Fi, the Personal Image Is in Bloom," *Audiovideo International,* November 1978, p. 44.

17. Pam Reynolds, "Big Rock Makes Big Impact," *Selling Sporting Goods,* October 1977, p. 90.

Chapter 9

1. Victor A. Lennon, *What Is the Best Selling Price?,* Management Aids No. 193 (Washington, D.C.: Small Business Administration, 1972), p. 2.

2. James C. Johnson and Louis E. Boone, "Fairwell to Fair Trade," *MSU Business Topics,* 24 (Spring 1976), p. 22.

3. Adapted from a list in Alfred R. Oxenfeldt, "A Decision-making Strategy for Price Decisions," *Journal of Marketing,* 37 (January 1973), p. 50.

4. William L. Lett (presenter), Achilles A. Armenakis, Samuel B. Pond, and David S. Newton (co-authors), "An Analysis of Factors Important in the Patronage Decision Process for Retail Pharmacies," *The World of Small Business: Problems and Issues,* Proceedings of the 27th annual conference of the International Council for Small Business, Quebec City, Quebec, Canada, 1979, article 19, p. 10.

5. Frank Moyer, "Help Customers Get Results, Boost Annual Sales 10–15%," *Sporting Goods Business,* January 1979, p. 46.

6. For example, see William H. Brannen, *Successful Marketing for Your Small Business* (Englewood Cliffs,

N.J.: Prentice-Hall, Inc., 1978), the appendix to Chapter 13, which contains an illustrative game called MARKUP, or see Delbert J. Duncan and Stanley C. Hollander, *Modern Retailing Management* (Homewood, Ill.: Richard D. Irwin, Inc., 1977).

7. Murray Krieger, *Creative Markdown Practices for Profit* (New York: Fairchild Publications, Inc., 1971), pp. 117–118.

Chapter 10

1. Alfred R. Oxenfeldt, "Product Line Pricing," *Managerial Marketing: Policies, Strategies, and Decisions,* ed. Eugene J. Kelley and William Lazer (Homewood, Ill.: Richard D. Irwin, Inc., 1973), p. 393.

2. For a discussion, see D. Maynard Phelps and J. Howard Westing, *Marketing Management* (Homewood, Ill.: Richard D. Irwin, Inc., 1968), pp. 359–361.

3. Richard H. Buskirk and Percy J. Vaughn, Jr., *Managing New Enterprises* (St. Paul, Minn.: West Publishing Co., 1976), p. 322.

4. John M. Rathmell, *Marketing in the Service Sector* (Cambridge, Mass.: Winthrop Publishers, Inc., 1974), pp. 80–81.

5. Appendix to Chapter 10 is from Bruce J. Walker, *A Pricing Checklist for Small Retailers,* Small Marketers Aids No. 158 (Washington, D.C.: Small Business Administration, 1976).

Chapter 11

1. William H. Brannen, *Successful Marketing for Your Small Business* (Englewood Cliffs, N.J.: Prentice-Hall, Inc., 1978), p. 286.

2. These items are available at most major libraries or may be obtained from the publishers. For SBA Publications, contact your local SBA field office listed in the telephone directory or mail your request to Small Business Administration, P.O. Box 15434, Fort Worth, Texas 76119. Or you may telephone your request at no charge by dialing 1-(800)433-7212. (Texas residents dial 1-(800)792-8001.) Items in the *Small Business Reporter* series may be obtained by sending $2 for postage and handling to Small Business Reporter, Bank of America, Department 3120, P.O. Box 3700, San Francisco, California 94137.

3. Robert E. Karp, "On Developing Good Advertising Practices," *Journal of Small Business Management,* 12 (April 1974), p. 2.

4. John W. Wingate and Seymour Helfant, *Small Store Planning for Growth,* Small Business Management Series No. 33, 2d ed.; (Washington, D.C.: Small Business Administration, 1977), p. 68.

5. Adapted from David W. Nylen, *Advertising: Planning, Implementation, and Control* (Cincinnati: South-Western Publishing Co., 1975), p. 261.

6. Dillard B. Tinsley and Danny R. Arnold, "Small Retailers in Small Towns: Is Marketing the Key?" *Journal of Small Business Management,* 16 (January 1978), pp. 7–12.

7. John W. Wingate and Seymour Helfant, *Small Business Planning for Growth,* Small Business Management Series No. 33, 2d ed. (Washington, D.C.: Small Business Administration, 1977), p. 77.

8. Karen E. Claus and R. James Claus, *Signs and Your Business,* Small Marketer Aids No. 161 (Washington, D.C.: Small Business Administration, 1977) pp. 3–4.

9. Karen E. Claus and R. James Claus, *The Sign User's Guide: A Marketing Aid* (Palo Alto, Calif.: Institute for Signage Research, 1978).

10. *Ibid.,* p. 193.

11. This description is quoted from a booklet of the Specialty Advertising Association International, *24 Karat Specialty Advertising,* which describes the Golden Pyramid Award winners of 1976.

12. "Lawn and Garden Co-op Ad Directory," *Hardware Retailing,* February 1979, p. 41.

Chapter 12

1. Delbert J. Duncan and Stanley C. Hollander, *Retailing: Modern Concepts and Practices* (3d ed.; Homewood, Ill.: Learning Systems Company, 1979), p. 116.

2. This discussion of theory is based on Robert F. Gwinner, "Base Theory in the Formulation of Sales Strategy," *MSU Business Topics,* 16 (Autumn 1968), pp. 37–44. Reprinted by permission of the publisher, Division of Research, Graduate School of Business Administration, Michigan State University.

3. Joseph C. Schabacker, ed., *Strengthening Small Business Management* (Washington, D.C.: Small Business Administration, 1971), p. 84.

4. Raymond A. Marquardt, James C. Makens, and Robert G. Roe, *Retail Management* (2d ed.; Hinsdale, Ill.: The Dryden Press, 1979), pp. 462–463.

5. For more discussion, see Robert W. Miller, *Profitable Community Relations for Small Business,* Small Business Management Series No. 27 (Washington, D.C.: Small Business Administration, 1961), pp. 29–33.

6. Elizabeth M. Sarbet, *Measuring the Results of Advertising,* Small Marketers Aids No. 121 (Washington, D.C.: Small Business Administration, 1972), pp. 2–3. For additional help in ascertaining the results of your advertising, see Elizabeth M. Serbet, *Do You Know the Results of Your Advertising?,* Small Marketer's Aids No. 169 (Washington, D.C.: Small Business Administration, 1979), 8 pp.

7. William Haight, *Retail Advertising* (Morristown, N.J.: General Learning Press, 1978), p. 494.

8. J. Wade Rice, *Advertising—Retail Store,* Small Business Bibliography No. 20 (Washington, D.C.: Small Business Administration, 1973), p. 2.

9. "National Advertising Comes to Hardware Retailing," *Hardware Retailing,* October 1978, pp. 218–219.

Chapter 13

1. Dillard D. Tinsley, "Competition, Consultants, and Completeness: Strategy in Small Retailer's Future," *Journal of Small Business Management,* 14 (July 1976), p. 13.

2. For a more detailed discussion of people strategy, see William H. Brannen, *Successful Marketing for Your Small Business* (Englewood Cliffs, N.J.: Prentice-Hall, Inc., 1978), Chapter 16.

3. "Radicia's Newsstand: Know Your Customer," *Channels,* 14:1 (1979), p. 15.

4. "It Lacks Computer and Cairo Branch—But Bank Has Parrot," *Wall Street Journal,* March 11, 1976, p. 1.

5. Theodore Cohn and Roy A. Lindberg, *How Management Is Different in Small Companies,* An AMA Management Briefing, 1972, p. 12.

6. Robert E. Levinson, "How to Make Your Family Business More Profitable," *Journal of Small Business Management,* 12 (October 1974), pp. 35–41.

7. Joseph C. Schabacker, ed., *Strengthening Small Business Management,* Selections from the papers of L. T. White (Washington, D.C.: Small Business Administration, 1971), p. 135.

Chapter 14

1. For the small retailer who is going to do his own marketing research some published materials are available. For example, see George Edward Breen, *Do-It-Yourself Marketing Research* (New York: McGraw-Hill Book Company, 1977).

2. Philip Kotler, "Atmospherics as a Marketing Tool," *Journal of Retailing,* 49 (Winter 1973–74), pp. 63–64.

3. Also see Roger D. Blackwell, *Knowing Your Image,* Small Marketers Aids No. 124 (Washington D.C.: Small Business Administration, 1972), 8 pp.

Chapter 15

1. G. E. Tibbets, "Small Business Management: A Normative Approach," *MSU Business Topics,* 27 (Autumn 1979), p. 10.

2. James L. Heskett, *Marketing* (New York: The Macmillan Company, 1976), p. 440.

3. Donald Stegall, Lawrence Steinmetz, and John Kline, *Managing the Small Business* (Homewood, Ill.: Richard D. Irwin, Inc., 1976), p. 152. Copyright © 1976 by Richard D. Irwin, Inc.

4. George W. Rimler and Neil J. Humphreys, "Successful Delegation—A Must for Small Business," *Journal of Small Business Management,* 14 (January 1976), p. 45.

5. For example, see the *Journal of Small Business Management,* the *American Journal of Small Business,* and the various small business management books whose titles appear in the notes to this book. For operational suggestions, see your trade publications and William L. Siegel, *People Management for Small Business* (New York: John Wiley & Sons, Inc., 1978), 130 pp.

6. For example, many security services are available. The SBA also provides help with such Small Marketers Aids as *Preventing Retail Theft* (No. 119), *Reducing Shoplifting Losses* (No. 129), and *Sweeping Profit Out the Back Door* (No. 138). These and many other materials are free from the SBA.

7. Curtis E. Tate, Jr., et al., *Successful Small Business Management* (Dallas: Business Publications, Inc., 1978), p. 209.

8. John W. Wingate and Elmer O. Schaller, *Management Audit for Small Retailers,* Small Business Management Series No. 31 (3d ed., Washington, D.C.: U.S. Small Business Administration, 1977), 61 pp.

9. Harold Shaffer and Herbert Greenwald, *Independent Retailing* (Englewood Cliffs, N.J.: Prentice-Hall, Inc., 1976), p. 389.

Index

DATE DUE

GAYLORD			PRINTED IN U.S.A.